THE HIGHLAND RAILWAY

Frontispiece 'Clyde Bogie' 4—4—0 No 76 Bruce and 'Loch' 4—4—0 No 125 Loch Tay pass *Welsh's Bridge* signal cabin with a heterogeneous collection of rolling stock bound for Perth. Bruce *was completed in 1886 and exhibited at the Edinburgh Exhibition before entering service in December of that year. Although it would appear that the signal posts on the left lack arms, this is a common illusion of early photographs.*

THE HIGHLAND RAILWAY

The History of the Railways of the
Scottish Highlands—Vol 2

by

H. A. Vallance

extra material by

C. R. Clinker

Anthony J. Lambert

British Library Cataloguing in Publication Data
Vallance, H.A

    The Highland Railway—5th ed.—(The History
    of the railways of the Scottish Highlands; 2)
    1. Highland Railway
    I. Title   II. Clinker, C. R.   III. Lambert,
    Anthony J.   IV. Series
    385'.09411'5   HE3040.H/

    ISBN 1 899863 07 9 (pbk)

First published 1938
Second edition 1963
Third edition 1969
Fourth edition 1985
Fifth extended edition 1996

Printed in Great Britain by Redwood Books, Trowbridge
for House of Lochar, Isle of Colonsay, Argyll PA61 7YR

Contents

Publisher's Note

For many years my favourite hotel has been The Station at Inverness. And when staying there, just before going to bed, a favourite ritual is to pace the platforms of the station itself, noting when the last trains are expected in, and what the loading is on the night service to Glasgow and Edinburgh. These days there are often Americans making last-minute enquiries about their 'trip', perhaps by observation car to Kyle of Lochalsh.

Many stations have their individual atmosphere, but Inverness is especially unusual and colourful. The sheer distance from London, the Highland Railway war memorial, the triangular layout (though by the time this appears in print passenger-carrying trains will no longer be seen backing into their platform), the railway crossroads of the Highland as yet suffering from few major withdrawals of service: there are many ingredients in the magic. Not only do all four main routes into Inverness survive, but such has been the pressure on the main line up from Perth that some sections that were singled have had to be redoubled.

Passengers still change trains here, with generous waits enabling them to make good use of the hotel that is part of the station fabric, if no longer under common ownership. And in the hotel lobby wherein much of Highland social life has been enacted over the generations, people still gaze in awe at the wrought ironwork of the double staircase—up which I always step thinking of the thoughts the directors of the railway company must have enjoyed when they first opened the doors to the public. The hotel, like the rest of the railway, was built to high standards for posterity. The Highland might have served a lightly-populated part of Britain, but it was a major railway in all senses, covering enormous distances and in peace and war carrying extraordinarily heavy traffic at peak times.

Missing from the bookstall on the station for some years has been this book, and it was after my 1984 visit to Inverness that I decided that the time had really come to relaunch it. The volume has enjoyed a long and distinguished career, beginning long before David & Charles's involvement.

(3) 'Clan' 4—6—0 No 14769 (HR No 57) Clan Cameron was the last locomotive to be built for the HR, being completed in August 1921, yet the first of the class of eight engines to be withdrawn, in October 1943. Under LMS ownership No 14769 has lost its cylinder tail rods and acquired an additional pair of guard irons. Clan Cameron is waiting to leave Inverness in 1928.

It had its origins in a paper read by H. A. Vallance, then editor of *The Railway Magazine,* to members of the Railway Club in the early 1930s. It was first published in 1938, but not widely circulated. David & Charles published a substantially-revised and totally re-set edition shortly after their founding in 1963, and such was the demand that a second impression followed the same year. In 1969 there was a further revision, this time by C. R. Clinker, since Mr Vallance had died. Mr Clinker undertook further revision for a Pan paperback edition a couple of years later, and more recently passed on himself, In his note to the 1969 edition he made the point that Vallance's name would remain as closely associated to the Highland as MacDermot's was to the Great Western.

This edition follows the original where possible, incorporating Mr Clinker's material both for the hardback and paperback editions where appropriate, and has been further revised by Anthony J. Lambert, author of two pictorial volumes on the Highland Railway. Mr Lambert has also added another chapter to bring the story up to date.

The Highland Railway was always among the most meticulous of railway histories, and with the extra details now added (even the opening and closing dates of individual signalboxes) it is almost unique in its coverage. Many of the original photographs are again presented, but it has not been possible to find good new prints of all of them and in any event we wished to add a rather wider range of subject matter, and also introduce colour for the first time.

Its dramatic scenery, splendid viaducts and other engineering works and unusual traffic arrangements still make the Highland routes among the most fascinating in Britain, and perhaps nowhere in the world do a higher proportion of the travellers enjoy their train journey for its own sake. This new edition is prepared to enhance that enjoyment—and to encourage more to travel to the Further North while it is still possible to do so.

David St John Thomas,
December 1984

Postscript by the ex-publisher – 1996

Much has happened in the dozen years since the above was written. Personally I am now the ex-publisher and, having sold David & Charles, unexpectedly find myself living on former HR territory at Nairn. The new publisher, though, living on an island, cannot make that claim! More seriously, the former Highland system saw dramatically improved services and passenger traffic in the late eighties, though the recession then resulted in the clock going substantially backward. The increase and then decrease in activity was especially noticeable at Inverness, which at the end of the eighties had many more daily trains than ever before.

Decades ago none of us could seriously have expected so much of the Highland system to be spared, now almost certainly into the twenty first century, and the railway traverses a terrain as dramatic as ever. The great sadness is that the vast majority of passengers have to use Sprinters with their limited vision (and many seats beside window posts), Sprinters indeed being universal even to Kyle of Lochalsh in the 1995 season. Yet rejoice that the system exists and by and large works effectively and of course far more economically.

As always there are two view points. Wick people are furious they are now sent via Thurso, but the enthusiast no longer has the problem of how to cover the branches to both termini in the same day. The loss of car-carrying trains is a huge loss for many including ourselves, yet having given up the ghost on the freight side there is once more occasional traffic even to the Far North and the daily freight through Nairn increasingly earns its keep.

In 1994 I was commissioned by Highlands & Islands Enterprise to produce the *Highland Railway Report*, which might be of interest to those considering social and economic aspects and liking details that traffic census reports do not provide. Readers of this book can obtain a copy for ten first class stamps: PO Box 4, Nairn IV12 4HU. And if you yourself are not yet familiar with the system, as un-English as it could be, do spare a few days you will never regret.

David St John Thomas
January 1996

CHAPTER 1

A Fight for a Railway

FIRST MOVES

In the years following the Industrial Revolution, when many parts of the country were experiencing a trade boom, with its consequent increase of wealth, the Highlands of Scotland were plunged in the depths of financial depression, and poverty was rife. It was an era of great changes. The old clan system had been completely shattered by the Rebellion of 1745; and the landowners were turning their attention to sheep-farming on a large scale. Many of their tenants were compulsorily evicted from their homes, and forced to emigrate overseas, or to make their way to the cities in search of a livelihood.

The absence of mineral wealth retarded, to a great extent, the development of the country; but the chief obstacle was the lack of good transport, which prevented such industries as did exist from securing a wide market and a ready outlet for their wares.

To facilitate the movement of troops, after the Rebellion of 1715, some 250 miles of road had been constructed at the expense of the Government; but General Wade, who carried out this work, had only considered the military aspect of the undertaking, and many of his roads were quite unsuited to the requirements of trade operating under peace-time conditions.

In 1803, the Government again took a hand in the betterment of the means of communication. Thomas Telford was appointed to survey for new roads and for the improvement of the existing highways. In the course of the next 17 years he constructed about 920 miles of road, and built some 1,200 bridges.

Following these improvements came the introduction of numerous stage-coaches, which radiated from Inverness in several directions. By this means the far north was linked with the Highland capital, whence other coaches connected with Aberdeen, and with the industrial districts of the Lowlands.

A partial trade revival resulted. Goods which had previously been borne in coasting vessels could now, in many cases, be sent by road. This meant a considerable saving of time, for the steamship was as yet in its extreme infancy, and bad weather, or contrary winds, often delayed sailing vessels. However, in the Highlands, as in most other parts of the country, it was the railway that most effectually solved the transport problem; but it was many years before the iron road penetrated into these remote districts.

As soon as the steam engine had been proved a success, a number of railways were laid down in the industrial areas of the Lowlands, where trade was good, and the nature of the ground permitted of fairly low constructional costs. There is, however, an old saying that 'The Forth bridles the wild Highlandman'. And just as this had been applied, with some measure of truth, to the raiding clansmen of old, so was it now applicable to the check that the railway received in its advance towards the north. Beyond the River Forth, the well-populated and relatively flat country of the Lowlands gives place to the sterner and wilder Highlands, where large districts are very sparsely inhabited, and where railway construction is a matter of considerable expense.

Along the east coast, however, there is a strip of much easier country, and it was not long before railways were projected in this district, having as their ultimate objective Aberdeen, the largest town on the east coast between Dundee and Inverness, and the trade centre for a wide district. The railway was opened to Perth, from Edinburgh and Glasgow, in 1848, and reached Aberdeen in 1850. For some years the route was made up of the lines of several companies; but eventually all were amalgamated with the Caledonian Railway.

PARLIAMENTARY BATTLE

In March 1845 the Great North of Scotland Railway Company was floated to build a railway from Aberdeen to Inverness. The proposed route went inland from Aberdeen to Elgin, whence it followed the coast, through Forres and Nairn. Branches were to serve Banff, Garmouth, Burghead, and other small fishing townships in Banffshire and Morayshire. This railway, together with the proposed line from Perth to Aberdeen, via Forfar, would have provided a through route, albeit circuitous, between Inverness and the south.

At once two rival schemes were in the field. The first, supported by the inhabitants of the fishing towns which the Great North was to serve by means of branches, was for a railway from Aberdeen to Elgin, passing through Ellon and Turriff to Banff, and following the seaboard from that point. A separate company, the Inverness & Elgin Junction, was to extend the line from Elgin to Inverness, following the same route as that already proposed for the Great North of Scotland Railway. At Inverness a short branch was to serve the harbour.

Neither of these schemes were regarded with any great favour in Inverness. Although both promised reasonably direct access to Aberdeen, the metropolis of the north-east coast, the outlet to the south was deemed unduly circuitous. Small wonder, therefore, that a desire to improve on these projects began to grow. On 9 April 1845 a prospectus was issued for a direct line across the mountains to Perth. The moving spirit was a civil engineer named Joseph Mitchell, who had worked for several years as Telford's assistant on road construction in the Highlands. Backed by influential Highlanders, he put forward a scheme which, regarded in the light of those early days, was bold in the extreme.

The proposed railway joined the line of the Inverness & Elgin Junction at Nairn, 15 miles east of Inverness, and turning sharply inland, followed the old coach road closely past Ardclach and Glenferness, crossing the Monadhliath Mountains at an altitude of 1,320 ft above sea level. The line then ran beside the River Dulnan to Carr Bridge, whence it turned south to Aviemore. The left bank of the Spey was followed as far as Kingussie, where the river was crossed; and from Etteridge the railway climbed, to cross the Grampian Mountains by the Druimuachdar Pass, almost 1,500 ft above sea level. Beyond the watershed, there was a steep descent beside the Garry to Blair Atholl, and the Pass of Killiecrankie. The Tay was crossed near Dunkeld, and the line trended slightly to the west through the villages of Waterloo and Auchtergaven. At Marthall, near Perth, it was proposed to join the line from Perth to Forfar (the Scottish Midland Junction Railway) for which a bill already had been deposited. In addition to the main line, there was to be a spur at Nairn to enable trains to run direct from Elgin to the south without reversing. Immediately this scheme was launched, the Inverness & Elgin Junction severed its connection with the Aberdeen, Banff & Elgin, and threw in its lot with the new undertaking.

When it is remembered that engineers were then still imbued with the idea that railways which were to be worked by pure adhesion must be easily graded, and that huge sums were frequently expended to attain this ideal, the boldness of Mitchell's

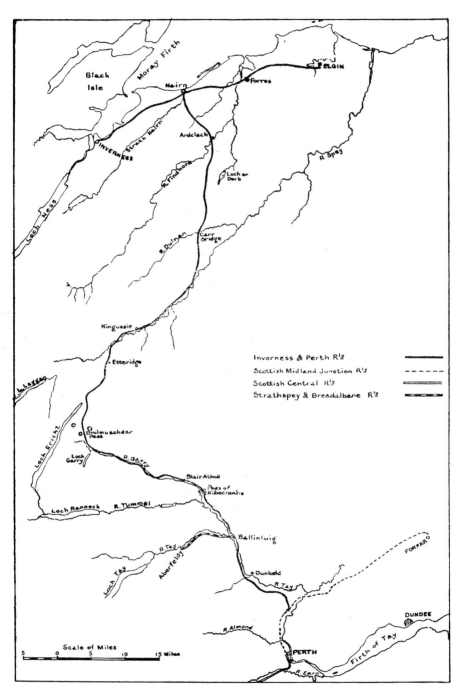

Map of the proposed Inverness & Perth Railway, 1845

scheme will be readily appreciated. Another fact that must not be lost sight of, is that between Nairn and Perth, a distance of almost 120 miles, there were no big towns. Much of this country was wild, desolate and sparsely inhabited.

All three companies introduced bills into Parliament. At this stage internal dissensions and grave financial difficulties brought about the complete collapse of the Aberdeen, Banff & Elgin, leaving a straight fight between the other two. The advantages of the direct route, as regards distance, were obvious; but the long and steep gradients proposed proved an insurmountable barrier. In the course of the evidence, Mr William Austen, one of the opposing Parliamentary counsel, is reported to have said:

> Ascending such a summit as 1,480 feet is very unprecedented, and Mr. Mitchell is the greatest mountain climber I have ever heard of. He beats Napoleon outright, and quite eclipses Hannibal. I read a book the other day, of several hundred pages, describing how Hannibal crossed the Alps. But after this line will have passed, I have no doubt that quartos will be written about Mr. Mitchell.

The result was that the bill was rejected. Mitchell was a fine engineer, and a bold thinker; but he was before his time. He lived to build his railway over the mountains, on a slightly altered route, it is true, but he had to wait many years before realizing his dream.

EXPENSIVE VICTORY

The first in the field, the Great North of Scotland Railway, was successful, and obtained its Act on 26 June 1846. It is estimated that the victory cost £80,000; and the Company was at once in financial straits, which were accentuated by the crash that followed the 'Railway Mania', then at its height. It was not until an extension Act had been obtained that work could be started, on 25 November 1852.

The railway was opened from Kittybrewster (1½ miles from Aberdeen) to Huntly, a distance of 39 miles, on 19 September 1854. Four years previously, the railway had been completed from Perth to Aberdeen. A through journey was then made possible between England and the south of Scotland, and Huntly. From this latter point coaches, running in connection with the trains, continued the journey to Inverness.

Here for some time the railway stopped short, want of funds preventing it from going farther. Subsequently, another Act was obtained to extend it to Keith, 53 miles from Aberdeen, and 55 from Inverness. The extension was opened on 11 October 1856. One year earlier, on 24 September 1855, the line had been extended from Kittybrewster to a terminus at Waterloo Quay, Aberdeen, where a passenger station was opened on 1 April 1856. This brought the Great North to within half a mile of the Guild Street terminus of the line from Perth, an omnibus conveying passengers between the two stations.

Despite frequent overtures to co-operate in the building of a joint station, the Great North remained at Waterloo for 11 years, to the great inconvenience of passengers. Finally, on 4 November 1867, a short branch was opened from Kittybrewster to the present joint station. It is only fair to add that this reluctance to participate was caused by the financial difficulties under which the Great North for so long laboured.

It remains to be recorded that in 1847 an Act was obtained for the amalgamation of the Great North and the Aberdeen Railway which formed the connection to the south. Owing to financial troubles, this was repealed in 1850; and the Aberdeen Railway was later absorbed by the Caledonian. Had this amalgamation Act stood, it is probable that the Highland Railway would never have been built under independent ownership, as the Caledonian would have had a monopoly of the country north of Perth and Aberdeen.

The Great North had won the day in the fight for a railway to the Highlands, but at so great a cost that it was unable to carry out its contract in full. For some years no attempt was made to extend the system west of Keith. Between that town and Elgin lies a stretch of difficult country, and the Company was unable to raise the necessary capital for constructing the railway. Connections by coach were provided to Inverness, but this was a slow journey, which caused dissatisfaction to all. The Inverness party soon took steps to improve communications in their district; steps that ultimately resulted in the formation of the Highland Railway.

STATION SCENES

(4)   *Strome Ferry in 1933 looking west, showing on the right the remains of the pier that was served by steamers owned by the Dingwall & Skye Railway, HR and Hutcheson & Co until the extension of the railway to the pier at Kyle of Lochalsh on 2 November 1897. Strome Ferry pier was then closed, although not dismantled until 1937.*

(5)   *Forres station looking east showing the line to Elgin and Keith on the left and the old main line to Aviemore and Perth on the right. The fine pair of bracket signals, like most signalling apparatus on the HR, was supplied by Mackenzie & Holland of Worcester; Dutton & Co, also of Worcester and later taken over by Mackenzie & Holland, supplied some equipment for the Wick line. Forres station was rebuilt in 1954–5.*

BRANCH TERMINI

(6)   *The delightful station at Strathpeffer Spa on 28 July 1913 with 0—4—4T No 25 Strathpeffer. Only the obduracy of the local landowner, Sir William MacKenzie, prevented the Dingwall & Skye Railway passing through the town on its way to Strome Ferry. After his death, the branch was built without opposition, opening on 3 June 1885. In 1908 Strathpeffer was served by a through carriage from King's Cross, changed to Euston in the following year. To serve the Highland's new hotel in the Spa, opened in June 1911, the 'Strathpeffer Spa Express' was inaugurated, providing a non-stop service from Aviemore to Dingwall; it was the only regular train to run through Inverness without stopping. The signal cabin, which can be seen on the right, closed on 27 September 1936 when the branch became operated by 'one engine in steam'.*

(7)   *The light railway from Wick to Lybster was the last section of the Highland system to be built, although work began on a light railway to Cromarty. Notice the Lybster station handbell on the window sill and the ornate weighing machine.*

CHAPTER 2

The Genesis of the Highland

THE MISSING LINK TO ABERDEEN

When it became evident that the Great North by its own efforts could not reach Inverness, steps were taken to provide the missing link in the railway to Aberdeen. The Earls of Grant and Seafield took a prominent part in the promotion of the scheme, and on 24 July 1854 powers were obtained for a railway between Inverness and Nairn, a distance of 15 miles, with a short branch, about half a mile long, to Inverness Harbour. The only real opposition came from Mr Welsh, of Milburn House, close to the terminus of the proposed line. This gentleman claimed that the railway would injure his policies; but his objections were overridden and the construction of the line proceeded.

The first sod was cut by the Countess of Seafield on 21 September 1854, in the midst of great rejoicings, the day being observed as a general holiday in Inverness. Towards midday a great crowd of people had collected at the Exchange, whence a procession of magistrates, tradesmen and directors of the Company was to proceed to the place where the first sod was to be cut. The scene of the ceremony was a field to the east of Milburn House. Wooden barricades had been erected, but such was the size of the crowd that these proved insufficient, and there was some confusion when many of the spectators broke through and filled up the seats reserved for the distinguished guests.

At length the Countess of Seafield arrived, in company with the young Lord Reidhaven, the Hon. Lewis Grant and Dr Edward Macdonald. They were received by Cluny Macpherson, of Cluny, the chairman of the directors. After Dr Macdonald had offered up a prayer, and Cluny had addressed the assembly, the Countess came forward to perform the ceremony of cutting the sod. The special wheelbarrow used for the purpose was made of mahogany, with a bright brass band round the wheel. When the Countess had performed her task, Cluny took the barrow, trundled it to the field, and tipped out the contents, afterwards returning with the empty barrow.

The contractors, Brassey & Falshaw, pushed forward the works with all possible speed, and it was hoped to have the line ready for opening by 1 August 1855; but many obstacles intervened. All the plant had to be brought by sea, and vexatious delays were frequent by reason of the uncertainty of this means of conveyance. Great trouble was experienced in obtaining delivery of the turntables and signals, and when these did arrive it was found that only part had been sent. There were, however, enough for the formal opening ceremony to take place on 5 November 1855, official sanction having been obtained on the second.

In honour of the opening, business in the town was almost suspended. The special train was to start at noon, but long before that time a great crowd had collected at the station, an unpretentious building, but described at that time as being neat and designed with the ultimate intention of through communication. The platform was 60 yards long, and it is not surprising that the accommodation was taxed to the utmost. The train consisted of 30 vehicles of various kinds, for the most part ordinary trucks fitted with seats.

Everything being in readiness, the signal to start was given, after the Provost and the magistrates and the directors had taken their seats, and, amidst deafening cheers, the first train left the Highland capital. For the first mile or so the train went very slowly, as vast crowds assembled at the sides of the line. According to one contemporary account:

> The people were ranged like a dense hedge on either side, and the welcome they gave the train was most encouraging. The bridges and heights flanking the seashore were studded with ladies who waved their handkerchiefs. The steep bank, on the summit of which stands the ruin of the Hut of Health, presented a very curious appearance, on account of the crowds of people collected upon it. The number of people could not have been less than two or three thousand, and as they swarmed to see the spectacle, they appeared to hang in black clusters from the banks.

Having passed these crowds, the train gathered speed and travelled at about 30 miles per hour, to the intense excitement and indeed, in some cases, no little fear of the passengers, many of whom had never travelled at this rate before. The train reached Nairn amidst scenes of general rejoicing, and the visitors marched through the town in procession. The return journey began at 3 p.m., and Inverness was reached about an hour later, when an immense crowd welcomed the travellers. Public traffic began the next day.

There were four intermediate stations: Culloden, Dalcross, Fort George, and Cawdor. The station at Cawdor served Cawdor Castle; it was renamed Kildrummie in 1857, and disappeared from the public timetables about a year later. Coaches continued to run in connection with the trains between Nairn and Huntly and later to Keith, when the Great North reached that town. Three train and coach connections were given in each direction between Inverness and Aberdeen. Between Inverness and Nairn there were three trains each way on weekdays, but this number was soon raised to five. The majority took 45 m. for the journey, calling at all stations; but one, the mail, called only at Fort George, and took 35 m.

Having reached Nairn, no time was lost in pushing on to the east. It was at first proposed to continue as far as Elgin, and wait for the Great North to complete the railway from Keith. As already said, the intervening country is hilly, necessitating some fair-sized earth works, and a costly bridge over the Spey. In consequence, the Great North objected to being left to carry out this section single-handed, and offered the promoters of the Nairn & Elgin £40,000 towards the expense of continuing their line to Keith. This offer was accepted.

The railway, under the title of the Inverness & Aberdeen Junction, was authorized between Nairn and Keith on 21 July 1856, and was to take over the working of the Inverness & Nairn. Amalgamation between the two took place on 17 May 1861.

The first section, eight miles long, was opened from Nairn to Dalvey on 22 December 1857. Dalvey station stood on the west bank of the Findhorn, near Forres. It was a temporary terminus, and was only in use pending the completion of the bridge over the river. When this was finished, the station was closed on 25 March 1858, on which date the line was opened to Elgin. On 18 August following, Keith was reached, and a through journey between Inverness and Aberdeen was for the first time possible.

The most noteworthy engineering feat on the line was the bridge over the Spey at Orton. For some time after the railway was opened to Keith, it was in an unfinished state, a temporary scaffolding carrying the rails, and the Board of Trade would not sanction its use for passenger trains. Accordingly, on the arrival of the train, the passengers got out and walked over the adjacent road bridge. The engine was detached, and the coaches hauled over by ropes. The passengers having re-entrained, a fresh locomotive was attached and the train continued its journey. The bridge was rebuilt in 1906.

THE MORAYSHIRE RAILWAY

Closely associated with the Inverness & Aberdeen Junction Railway was a local undertaking, the Morayshire Railway, which, after a somewhat chequered history, passed into the hands of the Great North of Scotland Railway. In 1841 a survey was made for a railway between Elgin and the fishing port of Lossiemouth, a distance of six miles. But the scheme failed for lack of support. Some years later it was revived under the title of the Morayshire Railway, and a bill was submitted to Parliament in 1846.

At the same time, the Great North of Scotland Railway was seeking powers for the line from Aberdeen to Inverness. It was proposed to connect the two railways at Elgin and to build an extension of the Morayshire from Orton, ten miles to the east, to Rothes and Craigellachie, in Strathspey, leaving the main line of the Great North to provide the connecting link. Powers for the complete undertaking were obtained on 16 July 1846, a few weeks after the Great North of Scotland Act had been passed.

When, owing to the financial crash, the Great North decided to limit its undertaking to a line from Aberdeen to Keith, the directors of the Morayshire applied to the Railway Commissioners for permission to abandon their extension to Craigellachie, and a warrant authorizing this action was granted on 10 July 1851. The first sod of the Elgin-Lossiemouth section was cut in the following November, and the railway was opened on 10 August 1852.

By 1856, proposals were afoot for the completion of the Craigellachie extension under the sole ownership of the Morayshire Company; but with the advent of the Inverness & Aberdeen Junction Railway it was decided to revert to the original scheme of 1846, and make use of that Company's track between Elgin and Orton. On 14 July 1856 the Company was once more authorised to construct the extension. The line was opened from Orton to Rothes, 3½ miles, on 23 August 1858, and to Craigellachie[1] on 23 December following.

For a few weeks Morayshire trains worked separately between Elgin and Orton; but soon it became the practice to attach the coaches to Inverness & Aberdeen Junction trains. In all probability, lightness of traffic was a deciding factor in this alteration; but it was subsequently alleged to have been necessary because of the

[1] Actually Dandaleith, on the west bank of the Spey.

serious delays to main-line trains, caused by the constant failure of the Morayshire engines.

The agreement for the common use of the line between Elgin and Orton involved the two companies in a serious dispute destined to have far-reaching results. The Morayshire claimed the right to carry passengers and goods from places on its own system to stations on the Inverness & Aberdeen Junction Railway, served by the trains of both companies, paying only a proportion of the fare for use of track and haulage. The latter Company retorted that such traffic should pass completely into its hands at Elgin or Orton, and that the proportional rates applied only to traffic from Lossiemouth to Rothes and Craigellachie, or *vice versa*. Matters came to a head when the Inverness & Aberdeen Junction Railway attempted to seize the traffic at the junctions, and the Morayshire Railway decided to seek powers for an independent line.

The Act authorizing the railway from Elgin to Rothes, through the Glen of Rothes, was passed on 3 July 1860. The junction at Elgin faced away from Lossiemouth, necessitating a reversal for through trains. The line was opened on 1 January, 1862. For some time connections were given between Rothes and Orton, but except for passengers proceeding eastwards towards Keith this section became redundant.

On 17 May 1861 the Morayshire Railway was empowered to extend its line over the Spey at Craigellachie and effect a junction with the Strathspey Railway, which was authorized on the same date from Dufftown to Grantown-on-Spey. At Dufftown this latter line joined the Keith & Dufftown, which was in effect an extension of the Great North of Scotland Railway. Now, that Company had contributed to the building of all three of the local lines, and ultimately concluded working agreements with them on 30 July 1866, thus providing for itself a through route to Elgin. In the case of the Morayshire, the Great North was to work the line at 45 per cent, and this arrangement continued until complete amalgamation in 1881.

On the day following the working agreement (31 July 1866), the Great North, without notice, closed the section between Orton and Rothes, as being no longer required. This action was the subject of some discussion between the two companies, but the dispute was finally settled to the satisfaction of both. The abandoned section remained for many years just as it had been left, and became much overgrown. The permanent way was not removed until 1907. The course of the line remained plainly visible, particularly at Orton, where the junction with the line to Keith was very clearly defined.

Mention must be made of the FINDHORN Railway, another small line now consigned to the limbo of forgotten ventures. It served the village of Findhorn, on the eastern shores of the bay of the same name, about five miles north-east of Forres.

On 19 April 1859 an Act was obtained for the construction of a railway, three miles long, from the village to a junction with the Inverness & Aberdeen Junction Railway at Kinloss. There were no constructional difficulties, as the surrounding country was level and sandy. The railway was opened on 18 April 1860, and was worked as an independent concern for two years. At the end of this period the Company found itself in financial difficulties, and on 1 March 1862 the line was taken over by the Inverness & Aberdeen Junction Railway, and worked as a branch of that system. Traffic still proved insufficient to pay operating expenses, and regular services were withdrawn on 1 January 1869.

For the time being, occasional goods trains were run, but the line was completely closed about 1880, and the Company was wound up. The permanent way was removed, but the course of the line remained clearly traceable, particularly at the northern end, where the railway ran in a shallow cutting between the main street of the village and the shore. The terminus was at the quayside, and to facilitate the loading of ships a siding, approached by a wagon turntable, was laid on the pier. The platform and station buildings were demolished, the site being eventually occupied by some sheds. One of the chief causes of the failure of the railway was the difficult approach to the harbour at Findhorn. At its mouth the river forms a huge landlocked bay, but the sea has thrown up a sand-bar, making the entrance difficult and restricting the size of ships. The sand subsequently accumulated to such an extent that the harbour was practically closed.

INCONVENIENCE AT ABERDEEN

At long last Inverness had secured a railway route to the south, but the undertaking left many things to be desired. By reason of the £40,000 subscribed, directors of the Great North of Scotland Railway attended the board meetings of the other Company. Despite the fact that they had failed in their original undertaking, and had only been able to render partial assistance in the building of more than half the line between Aberdeen and Inverness, they adopted a high-handed attitude which resulted in constant friction between the two companies. Finally, in 1860, the Inverness & Aberdeen Junction Railway bought out the Great North, and was left to manage its own affairs.

Far worse than those board-room quarrels was the inconvenience at Aberdeen, caused by the two stations at Waterloo and Guild Street being over half a mile apart. On arrival at Guild Street of the mail train from the south, the mails were at once transferred to a waiting van and taken to Waterloo. Passengers and luggage followed by omnibus. There was a margin of about three-quarters of an hour between the arrival of the train from Perth and the departure for Inverness, and if the train from the south was punctual, a good connection could be made. Frequently, however, the train from Perth arrived late. In this case, the mails were at once rushed over to Waterloo, and as soon as they were loaded, the Great North started the train.

If the passengers could reach Waterloo station as soon as the mails, for which the Great North was bound to wait, and could get into the train before they were loaded, they were certain of their connection. But the train was often started before the passengers could arrive, or before they could all transfer from the omnibus to the train, and travellers were stranded.

There is a picturesque story to the effect that on one occasion, when the train from the south was late, the omnibus was seen tearing along the quay in the wake of the mail van. As soon as this latter arrived, although it wanted still a few minutes to starting time, the officials shut and bolted the doors of the station against the omnibus, rather than delay their train, which was duly started, despite the knockings and clamourings of the furious passengers without. It is said that amongst these were certain influential Highlanders, and that, enraged by such high-handed treatment, they held an indignation meeting, and there and then decided to promote another direct line to the south, and obviate changing and discourtesy.

Whether or no the above story is true is a moot point. There is no question, however, that the connection was frequently missed through passengers arriving at Waterloo after starting time. The Inverness party was never satisfied with the circuitous route *via* Aberdeen, and it needed but little to revive the project for a direct line over the mountains to Perth. Joseph Mitchell was again called upon to survey a route, and, after much negotiation with the landowners, a bill was submitted to Parliament in November 1860.

CHAPTER 3

Across the Grampians

AGITATION FOR A DIRECT ROUTE

As early as 1845, the Scottish Midland Junction Railway promoted a branch through Strathtay to Dunkeld, but by mutual consent the proposal made way for the ill-fated direct line from Inverness to Perth. Although the Scottish Midland Junction reinstated its bill, which was duly passed, construction was never begun, and the scheme lapsed. Finally, on 10 July 1854, an independent company, the Perth & Dunkeld, obtained an Act for a line, 8¼ miles long, leaving the Scottish Midland Junction at Stanley, 7¼ miles from Perth, and terminating at Birnam, on the opposite side of the Tay from Dunkeld. The railway was opened on 7 April 1856, and was worked first by the Scottish Midland Junction, and subsequently by the Scottish North Eastern Railway.[1]

Four years later, with the renewal of the agitation for a shortened route from Inverness to the south, the importance of this purely local undertaking increased. The proposed new railway through the Central Highlands left the Inverness & Aberdeen Junction Railway at Forres, 24 miles east of Inverness, and turning sharply to the south, rose steeply for several miles to cross the hills separating the valley of the Findhorn from Strathspey. Beyond the summit at Dava, 1,052 ft above sea level, the approximate course of the route surveyed by Mitchell in 1845 was joined, and the line proceeded by way of Grantown and the west bank of the Spey to Kingussie. There followed a long, steep climb up the northern slopes of the Grampians to the head of the Druimuachdar Pass, and a corresponding descent to Blair Atholl and the Pass of Killiecrankie. Crossing the Tay near Dalguise, the line reached Dunkeld, where it made an end-on junction with the Perth & Dunkeld Railway.

Although the route was characterized by its severe gradients, and

---

[1] The Scottish North Eastern Railway was formed on 29 July 1856 by an amalgamation between the Scottish Midland Junction and Aberdeen Railways.

the summit level of 1,484 ft at Druimuachdar exceeded any pre-
viously sanctioned in the British Isles, such had been the advance in
locomotive design since 1845 that the arguments which had secured
the rejection of Mitchell's original plans now proved unavailing.
Despite determined opposition, the Act was passed on 22 July 1861.[1]
By the terms of the Act, the Company, under the title of the
Inverness & Perth Junction Railway, was to take over the Perth &
Dunkeld Railway. The two systems were amalgamated on 28
February 1864.

The first sod was cut on 17 October 1861, and so expeditiously
was the work carried out that the 13 miles from Dunkeld to
Pitlochry were opened on 1 June 1863. The 36 miles from Forres to
Aviemore followed on 3 August, and the final length over the
Grampians, from Aviemore to Pitlochry, was completed on 9
September.

The chief engineering works on the line were the seven-span
masonry viaduct over the Divie, near Dunphail, 477 ft long and
105 ft high; the girder bridge across the Tay, near Dalguise, 515 ft
long and 67 ft high; and the ten-span masonry viaduct, 54 ft high,
over a deep ravine in the Pass of Killiecrankie. Smaller masonry
bridges were required to carry the railway over the Bran, north of
Dunkeld, and the Garry, at Struan. The latter was remarkable in
that its main span crossed not only the river, but also the stone
bridge carrying the Rannoch Road over the Garry at the same
point. At Blair Atholl the Tilt was crossed by a single-span lattice-
girder bridge.

Only two short tunnels were found necessary—one in the Pass of
Killiecrankie (128 yd long), and the other north of Dunkeld (350 yd
long). South of Dunkeld there was a third tunnel (310 yd long), but
this had, of course, been constructed by the Perth & Dunkeld
Railway. (These, incidentally, were the only three tunnels on the
Highland Railway.)

Although the work of building the main line was completed as
soon as possible, some time elapsed before all the stations were
ready to be opened, a few of the smaller ones being left until communication between Forres and Perth had been established. Thus
accommodation was not provided at Dava until 1864, and Killiecrankie and Dalnaspidal until 1865.

[1] Druimuachdar remained the highest summit on a standard-gauge railway in the country until the opening of the Leadhills Light Railway (worked
by the Caledonian Railway). Between Leadhills and Wanlockhead this line
rose to a height of 1,498 ft above sea level.

On the other hand, two stations subsequently closed figured in the timetables. One was at Rohallion, between Murthly and Dunkeld, serving the castle of the same name. Opened by the Perth & Dunkeld Railway, the train service consisted, for some time, of one train in each direction, on Fridays only. Later on, this was increased to a daily train in each direction. It would appear, however, that the station was in the nature of a conditional halting-place, as the early timetables have the following note appended: 'Stops by request at Rohallion, Dunkeld fares charged'. The sparseness of the traffic brought about the closing of the platform in 1864. Almost all traces of the station have disappeared, and it is now difficult to identify the site.

The second station subsequently closed was at Rafford, between Dunphail and Forres, at a point where a side road from the village of Rafford crossed the railway. A complete station was established here, and not a conditional stopping-place as at Rohallion. However, traffic did not come up to expectations, and it was closed in 1865. Until 1871 the station subsequently known as Kincraig was named Boat of Insh, taking its name from the nearby 'boat', or ferry, over the River Insh.

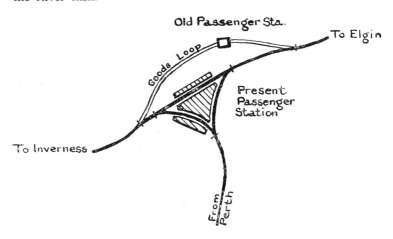

The Junctions at Forres

A new station was required at Forres. A double junction was provided with the line from Inverness to Keith, so that trains could be run in each direction without reversing. To give each train platform accommodation, a new station, triangular in form, was built to the south of the existing one. A new line was provided for the trains from east to west, leaving the original route as an auxiliary loop for goods trains and light engines. The old station building became the stationmaster's residence.

The 1861 Act also authorized a branch, nine miles long, from Ballinluig to ABERFELDY, along the valley of the Tay. Powers for a similar line had been obtained by a small independent company, the Strathtay & Breadalbane, in 1846, but the rejection of the bill for the direct line from Inverness to Perth had caused the scheme to fall into abeyance. Work on this section was considerably delayed, and it was not until 3 July 1865 that it was ready to be opened. It was an expensive line to construct. There were 41 bridges, including two over the river, and 800,000 cubic yd of cutting and filling were required.

THE IMPORTANCE OF PERTH

The advantages of the direct line were many. It eliminated the changing and discourtesy at Aberdeen, and gave a route virtually under one ownership between Inverness and Perth. The greatest benefit lay, however, in the shortening of the journey. Previously the distance by rail from Perth to Inverness had been 198 miles; it now became 144. This represented a saving of about $2\frac{3}{4}$ hours in travelling time, and a corresponding reduction in fares.

As early as 1848 Perth had become a railway centre of considerable importance; and by the Scottish Central Railway's Act of that year the railways converging on the town were authorized to contribute towards the provision of a general station on that Company's line. In 1861 the Inverness & Perth Junction Railway was granted running powers over the Scottish North Eastern Railway, between Stanley Junction and Perth, and the right of user of the general station. Four years later the interests of the various companies were vested in a joint committee, which took over the entire management of the station. As the result of the amalgamations in 1865 and 1866 between the Caledonian, the Scottish Central and the Scottish North Eastern Railways, the number of partners in the undertaking was reduced to three: the Caledonian, the North British and the Highland, with the predominant interest in the hands of the Caledonian. The Station Hotel was the subject of a separate Act in 1865.

Although the Inverness & Perth Junction Railway was assured of the right to use the station, both by the Act of 1861 and the subsequent setting up of the joint committee, some difficulty was experienced with the Scottish North Eastern Railway over the question of tolls for the use of the line between Stanley Junction and Perth. For some time after the line was opened, the Inverness & Perth Junction paid toll on each passenger, and as the traffic grew, this amount reached large proportions. The owning company was repeatedly approached with a view to a settlement whereby this toll could either be considerably reduced, or a fixed sum paid each year, but for some time the parties were unable to reach a basis of agreement.

At the half-yearly shareholders' meeting in 1866, it was reported that a survey had been made for an independent route between Stanley and Perth, which would not only obviate the necessity of paying anything, but which was slightly shorter than the existing line. This threat evidently brought the Scottish North Eastern into a more reasonable frame of mind, for, at the meeting in the following year, it was announced that after the tolls had reached the high total of £10,000 in the previous year, the two companies had come to an agreement whereby the Inverness & Perth Junction Railway was to pay the sum of £5,000 per annum in perpetuity, irrespective of the number of passengers that passed over the line. The Scottish North Eastern Railway also undertook not to divert an undue amount of traffic over the older route, *via* Aberdeen.

Some time prior to the opening of the direct line to Perth, a further addition was made to the Inverness & Aberdeen Junction Railway in the shape of a branch from Alves to the fishing port of BURGHEAD, a distance of $5\frac{1}{2}$ miles. It will be remembered that the original scheme of the Great North of Scotland Railway had included a branch to Burghead, but it was not until 17 years later that the village obtained railway facilities. Powers were obtained on 17 May 1861 to construct the branch, which was opened on 22 December 1862 to a station on Burghead Pier. In 1864 a station was opened at Wards between Alves and Burghead, at which trains called by request. In the following year the name was changed to Coltfield Platform.

THE HIGHLAND RAILWAY IS BORN

Following the opening of the direct line to Perth came a period of amalgamation and consolidation. Amalgamation had already taken place, on 17 May 1861, between the Inverness & Nairn and the Inverness & Aberdeen Junction Railways, and on 28 February

1864 between the Inverness & Perth Junction and Perth & Dunkeld Railways. One year later, on 1 February 1865, the Inverness & Aberdeen Junction and the Inverness & Perth Junction Railways were amalgamated. On 29 June following, the combined undertaking was authorized to be known as the Highland Railway, with headquarters at Inverness. At the time of its inception the Company owned, or worked, 242 route miles, made up as follows:

Inverness to Keith	...	...	...	55 miles
Forres to Stanley Junction		...	...	$111\frac{3}{4}$,,
[1]Inverness to Bonar Bridge		...	...	$57\frac{1}{2}$,,
Ballinluig to Aberfeldy	...	...	...	$8\frac{3}{4}$,,
Alves to Burghead	...	...	...	$5\frac{1}{2}$,,
[2]Kinloss to Findhorn	...	...	...	$3\frac{1}{2}$,,
		Total	...	242 miles

The $7\frac{1}{4}$ miles of Scottish North Eastern track between Stanley Junction and Perth should be added to obtain the total of $249\frac{1}{4}$ miles over which the Company's trains actually worked.

[1] See Chapter 4.

[2] Worked since 1862 by the Inverness & Aberdeen Junction Railway.

The Advance to the North

THE GEOGRAPHICAL OBSTACLE

In certain respects, the geographical position of Inverness is similar to that of Edinburgh. Immediately to the north of the latter is the Firth of Forth, about five miles wide directly opposite the city, but narrowing considerably towards the west. Beyond comes the somewhat isolated peninsula county of Fife, bounded on the north by the Firth of Tay, about two miles wide at Dundee.

To the north of the Highland capital is the Beauly Firth, about 1½ miles wide in most places, but narrowing to about half a mile, at Kessock Ferry, close to the city. The analogy to Fife is supplied by the peninsula of the Black Isle, while the Cromarty Firth corresponds to the Firth of Tay. Here, however, the similarity ends. In the south there are no more deep indentations of the coast as far as Aberdeen, but north of the Cromarty Firth is a third big opening, the Dornoch Firth, running deeper into the land than the other two. A few miles north of the Dornoch Firth is Loch Fleet, but this is a much smaller opening and does not constitute a particularly serious obstacle.

For many years a railway journey from Edinburgh to Dundee was a very roundabout business, and it was not until 1890 that both the Firths of Forth and Tay were bridged, and a direct line of communication established. Fortunately, the volume of traffic rendered such costly structures desirable. In the case of Inverness, however, not only did the original railways have to run round the arms of the sea, but subsequently the traffic did not increase to an extent to warrant the provision of any deviations to shorten the route. As the crow flies, the distance from Inverness to Wick is about 80 miles; by the railway it is 161 miles. Moreover, the only places of any size are situated on the east coast, so that any railway between Inverness and the far north would have, of necessity, to follow the coast, with its windings, in order to serve these trade centres.

(A) *Colour photographs of Highland engines at work are rare. This view of 'Clan' class 4—6—0 No 14767 (HR No 55) Clan MacKinnon was taken at Aviemore shed in 1946. The building in the background appears to be the corrugated-iron carriage shed, erected in Highland days*

THE INVERNESS & ROSS-SHIRE RAILWAY

Soon after the Inverness & Nairn Railway was opened, the possibility of an extension to the north was mooted. Some difficulty was experienced in the choice of a route, and several suggestions were put forward. The supporters of one scheme proposed to establish a steamer service between Nairn and the north side of the Cromarty Firth, whence one railway was to be built to Tain, and another to Invergordon, and possibly to Dingwall. It was not at that time considered practicable to build a railway from Inverness to Dingwall, *via* Beauly, because of the great expense of bridging the River Ness and the Caledonian Canal, and the Rivers Beauly and Conon. This scheme never came to fruition; and finally, an all-railway route between Inverness and the north was proposed.

The moving spirit of the undertaking was Sir Alexander Matheson, of Ardross, who worked unceasingly to obtain the line. His efforts resulted in the passing of the Inverness & Ross-shire Railway's Act, on 3 July 1860, for a railway from Inverness to Invergordon, a distance of 31 miles.

The ceremony of cutting the first sod was performed on 19 September 1860 by Lady Matheson, the day being observed as a general holiday in Inverness. At 3 p.m. the procession, headed by the Militia, started for the field, which was situated opposite the 'White House', on the outskirts of the town, where Meakin, the contractor for the Inverness-Dingwall section, was awaiting its arrival. After the ceremony, the party returned to the town, and in the evening the directors of the new line were entertained to dinner.

The construction of the railway was pushed forward with all possible speed. In December 1861, Miss Mitchell, daughter of the engineer, laid the keystone of the Ness Viaduct, and the swingbridge over the Caledonian Canal, at Clachnaharry, was completed shortly afterwards. The last of the big works to be finished was the masonry viaduct over the River Conon, although the foundation stone had been laid by Miss MacKenzie, of Seaforth, as early as November, 1860. The Beauly river was crossed by a timber bridge (renewed as a steel structure in 1909). In March 1861 the contract for the 13 miles from Dingwall to Invergordon was let to MacDonald & Grieve, with the stipulation that the work should be completed as soon as that between Inverness and Dingwall, so that the whole railway could be opened at the same time. The date fixed for the opening was 1 April 1862, but unforeseen delays occurred.

(B) *LMS Class 5 4—6—0 No 5014 passing the signal cabin at Slochd with a down freight in August 1939*

The opening of the section between Inverness and Dingwall took place on 11 June 1862. On the previous day the line had been inspected by Colonel Yolland, of the Board of Trade, who expressed entire satisfaction with all the works. The directors thereupon decided to open the line on the following day, Andrew Dougall, the secretary, announcing the fact by wire from Dingwall, and ordering a special train to leave that evening with all the officials, who were to be dropped at their respective stations in readiness for the opening on the morrow.

The existing terminus at Inverness was not adapted for conversion to a through station, as it faced south, with a frontage in Academy Street, whereas the new line approached the city from the west. It was therefore decided to enlarge the station by the provision of extra terminal platforms on the west side to accommodate the Ross-shire trains. The two railways diverged immediately beyond the station, passing on either side of the locomotive shops. The third side of the triangle, providing physical connection from east to west, was formed by part of the harbour branch. This line subsequently became known as the Rose Street curve.

Although further additions were made to the station from time to time, until there were four platforms in the southern section, and three in the northern, the layout remained practically unaltered. The somewhat unusual arrangement of lines proved convenient as, apart from a few through coaches, Inverness was the terminus of all trains arriving. To facilitate the interchange of passengers, it became the practice to send trains from the south *via* the Rose Street curve, whence they were reversed into the northern part of the station. A similar procedure was adopted with arrivals from the north, but trains from the Keith line usually ran direct to a platform in the southern section.

The completion of the line from Dingwall to Invergordon was much delayed by the opposition of Mr MacKenzie, of Findon, who claimed that his tenants would be placed in danger if they had to use the proposed level crossing on the Ferry Road. After much discussion, the Company decided on a bridge, and the railway was opened on 25 March 1863.

Shortly after the opening of the line to Dingwall, the Inverness & Ross-shire Railway was amalgamated with the Inverness & Aberdeen Junction Railway, the Act authorizing the union being dated 30 June 1862. By the Ross-shire Extension Act, passed on 11 May 1863, powers were obtained to extend the line to Bonar Bridge, 26½ miles from Invergordon, and 57½ from Inverness. The railway was

THE DUKE OF SUTHERLAND'S RAILWAY

(8) *The opening ceremony, 1 November 1870.*

(9) *The present Dunrobin station, from the south.*

(10) *Tank engine 'Dunrobin', built in 1870, beside the statue of the Second Duke at Dunrobin.*

BRIDGES

(11) *The commemorative plaques at Inverness station were removed from the box girder bridge over the River Spey near Orton which was replaced by this lattice girder bridge in 1905–6.*

(12) *The bridge over the River Tay at Dalguise soon after construction. The spans are of 141ft and 210ft and the total cost was £20,395, a price per lineal foot of £39 12s. The gentleman on the left appears to be practising his semaphore.*

opened to Meikle Ferry, 2½ miles from Tain, on 1 June 1864, and to Bonar Bridge on 1 October following.

The temporary terminus at Meikle Ferry provides another instance of stations that have subsequently been closed. It was situated at a point where a tongue of land juts out into the Dornoch Firth, and the narrow strait thus formed is crossed by a ferry. Some four miles to the north is Dornoch, the county town of Sutherland, and one of the smallest county towns in the country. The ferry not only gives easier access to Dornoch, but also to places lying farther to the north, as the nearest road bridge over the firth is at Bonar Bridge, some miles to the west.

When the railway reached Meikle Ferry, a coach connected, *via* the ferry, with towns and villages in Sutherland and Caithness. But the ferry was some distance from the station and a journey to the north by this route was naturally somewhat slow. When the railway was completed to Bonar Bridge, coach connections were still given *via* the ferry, but this lasted for a short time only as they soon began to operate from Bonar Bridge. In consequence, traffic at the ferry station dwindled almost to vanishing point. The station was closed in 1869.

Between Edderton and Bonar Bridge a station known as Mid Fearn was provided to serve Fearn Lodge. It remained open for only eleven months, after which it was withdrawn from the public timetables, although still used as a conditional stopping-place for the lodge and the wives and families of local railwaymen.

Another station worthy of mention is Clachnaharry, situated close to the bridge over the Caledonian Canal. Opened in 1869, it remained in continuous use until it was closed in 1913. There was no station at Clunes until 1864, and in 1869 Parkhill station was renamed Kildary, to avoid confusion with the Aberdeenshire station of the same name, on the Great North of Scotland Railway.

THE SUTHERLAND AND THE DUKE OF SUTHERLAND'S RAILWAYS

The village of Bonar Bridge is in two portions, one on each side of the Kyle of Sutherland, as the upper reaches of the Dornoch Firth are called. On the north, or Sutherland, side is Bonar Bridge proper, while on the Ross-shire side is Ardgay, and the railway station of Bonar Bridge. The two portions of the village are connected by a long road bridge which carries the main road to the north over the kyle. When an extension of the railway was proposed, it was decided to continue on the south side of the kyle for

Plan of Inverness Station

some three miles, crossing thence to the northern shore to follow the banks of the River Shin and the course of the River Fleet down to the coast, at the head of Loch Fleet.

On 29 June 1865 the Sutherland Railway was authorized from Bonar Bridge to Brora, a distance of 32¾ miles. Having crossed the kyle, the railway climbed through the hills to Lairg, at the south-eastern end of Loch Shin, whence roads radiate in several directions to the west and north coasts. Turning to the east, the line continued past the head of Loch Fleet to Golspie and Brora.

Despite a contribution of £15,000 by the Highland Railway, the promoters were unable to carry out the whole of their scheme. The works were heavy and expensive, especially the viaduct over the kyle, comprising five masonry arches and a girder span of 230 ft, and the rock cuttings near Lairg. On 13 April 1868, the 26 miles from Bonar Bridge to Golspie were opened. A service of coaches, running in connection with the trains, was established between Golspie and Wick and Thurso, and between the Mound (at the head of Loch Fleet) and Dornoch.

For some years there was no station between Bonar Bridge and Invershin, at the northern end of the bridge over the Kyle of Sutherland. The nearest road bridge was at Ardgay, and people living on the Ross-shire side of the kyle had to come into Bonar Bridge to join the train, although the railway passed almost by their doors. A great improvement was effected in 1871, when a platform was opened at Culrain, at the south end of the viaduct. For the time being, trains stopped by request to pick up or set down passengers; but by 1873 it figured in the timetables as an ordinary station. Although little more than a quarter of a mile apart, Culrain and Invershin served different districts, because of the lack of facilities for crossing the kyle. (Prior to 1 January 1917 a third-class single ticket between these stations cost one halfpenny, the lowest fare on the Highland Railway.) In contrast to this distance were the ten miles separating Lairg and Rogart.

The Sutherland Railway had stopped short at Golspie, and the next advance in the extension towards the north was made possible by the generosity of the Duke of Sutherland, the principal land-owner in the county, whose seat was at Dunrobin Castle, two miles north of Golspie. Since the creation of the title in 1833, successive Dukes had done much to better conditions in the county and expended considerable sums on various improvement schemes. Large tracts of moorland were reclaimed and turned into fertile farm lands, while in the west and north of the county new roads were made in the neighbourhoods of Durness and Lochinver.

As soon as the railway reached Golspie, the third Duke projected a privately-owned line along the coast for some 17 miles to Helmsdale, on the borders of Caithness. The railway was to come close to Dunrobin Castle, and pass onwards through Brora, the originally-intended terminus of the Sutherland Railway, serving a number of flourishing fishing villages. The Act authorising the transfer to the new undertaking of the six miles of the Sutherland Company's line from Golspie to Brora, and the extension of the railway from Brora to Helmsdale, was passed on 20 June 1870, but construction had begun before the powers were obtained.

Engineering difficulties at either end of the line delayed the completion of the works, but the section from Dunrobin (two miles north of Golspie) to a point about three-quarters of a mile short of Helmsdale was finished by the autumn of 1870. The Duke decided that the railway should be opened forthwith, and a temporary station, known as West Helmsdale, was built at Gartymore. An engine and some coaches were purchased for working the line, but since there was as yet no physical connection with the Sutherland Railway, at Golspie, the stock had to be placed on wagons and hauled along the road by a traction engine.

The opening ceremony was performed on 1 November 1870 by Princess Christian, and for the next seven months a service of two trains a day in each direction was run. By that time the works were completed, and on 19 June 1871 the railway was opened throughout, and the Highland Railway took over the working.

The temporary terminus at Dunrobin became a private station serving the castle, at which trains called by request to pick up or set down passengers. In 1902 the buildings were reconstructed to the designs of the estate architect.

ON TO THE FAR NORTH

Caithness, the most northerly county in Scotland, has only two towns of any size: Wick, situated on the east coast, and, some 20 miles away, Thurso, on the north coast. The former is a flourishing port for the herring fishery, while the latter, beside boasting a not inconsiderable connection with the fishing industry, is the nearest port on the mainland to the Orkneys.

In the early 1860s a railway was proposed between the two towns, and after many delays the line was authorized on 30 July 1866. The Company, under the title of the Caithness Railway, was

to build a line from Wick to Thurso, with a view to an extension
(to be authorized at a later date) to join the Sutherland Railway,
which had obtained its Act one year previously for a railway from
Bonar Bridge to Brora.

The line as authorized was only a local undertaking, isolated
from the railway system of the rest of the country. For the most
part, the proposed southern extension would have passed through
desolate country, boasting but few inhabitants. Despite the efforts
of local landlords to raise the money, the necessary funds were not
forthcoming, and for many years the whole scheme was in abeyance, the Company being unable to commence even the 21 miles
between Wick and Thurso, where the country is relatively fertile.

The distance from Helmsdale to Wick along the east coast is
about 35 miles, but the high land round the Ord of Caithness pre-
vents a railway from keeping to the shore and forces it inland. The
road, it is true, follows the east coast, but it is carried over the
Ord by means of long hills. There is also a precipitous drop into the
village of Berriedale, with a corresponding rise on the other side.
The proposed extension of the Caithness Railway was intended to
run inland from Helmsdale to a point about eight miles from
Thurso, where it was to join the already sanctioned railway from
Wick to Thurso.

Meanwhile, thanks to the efforts of the Duke of Sutherland, the
railway was being extended from Golspie to Helmsdale, and a new
company, the Sutherland & Caithness, was formed to carry the
railway on from Helmsdale to the north. The new concern proposed to take over the Caithness Railway, and to follow the same
route, both as regards the section already authorized, and the
southern extension. The latter joined the Thurso-Wick line at
Georgemas, which thus became the most northerly junction in the
British Isles. The Act authorizing construction was passed on 13 July
1871, and the railway was opened on 28 July 1874.* The Highland Railway subscribed £50,000 and the Duke of Sutherland
£60,000.

North of Helmsdale, in sparsely-inhabited Strath Ullie, the
stations were placed some distance apart. When the railway was
first opened, 9½ miles separated Helmsdale and Kildonan, and 8¼
Kildonan and Kinbrace. In 1877 a platform was opened to serve
Borrobol shooting lodge, which lies close to the railway, about two
miles north of Kildonan; trains called by request to pick up or set
down. In July 1907 a second platform, similar to Borrobol, was

* Hoy Station was not opened until 1 October.

opened at Salzcraggie, between Helmsdale and Kildonan, to serve Salzcraggie Lodge. Both were advertised as normal public stopping places, although Salzcraggie was officially a private station, maintained at the expense of the owner of Salzcraggie Lodge.

THE DINGWALL & SKYE RAILWAY

Although no efforts were spared to carry the railway through to the shores of the Pentland Firth, the possibilities of a branch to the west coast, north of the Caledonian Canal, were not overlooked. Because of the mountainous configuration of the country, there are only certain routes along which a crossing from east to west can be made. From very early times, these passes through the hills have been used for roads, and any railways crossing the country must of necessity follow approximately the same route. One of these natural highways runs westwards from Dingwall, the county town of Ross-shire, up Strath Conon and Strath Bran. Thence it passes over the watershed into Strath Carron. The coast is reached at a point opposite the Isle of Skye, on the sheltered waters of the Inner Sound. The distance from sea to sea is a little over 60 miles. The western end of this road forms a convenient port for the Isle of Skye and the Outer Hebrides.

About 1863 a proposal was made for a railway along this route to the west coast. Two years later the idea took definite shape, and powers were granted on 5 July 1865 for a railway 63 miles long, from the Highland Railway at Dingwall to Kyle of Lochalsh. The route ran due west for about four miles to the village of Strathpeffer Spa, whose mineral springs had already become widely known. The high ground lying to the north-west of Strathpeffer was to be avoided by trending somewhat to the south, through the village of Contin, to the banks of the Blackwater River, and the line then passed through Garve, and along the side of Loch Luichart to Strath Bran, whence it ran westwards to the coast. The Highland Railway was to subscribe £50,000 and the Caledonian Railway £100,000.

Unfortunately, the landowners in the Strathpeffer district put up the most determined opposition. Foremost among them was Sir William MacKenzie, of Coul House. The proposed railway passed through his lands for about four miles, and came to within a quarter of a mile of the house. At the Company's meeting in October 1866 it was reported that unexpected difficulties with regard to the purchase of the land had arisen, and that pending a settlement of these disputes nothing would be done towards the construction of the line. Matters remained at this impasse for some three years. Finally, on 29 May 1868, a further Act was obtained which sanctioned various deviations.

The Strathpeffer difficulty was overcome by diverting the railway somewhat to the north, so that it passed about two miles from the spa. Not only did this deprive Strathpeffer of a railway station in a central position, but the new location gave the railway a four-mile climb, for the most part at 1 in 50, to the Raven Rock Summit, whereas the original route would have been less severely graded. There is a tragic side to the story. Sir William MacKenzie did not enjoy his victory, as he died shortly before the line was finished.

The other alteration sanctioned by the Act of 1868 was at the western end of the railway. Because of the enormous cost of construction between Strome Ferry and Kyle of Lochalsh, it was decided to abandon that section. This had the effect of moving the terminus some ten miles up the sea-water Loch Carron. Ships could reach Strome Ferry, but Loch Carron was not such an ideal harbour as Kyle, being subject to strong currents and tides. There can be no doubt, however, that for the time being the Company was justified in taking this step.

The railway was opened throughout in 1870—for goods on 5 August and for passengers on 19 August. On the same day steamers began to run from the new pier at Strome Ferry to Portree, in the Isle of Skye, and to Stornoway in Lewis. The new railway opened up a quicker route between the islands and the south. Previously, passengers and goods had to go right round by sea to the Clyde, but the journey time was now reduced by many hours. In addition, the north-east of Scotland was for the first time made easily accessible from the Hebrides.

Several years elapsed before all the stations on the Skye line were open. Lochluichart and Achnashellach were added in 1871; Glencarron Platform followed in 1873; but Attadale was not opened until 1880.

To complete the early history of the northern lines, mention must be made of the branch to the MUIRTOWN Basin of the Caledonian Canal, about one mile from Inverness. To facilitate traffic between the basin and the town, a branch 58 chains long was constructed from Canal Junction, on the northern main line, to the wharf, and opened on 9 April 1877. Not until 4 July 1890 was official sanction obtained. Although the branch was extensively used by goods trains, the proposed passenger service, running in connection with the steamers on the canal, was never provided.

AMALGAMATION OF THE NORTHERN LINES

Twelve years had sufficed to bring the railway from Inverness up the east coast to the extreme north of the mainland and across the country from sea to sea. When the sparseness of the population and the meagre traffic are considered, this represents no mean achievement. From its inception, each extension of the railway was worked by the Highland Railway, which subscribed to the funds of the local companies, save the Duke of Sutherland's Railway, which was entirely a private venture. However, with the exception of the Ross-shire Railway, which by its amalgamation with the Inverness & Aberdeen Junction Railway became part of the Highland Railway in 1865, the remaining four nominally retained their independence for a number of years.

The Dingwall & Skye Railway was merged on 2 August 1880, but it was not until 28 July 1884 that the northern lines lost their identity. The new mileage added to the Highland Railway in these two years was as follows:

Dingwall & Skye Railway	53	miles
Sutherland Railway	26½	,,
Duke of Sutherland's Railway	17¼	,,
Sutherland & Caithness Railway ...	67¾	,,
Total ...	164½	miles

The year 1884 is one of the most important in the history of the Company, because the Act of that year consolidated the system almost into its complete form. With one highly important exception, the subsequent additions were in the nature of branch lines, most of them fairly short, which acted as feeders to the main routes. Save for two nominally-independent light railways, the whole of the lines built after 1884 were authorized as part of the Highland Railway, and not as separate undertakings to be amalgamated at a later date.

CHAPTER 5

Expansion 1884-1903

THE DIRECT LINE TO INVERNESS

Of the additions made to the Highland Railway subsequent to 1884 by far the most important was that which shortened the main line from Inverness to the south. Although the route *via* Forres was a great improvement on that *via* Aberdeen, which it superseded, it was by no means as direct as could be desired. Leaving Inverness, it ran almost due east for 24 miles before turning to the south. In consequence, the village of Aviemore, in Strathspey, was over 60 miles by rail from Inverness, whereas the distance measured in a straight line was little more than 30 miles.

Despite this disadvantage, the promoters of the Inverness & Perth Junction Railway had good reasons for choosing the route that they did. Forres is situated almost midway between Inverness and Keith, and it was their intention to leave the Inverness & Aberdeen Junction Railway at the most central point possible, so that no place should be unduly side-tracked. Had a direct line been made to Inverness from Aviemore, or even from Grantown, it would have placed the whole of the Inverness & Aberdeen Junction Railway virtually on a branch line. Although Inverness itself would have benefited, passengers from places further to the east would have had to make a considerable detour to reach the main line.

Nevertheless, it was realised at an early date that eventually steps would have to be taken to provide a shorter route to Inverness. For many years, however, the Highland Railway made no definite progress towards this. The country lying between Loch Ness and the Spey is composed of moorland, mostly well above sea level, with the Monadhliadh Mountains in the south-east. The whole district is wild, and much of it uninhabited. The building of a railway through such country would have been a costly undertaking, with almost negligible prospects of an adequate return from local traffic. In addition, the shortening of the route would have necessitated a substantial reduction in the rates for through traffic to Inverness.

Finally, the Company's hand was forced by a threat of an independent and shorter route to Inverness from the south, promoted in close association with the North British Railway. (See Chapter 6.) Powers were obtained on 28 July 1884 for a new line leaving the existing route at Aviemore, and passing through Carr Bridge and Moy to Inverness. On 23 May 1887 an Act authorizing a deviation near Inverness was obtained, and a third Act, dated 27 June 1892, again slightly altered the location of the railway. The first section, from Aviemore to Carr Bridge, 6¾ miles, was opened on 8 July 1892; the 17 miles to Daviot followed on 19 July 1897; and the final 11 miles to Inverness were completed on 1 November 1898.

The engineering works were exceptionally heavy, and included two large viaducts over the rivers Findhorn and Nairn. The former, 445 yd long, and constructed on a curve of half a mile radius, consisted of nine steel spans, supported on masonry columns, with a maximum height of 143 ft; and the Nairn viaduct, 600 yd long, and built entirely of red sandstone, was composed of 28 arches of 50 ft span, and one span of 100 ft over the river. The maximum height was 128 ft. Near Slochd Mhuic Summit, where the line reached a height of 1,315 ft above sea level, were two deep cuttings and a masonry viaduct of eight arches, over 100 ft high. The ascent to the summit from Inverness was severe, including several miles at 1 in 60, or little easier. The rise from Aviemore, although shorter, was almost as hard.

When the works were nearing completion, the Highland Railway was robbed by death of one of its oldest officers, Murdoch Paterson, the chief engineer. Paterson had been in the service of the Company since its earliest days, and had held the position of chief engineer since 1875. He died in the house provided for the stationmaster at Culloden Moor[1], whither he had gone to superintend the building of the Nairn viaduct. Paterson was succeeded by his resident engineer, William Roberts, who held office until 1914, being succeeded in his turn by Alexander Newlands.

The distance from Perth to Inverness *via* the new line was 118 miles, as against 144 *via* Forres. A substantial reduction in journey times was at once secured. The principal trains were diverted to the Carr Bridge line, and the older route became a secondary main line.

---

[1] When the new line was opened, Culloden Station on the original Inverness & Nairn Railway was renamed Allanfearn.

With a view to participating in the lucrative fishing trade of the towns of BUCKIE and PORTESSIE, and to tap the farming district lying between Keith and the coast, known as the Enzie, the Highland Railway obtained powers, on 12 July 1882, to construct a branch from Keith to a junction with the Portsoy-Elgin line of the Great North of Scotland Railway (authorized on the same day) at Portessie, a distance of 13¾ miles. The two railways ran parallel for some distance between Buckie and Portessie, and at the latter town the Highland Railway used the GNSR station. The line was opened on 1 August 1884.

The railway remained in use until 9 August 1915. Subsequently the track was removed between Aultmore (near Keith) and Buckie, and used elsewhere. No buildings were demolished, as it was intended to re-open the line after the war. Restoration of the permanent way was delayed because for many years the traffic had been light, and it was not considered expedient to re-open the branch for the time being. It was still closed when the Highland Railway became part of the LMSR in 1923.

With the growth in popularity of STRATHPEFFER as a spa, the need for better railway facilities became apparent, as the station on the Dingwall & Skye Railway, known as Strathpeffer, was about 1½ miles from the village, at the top of a steep hill. In the early 1880s representations were made to the Highland Railway, with a view to the construction of a branch from Dingwall to a centrally-situated terminus.

Powers for the new railway were obtained on 28 July 1884, and the line was opened on 3 June of the next year. From Dingwall, the older line was followed for 2¼ miles to Fodderty Junction, where the Dingwall & Skye Railway turned sharply towards the hills, to begin its long climb to Raven Rock Summit. The branch kept to the lower ground, and reached its terminus after a further run of 2½ miles. On the opening of the new line the existing station was renamed Achterneed.

On 4 July 1890, powers were obtained to extend the Burghead branch to the fishing village of HOPEMAN, a distance of two miles. The extension diverged from the original branch at a point a little to the south of the terminus. A new station, at the eastern end of the town, was provided to serve Burghead.

The extension was opened on 10 October 1892. On that date the old terminus was closed for passenger traffic, but goods trains continued over the line to serve Burghead pier. About half a mile from Hopeman the railway passed near to the large stone quarries of Cummingston. For some years a station was provided at this point, but it was closed on 1 April 1904.

Some eight miles east of Elgin lies the small town of Fochabers-on-Spey. When the Inverness & Aberdeen Junction Railway was opened to Keith, the second station east from Elgin was named FOCHABERS. This was, however, a decided misnomer, because the town was some four miles distant, along an indirect road.

Five years later, on 8 June 1863, a nominally-independent Company, the Fochabers & Garmouth, obtained an Act for a line from Fochabers station to Garmouth, passing some distance to the west of the town. The scheme was virtually a resuscitation of one of the branches included in the ambitious programme of the Great North of Scotland Railway in 1846. Both the Inverness & Aberdeen Junction and the Inverness & Perth Junction companies were empowered to subscribe towards the construction of the railway, and the former undertook to work it. The necessary capital was not forthcoming, and the powers lapsed before any construction could be undertaken.

When the Great North of Scotland Railway opened its line from Keith to Elgin, *via* the coast, a station named Fochabers was provided on the east bank of the Spey, opposite Garmouth. Here again the name was misleading, as the distance from the town was about four miles, and Fochabers acquired the doubtful distinction of possessing two of the most inconveniently-situated stations in the country.

On 27 June 1892 the Highland Railway obtained powers for a branch, three miles long, from Fochabers station to a point on the west bank of the Spey, about half a mile from the town. The Spey is very wide here, and to avoid a costly bridge, the railway was not carried over the river. The branch was opened on 16 October 1893, on which date the original Fochabers station was renamed Orbliston Junction. To avoid confusion with the GNSR station, the terminus of the new line was renamed Fochabers Town on 1 July 1894. The GNSR station was renamed Spey Bay in 1918.

The peninsula lying between the Beauly and Cromarty Firths is known as the BLACK ISLE. The district boasts much rich farm land, while on the south coast is Fortrose, a thriving fishing centre. Owing to its peculiar geographical position the isle is somewhat isolated, and was not placed on the main railway route to the

(C) *The last Highland Railway engine to remain in regular service was 0—4—4T No 55053, built at Lochgorm Works in 1905 and bearing the odd power classification of 'OP'. She is seen here at Dornoch station in July 1955, two years before her demise with a broken leading axle*

north. The nearest point on the Highland Railway's main line was Muir of Ord, some 13 miles from Fortrose.

To tap this district, and to provide transport for the fishing industry, powers were obtained on 4 July 1890 for a branch line on the south side of the isle, from Muir of Ord to Rosemarkie, a distance of 15¾ miles. On 1 February 1894 the railway was opened as far as Fortrose, but the extension to Rosemarkie was never begun. The journey to Inverness was indirect, but short of a costly bridge over the Beauly Firth at Kessock Ferry, a better route could not be secured.

Strome Ferry, the original western terminus of the Dingwall & Skye Railway, is not an ideal place for a pier. Loch Carron is subject to strong currents and it is frequently difficult to bring a ship alongside. The extension of the railway to KYLE OF LOCHALSH was often suggested, but for many years nothing was done. At length it became clear that Strome Ferry was in danger of losing its monopoly of the traffic to the Isle of Skye and the Outer Hebrides. The West Highland Railway had been authorized in 1889 from a junction with the North British Railway at Craigendoran (24 miles from Glasgow) to Fort William, and there was every possibility that the Company would soon seek powers to extend the line westwards to the Sound of Sleat. The establishment of a new port in this vicinity would have robbed Strome Ferry of much of its trade, as quite apart from the difficult approach to the pier, the railway journey to the south, *via* Inverness, was somewhat roundabout.

On 29 June 1893 the Highland Railway obtained powers to extend the railway from Strome Ferry to Kyle of Lochalsh, and to provide a pier there. The engineering works were heavy, as the line wound in and out along the shore through a series of deep rock cuttings. The site for the station at Kyle had to be blasted out of the solid rock.

The extension was opened on 2 November 1897, on which date the old pier at Strome Ferry was closed, and the ships transferred to Kyle of Lochalsh. Between Strome Ferry and Plockton a private station to serve Duncraig Castle was provided. There were intermediate stations for public traffic at Plockton and Duirinish.

Powers for the West Highland Extension Railway from Fort William to Mallaig had been obtained on 31 July 1894, and the competitive port, situated 22 miles south of Kyle of Lochalsh, was opened in 1901. Although a considerable share of the Hebridean traffic passed into the hands of the North British Railway, the

(D) *Former Caledonian Railway Pickersgill 4—4—0 No 54471 (CR No 932), built by the NB Loco Co in 1916, passes Conon with an Inverness to Tain local in May 1957*

Highland Railway retained the valuable mail contract, as well as the monopoly of traffic destined for Inverness and the north-east of Scotland.

The original line from Inverness to Nairn had provided a station to serve the military post of FORT GEORGE. This was only Fort George in name, as the depot itself was some $3\frac{1}{2}$ miles to the north, at the end of a sandy tongue of land jutting out into the Moray Firth. It was felt that the fort should be made more accessible by rail, and powers were granted on 4 July 1890 for the construction of a branch, $1\frac{1}{2}$ miles long, from the existing Fort George station to the village of Ardersier, which lies some two miles south of the depot proper. The terminus of the new line was to be called Fort George.

The surrounding country is level and sandy, and no difficulties were experienced in the construction of the line, which was opened for traffic on 1 July 1899. The junction station was renamed Gollanfield Junction, from the farm of the same name in the neighbourhood.

As has been mentioned already, the county town of DORNOCH was left some seven miles from the railway, the connection being supplied by a coach which plied to and from the railway station at The Mound. This means of conveyance was inconvenient, and towards the end of the century the desire to obtain better railway communication began to grow in the district.

The Highland Railway was in favour of the scheme, and on 13 August 1898 an order was obtained for a standard-gauge light railway, $7\frac{3}{4}$ miles long, leaving the Highland Railway at The Mound, and following the coach road closely. Although the Highland Railway agreed to work the line, the local Company remained nominally independent until the grouping.

The railway was opened for traffic on 2 June 1902. Although theoretically a light railway, the line was substantially built, and differed but little from the main line. The Board of Trade imposed many restrictions, which resulted in a much heavier expenditure than would otherwise have been necessary. Unlike many light railways, the line was fenced throughout, and gates were provided at the numerous level crossings. But the permanent way was lighter than that on the main line, and the rails were spiked direct to the sleepers.

Although Dornoch was reached from the south by a very circuitous route, the light railway was a great benefit to the town. It was possible to complete the journey without change of carriage, but such facilities were only provided for one summer, some years after the railway was opened (see Chapter 9).

The indirect course adopted by the Sutherland & Caithness Railway between Wick and Helmsdale deprived the coastal villages

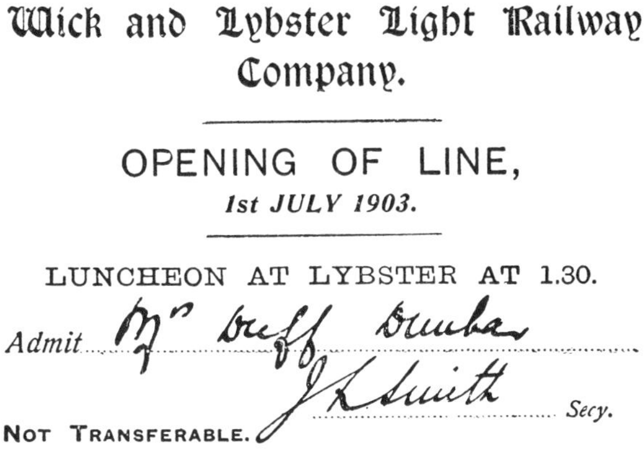

Wick and Lybster Light Railway Company.

OPENING OF LINE,

1st JULY 1903.

LUNCHEON AT LYBSTER AT 1.30.

Admit Mr Duff Dunbar

J L Smith *Secy.*

NOT TRANSFERABLE.

lying to the south of the Caithness fishing port of a railway for many years. With high-speed mechanical road transport still a dream of the future, this was a serious disadvantage to places where inhabitants depended for their livelihood on the quick disposal of such a perishable commodity as fish.

On 27 November 1899 powers were obtained for a light railway, 13¾ miles long, from Wick to LYBSTER. A Treasury grant of £25,000 was obtained, and the remaining capital was subscribed partly by the Highland Railway and partly by local subscription. The chief shareholders were the Caithness County Council and the Duke of Portland, who owned large estates in the neighbourhood. The total capital subscribed was £72,000.

The contractor for building the line was William Kennedy, of Glasgow. No special difficulties were encountered, and the railway was opened on 1 July 1903. The Highland Railway undertook to work the line at cost price. In many respects the undertaking was similar to the Dornoch Light Railway. The rails were spiked direct to the sleepers, the line was fenced throughout, and gates were provided at most of the numerous level crossings.

Although the route to the south was by no means direct, the line was of great service to the district through which it passed, and the fishing industry reaped the benefit, especially at Lybster, where the Duke of Portland spent large sums on improvements to the harbour.

THE EXTENT OF THE SYSTEM

The opening of the Wick & Lybster Light Railway marks the limit of growth of the Highland Railway. In the 18 years following, during which the Company maintained its separate existence, no new lines were opened. The system was now complete, and was made up as follows:

From	To			
Stanley	Inverness station	110	60	via Carr Bridge
Aviemore	Inverness, Rose Street	60	43	via Forres and Inverness Loop
Inverness station	Wick	161	16	
Forres	Keith	30	20	
Dingwall	Kyle of Lochalsh	63	50	
Keith	Portessie	13	71	
Muir of Ord	Fortrose	13	45	
Ballinluig	Aberfeldy	8	59	
Alves	Hopeman	7	37*	
Georgemas	Thurso	6	52	
Orbliston Junction	Fochabers Town	3	00	
Fodderty Junction	Strathpeffer	2	38	
Gollanfield Junction	Fort George	1	38	
Inverness Harbour branch		0	69	
Muirtown Basin branch†		0	58	
Wick & Lybster Light Railway‡		13	44	
Dornoch Light Railway‡		7	51	
Total		506 miles	31 chs	

* Including Burghead Pier Branch, 32 chs.
† Goods traffic only.
‡ Nominally independent lines worked by the Highland until Grouping.
Invergarry & Fort Augustus Railway, worked by the Highland from July 1903 to April 1907—24 mls 16 chs.

BRIDGES

(13)   *The beautiful bridge over the River Garry at Struan also spans the road to Rannoch, which is itself carried over the river at the same point. The siting of the Garry bridge was determined by the prohibition of crossing the river at any other point within the parks of Blair Castle. The bridge cost £5,100, or £18 12s 3d per lineal foot.*

(14)   *Joseph Mitchell believed that the arches of the bridge over the River Conon in Ross-shire were the largest spans of any skew bridge at that time. It crosses the river at an angle of 45 degrees to the stream, the five 73ft span arches being at right angles from pier to pier.*

SNOW SCENES

(15)   *Train snowed up at Ardullie (Dingwall), December* 1906.

(16)   *Snow-plough at Achterneed, December* 1906.

(17)   *Deep drifting at Fairy Hillocks (Altnabreac), January* 1895.

CHAPTER 6

The Invergarry & Fort Augustus Railway

In some remote, prehistoric age, a great earth-movement took place in what is now the North of Scotland, and the land was split by an immense rift running across the country from north-east to south-west. Subsequently, there was formed in this hollow a chain of lochs whence rivers flowed to the North Sea or the Atlantic.

Coming to historical times, we find at the north end of the rift the Highland capital, Inverness, and at the other, the one-time military post of Fort William. The rift, or Great Glen, as it is usually called, has always been a natural highway across the country.

Early in the 19th century, the chain of lochs was connected by means of canals to afford a waterway for the passage of ships. Unfortunately, the shallowness of the canals and the cramped dimensions of the locks imposed drastic limitations on the size of the ships passing through, and the undertaking never justified the enormous expense of its construction. The canal is still used by trawlers passing between the east and west coast fishing grounds, but regular passenger services have been withdrawn.

For many years the water and roadways through the glen remained unchallenged by the railway. At length, when a line was suggested, the proposal came not, as might have been expected, from the Highland Railway, but from the North British Railway, the bulk of whose system was in the densely-populated industrial area of the Lowlands. To understand how this Company came to penetrate into a district so far removed from the scene of its main activities, it is necessary to consider briefly certain aspects of its early history and development.

In 1842, railway communication was established between Edinburgh and Glasgow. Sixteen years later, a separate company made an extension along the north bank of the Clyde to Helensburgh, some 25 miles from the city. The Helensburgh Railway was ab-

sorbed by its larger neighbour in 1862. Four years later the Edinburgh & Glasgow and North British Railways were amalgamated.
North of the Firth of Clyde the country becomes wild and mountainous, and many years elapsed before an attempt was made to
carry a railway through this district.

In 1884, an independent company, under the title of the Glasgow
& North Western Railway, was formed to build a line from the
North British Railway at Maryhill (in the northern suburbs of
Glasgow), through Strathblane and Drymen, to the eastern side of
Loch Lomond. From the head of the loch, the railway was to pass
through Crianlarich and Tyndrum, and thence by way of Rannoch
Moor and the Pass of Glencoe to Loch Leven. That loch was to be
crossed at its narrowest point, near Ballachulish, and the line then
followed the coast, through Onich, to Fort William. It was also
proposed to extend the railway through the Great Glen to Inverness,
to join the Highland Railway. The total length of the undertaking
was about 155 miles, and the distance from Glasgow to Inverness
would have been about 160 miles. The distance by the Caledonian
and Highland Railway was 207 miles.

Although the Company was nominally independent, it was
backed by the North British. The Highland Railway realised that
not only was it in danger of losing traffic, but it would also have
to lower charges. Even had the threatened competition been countered by the shortened main line from Aviemore, the Highland
Railway would still have been at a disadvantage by some 20 miles.

When the bill came before Parliament, the Highland Railway
submitted that there was only traffic in paying quantities for one
railway to the Northern Highlands. If the new route was constructed, it would lose valuable revenue, and this loss would prove
an effectual barrier to further extensions of its own system in other
directions. This argument was convincing enough to secure the
rejection of the proposed new line, for the time being.

Some three years later the project was revived, under the title of
the West Highland Railway, for a line from the North British Railway at Helensburgh to Fort William, via Loch Lomond, Rannoch
Moor, and Spean Bridge. The branch through the Great Glen to
Inverness was not included. The NBR was to work the line. For the
moment there was no threat to Inverness, but the Highland opposed
the bill. This time its efforts were unavailing, and the Act was
passed in 1889. The railway was opened in 1894.

In 1893 two schemes were put forward for the connecting link
to Inverness. The first was proposed by the Highland Railway,

which naturally desired to control any line in the Great Glen. No sooner was this project in the field than a rival appeared, promoted by the West Highland Railway. After a great deal of argument, the two companies agreed to abandon the idea and the bills were withdrawn.

Two years later the West Highland and North British Railways brought forward a bill to extend the railway from Fort William to Mallaig, on the Sound of Sleat, a distance of 41 miles. The Highland Railway opposed the measure, because it would deflect the traffic from Strome Ferry, and the recently-sanctioned extension to Kyle of Lochalsh. Ultimately it was induced to withdraw its objection, and the bill passed. The West Highland and the North British Railways agreed not to promote directly, or indirectly, any railway through the Great Glen for at least ten years. The Highland Railway received £500 for its Parliamentary expenses.

A short time later, a local company, under the title of the Invergarry & Fort Augustus Railway, was floated to build a railway from Spean Bridge, on the West Highland Railway, to Fort Augustus, at the south end of Loch Ness, a distance of 24 miles. This proposal left a gap of about 30 miles between Fort Augustus and Inverness. After much opposition, the Act for the line was passed on 14 August 1896.

It soon became evident that both the Highland and the North British companies considered that the authorisation of the railway from Spean Bridge to Fort Augustus had cancelled the agreement of 1895, for in 1897 three schemes were launched for the connecting link between Fort Augustus and Inverness. The first was for an extension of the Invergarry Company's line, and the other two were put forward by the West Highland and the Highland Railways respectively. These latter sought to obtain running powers over the already-sanctioned portion of the Invergarry Railway. A fierce Parliamentary contest ensued. The Highland was anxious, at all costs, to keep its rivals out of Inverness; and the West Highland and North British Railways were desirous of keeping Fort William a close preserve. After a great deal of costly litigation, the preamble to the Highland Railway's bill was proved by the Commons, but the measure was thrown out by the Lords.

THE ISOLATED BRANCH

The local Company was therefore left to go ahead with the line from Spean Bridge to Fort Augustus. The works were completed towards the end of 1901, but then a fresh trouble arose. The construction of the line had been very costly. The number of culverts required to carry off mountain streams was enormous, and the earth works were heavy. The Company exhausted its funds in bulding the track, and had no money left for the purchase of rolling stock.

As the railway made physical connection with the West Highland at Spean Bridge, the North British was approached with a view to working the line. That Company declared itself willing to do so at cost price—a good offer, considering that traffic would be light. However, the directors of the Invergarry Company demanded a guarantee of personal indemnity. When this was refused, they offered their railway to the Highland.

This action aroused a fresh Parliamentary storm, every whit as fierce as that which had raged in·1897. Both the Highland and the North British were anxious to obtain control of the Invergarry line to the exclusion of the other. The result was that the opening of the line was delayed for some months. Finally, under the Act of 30 June 1903, the Highland Railway was empowered to enter into an agreement to work the line for an annual payment of £4,000. At the same time it gave the North British a guarantee that it would never try to penetrate nearer to Fort William. The latter Company gave a similar promise with regard to Inverness. These undertakings practically destroyed all hope of the connecting link from Fort Augustus to Inverness being built. The railway was opened on 22 July.

Under the agreement of 1903, the Highland Railway was to work the line for ten years, with the option of renewal. But traffic did not come up to expectations, and the line was entirely separated from the rest of its system. On 1 May 1907 it withdrew in favour of the North British, which worked the railway for the next four years. At length, on 31 October 1911, the services were completely suspended, at the instigation of the local Company. After remaining closed for almost two years, the line was reopened on 1 August 1913, and again worked by the North British Railway, which in the ensuing year purchased the undertaking for £27,000.

Originally, the railway extended about three-quarters of a mile beyond Fort Augustus village to a pier on Loch Ness, at which steamers called. This extension included a hand-operated swing-bridge over the Caledonian Canal, and a viaduct over the River Oich. Until 1906 certain trains ran forward to the pier, during the summer only, but from 1 October of that year the service was suspended, and the line fell into decay. But some goods traffic continued until July 1924 after which most of the rails were removed, and the swing-bridge was kept permanently open for the passage of ships. The station buildings at the pier were demolished, and the boats ceased to call.

In 1905, while still working the Invergarry Railway, the Highland Railway applied for powers to own and operate steamships on Loch Ness. It was proposed that these ships should run in connection with the trains, and supplement the existing service on the canal between Fort Augustus and Inverness.

The bill was strongly and successfully opposed by David MacBrayne, whose steamers held a monopoly on the northern part of the canal. Objections were also raised by the Invergarry Railway, which maintained that the establishment of such a steamer service would effectually enable the Highland Railway to block any attempt to complete the railway through the Great Glen.

Eventually, disaster once more overtook this waif of the railway world. Merged into the London & North Eastern Railway under the Railways Act of 1921, the line was worked by that Company for several years. At length traffic fell to such an extent that it was decided to suspend the passenger services from 1 December 1933. Arrangements were made for passengers and light goods traffic to be carried by road, but one coal train was scheduled on Saturdays. After the end of the second world war, this occasional use of the railway was no longer justified. All traffic closed from 1 January 1947, and the dismantling of the track followed.

Such is the chequered and stormy history of this little railway, a history that is probably without parallel in railway annals. It is greatly to be deplored that saner counsels did not prevail in 1897, which might have led to the railway being completed to Inverness, and placed in the hands of a joint committee. Admittedly, the Highland Railway would have had to lower its rates to Inverness, but the new route would, doubtless, have brought additional traffic to other parts of the system. The prospects of the Invergarry Company would have been far brighter, and the line might well have become a paying concern, instead of a dead loss to its promoters.

CHAPTER 7

Some Schemes That Failed

ULLAPOOL AND GAIRLOCH

Despite a sparse population, and relatively limited resources, the Highlands of Scotland have received their full share of attention from the railway promoter, and in addition to the existing lines a number of schemes have been mooted which have failed to materialise. Most belong to the decade between 1890 and 1900, although some of them come within the present century. Many of the proposed railways, although nominally independent, were backed by the Great North of Scotland Railway, in its attempts to secure an entry into Inverness. On the other hand, some were put forward, without the spur of competition, by the Highland Railway, or by an independent company.

The coasts of Wester Ross and Sutherland, although boasting no big towns, have in addition to Kyle of Lochalsh some harbours which might be developed as centres for the fishing industry. There are also certain other places that enjoy considerable favour as tourist resorts in the summer months. Chief among these is Ullapool, situated on sheltered Loch Broom. Established in 1788 by the British Fishery Society, as a base for the west coast herring fishery, the village decayed with the decline of its industry. For many years there was a hope that it would be adopted as a naval base, for which its land-locked harbour is well adapted. There was also the possibility that the fishing would revive, given adequate means of transport to the markets of the south.

Ullapool is the nearest port on the mainland for the Isle of Lewis. Indeed, at one time a steamer plied regularly to Stornoway. A direct road connects Loch Broom with Garve, on the Dingwall & Skye Railway, 32 miles distant.

With the possibility of securing a great increase of trade, it was deemed feasible, about the year 1890, to construct a railway to the village, and on 14 August of that year the Garve & Ullapool Railway was authorised. It was arranged that the Highland Railway should work the line, which would virtually become part of that system. The Company was unable to raise the necessary capital, and the scheme was shelved.

Two years later the Great North of Scotland Railway sought to obtain running powers over the Highland Railway from Elgin to Garve, and to work the Ullapool Railway. The Highland secured the defeat of this scheme, but no further progress was made with the original proposal, and the powers of the Company ultimately lapsed.

At Achnasheen, some distance west of Garve, there is another road from the railway to the west coast, serving the districts of Gairloch, Poolewe and Aultbea. In 1893, a railway, some 35 miles long, was proposed from Achnasheen to Aultbea. Once again, the Great North was behind the bill, and proposed to work the line, and secure running powers over the Highland Railway from Elgin to Achnasheen. The bill was presented and rejected in the 1893 session of Parliament.

In 1897 the Highland Railway came forward with a big programme for new lines, totalling 247 miles in all. The Ullapool and Gairloch schemes were revived, and two additional routes to the west coast were proposed. The first of these left the main line at Culrain, 60 miles north of Inverness, and keeping to the south bank of the River Oykell, ran by way of Rosehall and Oykell Bridge to the head waters of the river. Passing over the hills to Aultnacaelgach the Kirkaig River was followed to the west coast, whence the railway turned northwards to terminate at Lochinver, a total distance of 41 miles from Culrain.

Lochinver, with its fine land-locked bay, forms a good harbour, convenient for the Outer Hebrides. There were hopes that with the coming of the railway a port of call for ships serving the islands would be established. As is the case with Ullapool and Gairloch, the district is rich in natural beauty and the trout-fishing is good.

The second route to the west left the main line at Lairg, and went by way of Loch Shin and Loch More to the coast at Loch Laxford, a distance of 42 miles. In common with all the other proposed lines, it suffered from the disadvantage of crossing a tract of country that, for the most part, consists of barren moorland, sparsely inhabited and unproductive, where local traffic would have been of the scantiest.

Despite great efforts by the local landowners, neither of these schemes ever came to fruition. It is difficult to see what hopes the promoters had of securing an adequate return for their money.

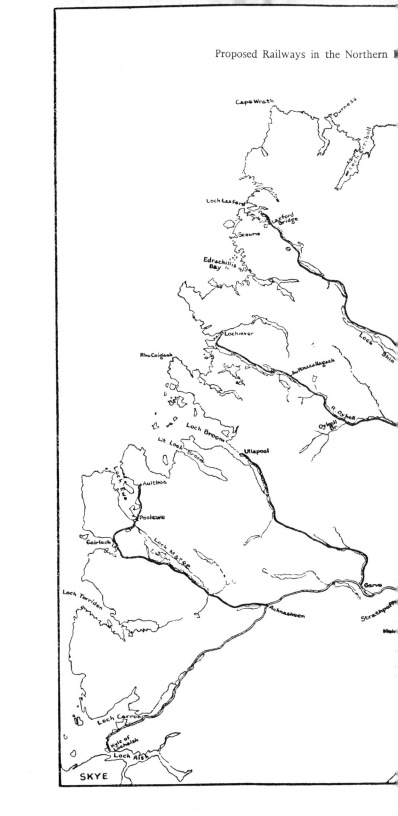

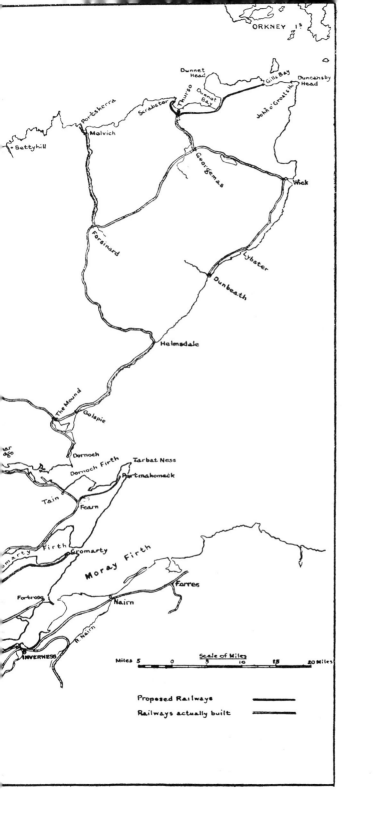

ORKNEY I^s

Dunnet
Head

Gills Bay

Duncansby
Head

Thurso

Dunnet
Bay

John o'Groats Ho.

Scrabster

Portskerra

Malvich

Bettyhill

Georgemas

Wick

Forsinard

Lybster

Dunbeath

Helmsdale

The Mound

Golspie

Dornoch

Tarbat Ness

Dornoch Firth

Portmahomack

Tain

Fearn

omarty Firth

Cromarty

Moray Firth

Forres

Fortrose

Nairn

R. Nairn

INVERNESS

Miles 5   0   Scale of Miles   5   10   15   20 Miles

Proposed Railways ——————

Railways actually built ══════

True, the west coast attracts a large number of tourists and, doubt-less, the railway would have increased this traffic. Beyond this, however, the source of revenue would have been meagre, although it is possible that a new fishing port might have been established at some point along the coast.

NORTH AND EAST COASTS

In addition to the routes to the west coast, there were proposals for new railways in the north of Sutherland and Caithness. In 1896 the Duke of Sutherland and certain other landowners formed them-selves into a company for the construction of a standard-gauge light railway from Forsinard Station, on the Highland Railway's northern main line, down Strath Halladale to Melvich and Port Skerra, a distance of about 14 miles. A pier was to be built at the northern terminus at which coasting steamers were to call.

Powers for the construction of the railway were obtained under the Forsinard Melvich & Port Skerra Light Railway Order of 13 July 1898. Certain materials and plant for the construction of the line were taken to Forsinard station by the Highland Railway, which was to have built and worked the line, but construction was not started and powers for the line ultimately lapsed.

The Highland Railway also proposed to extend its Thurso branch along the coast for 17 miles to Dunnet and Gills Bay. Further to the south, there was to be a light railway from Wick to Lybster (13 miles), with a possible extension of seven miles, to Dunbeath, to link up several fishing villages with the main line. The light railway from The Mound to Dornoch was also included in this programme. The line from Thurso to Gills Bay never materialized, but, as has been seen, the Lybster and Dornoch lines were built. The suggested extension from Lybster to Dunbeath was ultimately abandoned.

Certain outlying parts of Easter Ross were to be connected with the Highland Railway by means of light railways. One proposal was for a line from Fearn (near Tain) to Portmahomack on the southern shore of the Dornoch Firth, a distance of nine miles. A great deal of discussion took place as to whether the railway should come right into Tain or not, with the result that no definite steps were taken for many years. Ultimately the scheme fell into abeyance.

By far the most interesting of the proposed lines is the light rail-way that was to have connected the town of Cromarty with the main line. Cromarty is situated on the north coast of the Black Isle, on the shores of the firth of the same name. A railway had already been built from Muir of Ord to Fortrose, but the line served the southern coast of the Isle, leaving the northern portion somewhat off the beaten track. It was to remedy this that the light railway was proposed in 1897.

The original scheme was for a line from Cromarty to Dingwall, the county town. The Conon River was to be crossed at Alcaig Ferry, by a bridge of considerable size. A fierce discussion raged for a long time amongst those interested as to whether the proposed route was the best. It was felt in certain quarters that the railway should not include the expensive bridge at Alcaig, but should join the Highland Railway at Conon, to the south of Dingwall. Equally strong was the opinion that the line would be at a disadvantage if this route were adopted, and that the terminus should be at the county town.

The Light Railway Commission refused all assistance if the direct route to Dingwall was adopted, since it considered the bridge at Alcaig unnecessary. Ultimately, the Conon route was adopted. A further delay occurred at once while the promoters were trying to come to terms with the Highland Railway, so that the trains could run forward from Conon to Dingwall. This matter was still undecided when the Order was obtained on 1 August 1902.

Some time elapsed before construction was begun. Eventually a start was made, not, as might have been expected, from the junction at Conon, but from Cromarty. Considerable difficulty in the acquisition of certain lands led to this plan being adopted. Progress was by no means rapid, and Extension of Time Orders were obtained on 4 November 1907 and 7 April 1910. By 1914 the track had been laid for about six miles, at the side of the main road from Cromarty, and the works, including a substantial bridge at Cullicudden Farm, were well in hand for a further two miles. The remaining 11 miles had not been started.

On the outbreak of the first world war, all work was suspended, and about a year later the track was taken up and used elsewhere. Subsequently, nothing was done towards reinstating or completing the line, and the works lay derelict. The course of the abandoned cuttings and embankments remained clearly to be seen. In addition to the bridge at Cullicudden, which was built in concrete, several other smaller bridges and culverts had been constructed, but no permanent buildings had been erected. It is strange that the line should have been allowed to lie derelict in this way after so much money had been spent, particularly as the district served is far richer than is the case with most of the other lines previously mentioned.

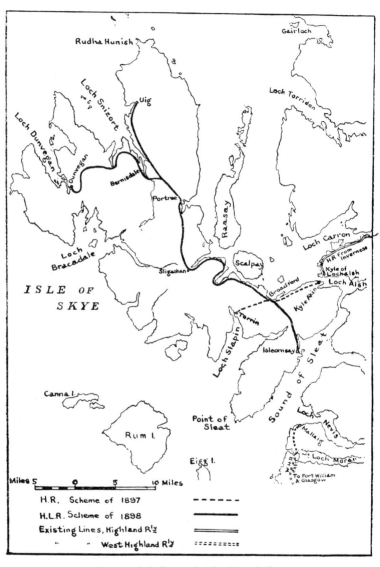

Proposed Railways in the Isle of Skye

SKYE AND LEWIS

The remainder of the Highland Railway's programme for 1897 comprised proposals for light railways in the islands of Skye and Lewis. For some years there had been much vague talk of providing the larger Hebridean Islands with railway facilities, but the proposals had never taken concrete shape. At length, the approaching completion of the railway from Strome Ferry to Kyle of Lochalsh led the various landowners to come to the Highland Railway with definite schemes.

On the Isle of Skye, one terminus of the proposed railway was to be at Kyle Akin, situated immediately opposite to the new pier at Kyle of Lochalsh, and separated from the mainland by a narrow strait, less than half a mile wide. Thence the line was to run by way of Broadford to Torrin, on Loch Slapin, on the west coast. The total length of the railway was 14½ miles.

In Lewis, the railway was to run from Stornoway, the chief town, westwards to Breasclet, and thence slightly north to Carloway, on the west coast, a distance of 21 miles.

Early in 1897 a party of Highland Railway officers crossed over to both islands, and went over the ground with the local landowners. In each case it was proposed to obtain an order under the Light Railways Act, and to apply for a Government grant. The Highland Railway was asked to subscribe a certain amount of the capital, and to build and work the lines. The remainder of the money was to be raised by local subscription. After a lengthy discussion the Highland directors decided not to proceed further with the scheme, as in their opinion there was not enough traffic for the railways to pay. Both schemes fell into abeyance.

In the following year a London syndicate, known as the Hebridean Light Railway Company, was formed. The support of the North British Railway was sought, as that Company was to work the West Highland Extension Railway, from Fort William to Mallaig, at that time under construction. A fresh terminus was selected in Skye, at Isle Ornsay, on the Sound of Sleat, whence it is an easy crossing of about ten miles to Mallaig.

Surveys were made for a railway from Isle Ornsay through Broadford and Sligachan to Portree, whence the line crossed the island to terminate at Uig, on Loch Snizort, where there is a large fish-curing station. A branch of the railway was to run from Portree to Bernisdale and Dunvegan.

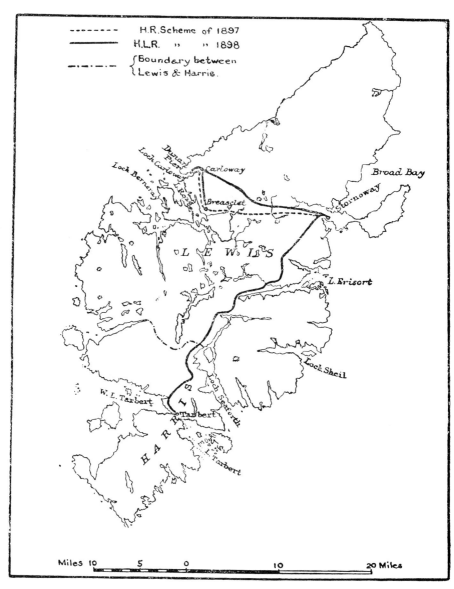

Proposed Railways in the Isle of Lewis

In Lewis it was proposed to build a railway from Stornoway to Tarbert (Harris), and from Stornoway to Carloway and Dunan Pier (on Loch Carloway), with a branch to Breasclet. The total length of these proposals was about 130 miles, of which rather more than one-half was in Skye.

On 23 April 1898 the Company gave notice that it proposed to make application under the Light Railways Act for powers to construct all of the above lines, except that from Stornoway to Tarbert. The gauge of the railways was to be 3 ft 6 in., and the estimated cost was £500,000. It was proposed to apply for a grant of £150,000, and for a loan of £60,000, from the Government. The remainder of the capital was to be raised by subscription.

In the Hebrides the proposals met with a very mixed reception. In certain quarters they were hailed as the salvation of the islands. On the other hand, grave doubts were expressed as to whether the crofters were in a position to carry the burden of the increased rates that would have had to be imposed. Many people, while admitting the usefulness of the railways, were convinced that they could never pay. Dissatisfaction was expressed because the lines in Skye did not run to Kyle Akin, to link up with the Highland Railway. It was feared that the coasting steamers would cease to run after the railways had been built, and leave some places entirely without transport facilities. Finally, a certain section maintained that the steamers were providing adequate facilities, and that the railways were not required.

The upshot was that the necessary capital was not forthcoming, and in the long run this was just as well. It is highly improbable that the lines would ever have repaid the cost of construction. In addition, the schemes of 1898 were under the tutelage of the North British Railway, and any attempt to carry them out would have led to the most determined opposition on the part of the Highland Railway, and the west coast shipping interests. Such a contest might easily have resulted in the unhappy history of the Invergarry & Fort Augustus Railway being repeated in the Hebrides.

LOCH NESS AND STANLEY—DUNDEE

In 1897 a company was floated to build a light railway from Inverness to the head of Loch Ness, a distance of about eight miles. It was proposed that the new line should branch from the Highland Railway, a short distance west of Inverness station, cross the Caledonian Canal by a swing-bridge, and run by way of Dunain to

Lochend. Although there was to be a junction with the Highland Railway, no arrangements had been made either for that Company to work the line, or for the trains to enter Inverness station. It was hoped, however, that running powers would be granted.

The promoters applied for an order under the Light Railways Act, and the Commissioners heard the case on 23 May 1899. It was urged for the Company that besides benefiting the district through which it would pass, the line would improve communications to Fort Augustus and Fort William. The chief opposition came from the Invergarry & Fort Augustus Railway, which claimed that the railway was only a block line, and would prevent the completion of its undertaking to Inverness. This opposition, and the fact that no settlement had been reached about the use of Inverness station, brought about the rejection of the scheme. The idea was never revived.

From time to time the possibility of building a direct railway from Dundee to the Highland Railway at Stanley Junction had been discussed, but no definite steps had ever resulted. In 1901, however, a route was surveyed. It was proposed to use the Caledonian station at Dundee, whence the line passed to the west, through the village of Balbeggie, to Stanley, a distance of about 15 miles. This represented a saving of some 12 miles over the route via Perth.

Early in 1902 a meeting was held in Dundee to discuss the proposal. Although the Highland Railway was represented, the Company made no definite promises, beyond agreeing to give the question of working the line full consideration at the appropriate time. It was, however, agreed that the promoters should go ahead with the scheme, and gain as much support as possible. The plans were given a great deal of publicity in the press, certain journals waxing enthusiastic over the possibilities of the new line, both as regards the desirability of a much shortened route to the Highlands, and the opening up of a new district hitherto untouched by railways. But the eulogies were the only support that the promoters ever received. Financial assistance was conspicuous by its absence, and the scheme was dropped.

1918 AND AFTERWARDS

In February 1918 a committee was appointed by the Secretary of State for Scotland to consider and report on the rural areas of the country that were in most need of improved transport for the

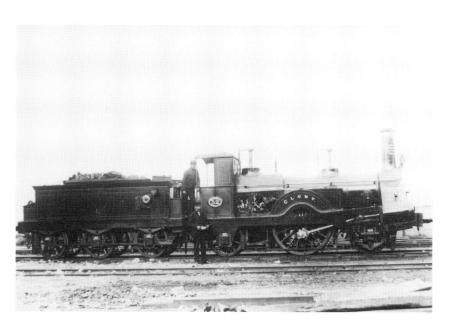

LOCOMOTIVES

(18) *'Glenbarry' class 2—2—2 No 32* Cluny, *originally* Sutherland, *was the only one of eighteen engines not to be rebuilt as a 2—4—0, surviving as the last Highland Single tender locomotive until September 1898.*

(19) *A 'Glenbarry' class 2—2—2 as rebuilt by Jones in September 1874 as a 2—4—0. Built in 1864 by Neilson & Co, No 55 bore the names* Cluny *and* Sutherland *before being dubbed* Invergordon *in 1884.*

LOCOMOTIVES

(20) '*Duke*' *class* 4—4—0 *No* 65 Nairnshire *stands by Inverness shed. The ten engines of this class were David Jones's first new design, and when introduced in 1874 were the most powerful locomotives in Britain. No 65 was withdrawn in January 1909.*

(21) *Jones's 'Big Goods' was the first* 4—6—0 *design to run on a British railway, all fifteen locomotives being built in 1894. The penultimate member of the class, No 114, is seen here passing Luncarty with a northbound goods. When these engines were built, the HR was again able to claim the most powerful as well as the heaviest locomotive in Britain.*

promotion of local industries. The committee considered not only schemes for extending and improving the railway system, but also went into the question of new roads and additional steamer services. As the result of its deliberations a number of proposals affecting the territory of the Highland Railway were made. Many of them were, however, only resuscitations of the Highland Railway's programme of 1897.

The schemes for railways to Lochinver, Ullapool, Gills Bay and Portmahomack were revived, as was the proposal to extend the Wick & Lybster Light Railway to Dunbeath. It was also proposed to relay and complete the Cromarty Railway. An entirely new proposal was for the extension of the Thurso branch to Scrabster harbour, a distance of two miles. The need for bridging this awkward gap in the short sea route to the Orkneys had become more than ever apparent with the outbreak of the first world war, when a constant stream of special heavy traffic began to pass to and from the naval base at Scapa Flow. The committee also considered the possibility of constructing a narrow-gauge light railway, primarily intended for the carriage of timber, from Beauly to Invercannich, and of linking up the Highland and West Highland Railways by means of a new cross-country line from Newtonmore to Tulloch. The latter was by no means a new proposal. As far back as 1861, a preliminary survey had been made for a railway from Kingussie to Fort William by virtually the same route. Although the scheme proved abortive, it undoubtedly hastened the promotion of the Dingwall & Skye Railway.

The committee issued its report before the war had ended. After the cessation of hostilities it was not deemed advisable to embark on the construction of any new railways, although many of the committee's suggestions for new roads were subsequently carried out.

Although many attempts have been made to open up the more distant parts of the Scottish Highlands by means of railways, adverse economic conditions have proved an insurmountable barrier. Even while the horse still reigned supreme on the roads, it had become obvious that neither the Highland Railway nor an independent company could undertake the construction of railways in those thinly-populated and largely unproductive districts unless a very generous measure of state aid was guaranteed. And that is a step which the Treasury has never felt justified in taking.

CHAPTER 8

Attacks from the East

KEITH AND ELGIN

The disputes and friction with the Great North of Scotland Railway which characterized the early history of the Highland Railway were destined to continue and play a prominent part in the course of subsequent events. Relations between the two Companies continued strained; and the position was made much worse when the Highland secured its own route to the south. At a comparatively early date steps were taken to extend the Great North from Keith to Elgin, but many years elapsed ere that Company began to cast covetous eyes on Inverness.

On 27 July 1857 an independent company, the Keith & Dufftown, obtained its Act for a railway between those two towns. The Great North contributed towards the building of the line, which was opened on 12 February 1862, and arranged to work it. The GNSR also helped to build, and worked, the Strathspey Railway, authorised 17 May 1861, from Dufftown to Nethy Bridge, and opened on 1 July 1863. A continuation of the railway beyond Nethy Bridge, authorised on 5 July 1865, and opened on 1 August 1866, joined the Highland Railway at Boat of Garten.

At Craigellachie, four miles from Dufftown, the Strathspey Railway joined the Morayshire Railway, whose history has already been noted. By means of these local lines the Great North gained an entry into Elgin on 1 July 1863. The distance from Keith to Elgin, via Craigellachie, was 27½ miles, as against 18 by the Highland Railway's route.

The Great North's alternative route, via the coast, was made much later, although the first portion, from Grange to Portsoy, was authorised under the Banffshire Railway Act of 27 June 1857, and opened on 2 August 1859. An extension from Portsoy to Buckie, authorised on 21 July 1863, was abandoned by the Act of 12 July 1867. One year previously (30 July 1866) the Banffshire Railway had been amalgamated with the Great North.

It was not until 12 July 1882 that powers were obtained for the railway from Portsoy to Elgin.[1] This extension was bitterly opposed by the Highland, which succeeded in obtaining running powers between Buckie and Portsoy (11½ miles). In return for this facility, the Great North secured running powers over the Highland Railway

[1] The Highland Railway branch from Keith to Portessie was authorised on the same day.

HIGHLAND RAILWAY COMPANY.

W. ⟨illegible⟩

STAFF NOTICE.

Office of Superintendent of Line,
INVERNESS, 18th December 1884.

KEITH STATION.

The following are the working arrangements for the above :—

SIGNALS WROUGHT FROM INTERLOCKING CABIN.

1. The Down Distant Signal for Main Line, situated on right side of Line, 1150 yards west of Cabin.

2. The Down Home Signal for Main Line, situated on same side, 150 yards west of Cabin.

3. The Distant Signal from Buckie Section, situated on left side of Line, 1150 yards west of Cabin.

4. The Home Signal from Buckie Section, situated on left side of Line, 150 yards west of Cabin.

5. The Signal for Trains from Keith for Mulben and Buckie is situated on left side of Line, 160 yards east of Cabin. (The top arm on Post controls Trains from Keith to Mulben, the middle arm controls Trains to Buckie Section, and the lower arm controls Trains from Goods Yard.)

6. The Signal to admit Up Trains from "Loop" Line to Main for Mulben is situated on left hand side, 54 yards west of Signal Cabin.

7. The Signal to admit from New Siding at back of Engine Shed to Up Main is situated at the Fouling Point thereof.

SIGNALS NOT WROUGHT FROM INTERLOCKING CABIN.

To admit to Passenger Station.—The Single Disc immediately west of Passenger Arcade.

For Exchange Trains between Highland and Great North of Scotland Companies.—Two single armed Semaphore Signals immediately west of Passenger Arcade.

The Exchange Signal admitting from Great North to Highland is interlocked with Signal Cabin, but under charge of Station-Master.

POINTS.

1. The Down Main Line Facing Points, situated 150 yards west of Cabin.

2. The Buckie Section Facing Points, situated 150 yards west of Cabin.

3. The Facing Points from Keith for Up Main Line, or for Buckie Section, situated 46 yards east of Cabin.

4. The Trailing Points from Buckie Section, situated 46 yards east of Cabin.

5. The Siding Points from Goods Yard for Up Main Line, or Buckie Section, situated 160 yards east of Cabin, and which are controlled by the lower arm on the Three Armed Signal Post, close by them.

6. The Cross-over Points from Up to Down Main Line, or vice versa, situated 166 yards east of Cabin.

7. The Points from Up Main Line to new Siding at back of Engine Shed, and which are controlled by a small Siding Signal at Fouling Point.

ENGINE WHISTLES.

From Passenger Station for Main Line, and from Main Line for Passenger Station	1 Whistle.
From Passenger Station for Buckie Line, and from Buckie Line for Passenger Station	2 Whistles.
From Goods Yard for Main Line, and from Main Line for Goods Yard	3 do.
From Goods Yard for Buckie Line, and from Buckie Line for Goods Yard	4 do.
Exchange Trains between Highland and Great North of Scotland Companies	5 do.

Bell Communication between the Passenger Station and Interlocking Signal Cabin.

The Bell Beats for the respective Trains to be the same in all cases as the Engine Whistles ; and must *in every instance be acknowledged by repetition.*

N.B.—The starting of *all* Trains—that is to say, both from Passenger and Goods Department—*is solely under the charge of the Passenger Station Master.*

Guards of all Trains from Goods Yard must intimate personally to the Passenger Station-Master when their Train is ready to start.

To come into operation on Monday, the 22nd current.

This cancels all previous notices with respect to the foregoing.

Please acknowledge receipt.

By order.

THOMAS ROBERTSON,
Superintendent of Line

between Elgin and Forres (12¼ miles). It was, however, laid down that neither Company should exercise its powers if the other refrained from so doing. Since the Highland never attempted to run to Portsoy, the powers of the Great North were completely useless. The extension was opened in sections : from Portsoy to Tochieneal on 1 April 1884; from Elgin to Garmouth on 12 August of the same year; and from Tochieneal to Garmouth on 3 May 1886.

For many years all traffic between the Highland and the Great North of Scotland Railways was exchanged at Keith, and no attempt was made to provide connections at Elgin. In 1880, however, William Moffatt was appointed general manager at Aberdeen, and a vigorous policy of improvement and expansion was at once instituted. Previously the Great North had never attempted to run any expresses, but it was not long before some quite creditable trains were provided between Aberdeen and Elgin, and representations were made to the Highland Railway with a view to expediting the service between Elgin and Inverness.

The Great North desired the exchange of traffic to take place at Elgin, so that it could secure the greater mileage, but the Highland opposed any alteration. For the time being, open warfare was avoided by means of 'Facility Clauses' in certain Acts, which still left Keith as the chief point of exchange, but the directors of the Great North were by no means satisfied, and determined to seek independent access to Inverness.

In 1884 a company was floated, under the title of the Strathspey, Strathdon & Deeside Junction Railway, to build a line from Ballater, the terminus of the Great North's Deeside branch, to Nethy Bridge, on that Company's Strathspey line. The route passed over the hills to Cock Bridge, in Strathdon, and thence through the village of Tomintoul, a distance of about 30 miles. The Great North supported the proposal, and at the same time came forward with a scheme for a line from Nethy Bridge to Inverness, via Carr Bridge. The distance from Aberdeen to Inverness by this route would have been about 115 miles. As has been seen, the Highland countered this proposal with a bill for its direct line from Aviemore to Inverness, which was successful. Both the schemes backed by the Great North were thrown out.

The opening of the railway from Portsoy to Elgin brought the question of the exchange of traffic at the latter town to a head The new line served a number of prosperous fishing towns on the Banffshire coast, and it was desired to run through trains from Aberdeen to Inverness by this route. In the opinion of the Great

North, the Highland would not offer sufficient facilities for exchanging the traffic at Elgin. In 1886, after much argument, the two companies entered into a seven-years agreement with regard to the through traffic, but this was by no means a success.

The dispute dragged on for years, and as frequently happens in this type of contest, it was the customers of the two railways who suffered the most. To them the outward signs of the struggle were a lamentable lack of facilities, both for passengers and goods, which frequently resulted in vexatious and costly delays. Both sides were high-handed and uncompromising. Added to this was the determination of the Great North to reach Inverness with its own trains.

The Great North was not satisfied with the traffic agreement, and in 1890 it applied for powers to build its own line from Elgin to Inverness. The proposed route ran more or less parallel to the existing Highland Railway, which was to be crossed in several places. A branch from Elgin to Burghead was included in the proposals, as were also running powers over the Highland Railway from Inverness to Muir of Ord, whence a branch was to run to Fortrose. The Highland was able to bring sufficient opposition to secure the defeat of all these schemes, but immediately afterwards obtained powers for the Black Isle branch and the extension from Burghead to Hopeman.

Foiled in its direct attempts to reach Inverness by means of an independent line, the Great North next tried to secure running powers over the Highland Railway from Elgin to Inverness. As has been noted already, it came forward in 1892 behind the revival of the Garve & Ullapool Railway, and again in the following year in support of the Achnasheen, Gairloch and Aultbea scheme. (See Chapter 7). In both cases the Great North proposed to reach the new lines by means of running powers from Elgin. These powers would, of course, have included access to Inverness. Both schemes were defeated.

In 1893 the seven-year agreement with regard to the through traffic came to an end. The Highland at once made certain alterations in the through trains, alleging that there was not enough traffic for them to omit all the local stations between Inverness and Elgin. The Great North maintained that the Highland was not justified in making these changes. An appeal to the Railway Commissioners resulted in the drawing-up of a timetable, which was supposed to get rid of the difficulties, but the Great North was by no means satisfied.

In 1895 it applied for running powers over the Highland track from Elgin to Inverness. In the course of the evidence an interesting piece of railway history came to light, which might have had an important bearing on the case, but it was ruled out of court. It will be remembered that the original Great North of Scotland Railway Act of 1846 authorised a line from Aberdeen to Inverness, but this was only completed as far as Keith. When the Inverness & Nairn Railway was promoted, the Great North gave notice of opposition, on the grounds that it was an invasion of the territory assigned to it by Parliament. It was, however, induced to withdraw opposition by a promise of running powers between Inverness and Nairn when it had extended its line to Nairn. By some oversight this agreement was never included in the Act authorising the railway. Counsel for the Great North urged that the agreement was still binding in 1895, but the point was not allowed.

The Great North complained that the Highland trains were constantly unpunctual, and that delays occurred to its services at Elgin. It also alleged that the Highland would not take through coaches from the Craigellachie line, and only one set from the coast line. It contended that it had the right to run the through coaches by whichever route it pleased, and that it would be able to work the trains more punctually and expeditiously if it secured running powers.

The Highland Railway opposed on the grounds that there was not enough traffic for separate trains to be run, and that as the line was single, delays were liable to occur if more trains were run. Opposition also came from the town of Inverness, on the ground of unhealthy competition.

After a long hearing, the bill was thrown out. The findings of the parliamentary committee were, however, somewhat incongruous. While admitting that the Highland had not given sufficient facilities for the through traffic, and that unnecessary delays had occurred, it did not consider that the position warranted the granting of running powers, as it held the opinion that an amicable settlement under the existing régime was all that was needed. The committee expressed the hope that the two companies would be able to settle their differences to the improvement of the service.

In the midst of these troublous times, the Highland Railway suffered the loss of Andrew Dougall, the general manager, who retired at the close of the year 1896. A native of Perthshire, Dougall had gained railway experience, as a young man, in the south of Scotland, before entering the service of the Inverness & Nairn Railway in 1854. On the completion of that undertaking in the following year, he was appointed general manager, and shortly afterwards assumed the dual office of general manager and secretary. As the years passed by, his duties were increased to embrace the secretaryship of the nominally independent lines, subsequently amalgamated with the Highland Railway. He had seen the system grow, and none knew better than he its particular needs or the peculiar difficulties under which it laboured.

The acrimonious joint board meetings of the early days were for him a vivid memory, and 35 years later his energies were devoted to maintaining the Highland capital as a close preserve of the company he served. In Andrew Dougall, William Moffatt found a worthy adversary, who successfully resisted all attacks, although it was left to his successor, Charles Steel, to lead the Highland to victory in the last battle for Inverness.

The findings of the parliamentary committee of 1895 gave satisfaction to neither side. The Great North alleged that the through coaches between Inverness and Aberdeen were monopolised, on the Highland Railway, by local passengers, with the result that through passengers frequently had to change at Elgin or Keith. After a great deal of argument, it was allowed to send an attendant with the through trains, to ensure that only passengers for its line used the through coaches.

The Great North also stressed the point that the population on the Craigellachie line was greater than that on the Highland Railway's route, *via* Mulben, and that most of the through trains should take this route. The Highland, for its part, took the view that its route was the shorter, and as the primary function of the through trains was to serve passengers travelling between Inverness and Aberdeen, they should go by the most direct route.

Complaints were received that the Great North was unnecessarily diverting traffic over its line by refusing to stop the best trains at Keith. In defence of this action, it was argued that the junction station at Keith was not so centrally situated as Keith Town, on the Craigellachie line For whatever reason the stop at Keith was omitted, it had the effect of causing through traffic to be handed over at Elgin in many cases.

Matters were in this unsatisfactory state in 1897, when the Great North came forward with a second bill for running powers between Elgin and Inverness. On this occasion it sought to overcome the obstacle of single-line working by offering to bear the expense of doubling the Highland Railway from Elgin to Dalcross, from which point it was already double into Inverness. The hearing of the bill occupied several days. At first it appeared that the promoters were making a good impression but, in the end, the tide turned in favour of the Highland, and the measure was rejected.

After the defeat in 1897, the Great North made no further attempts to enter Inverness. A basis of agreement was reached with regard to the through trains, and Elgin became the chief point of exchange. For some years engines were changed at the junction station, but in 1908 it was agreed that certain trains should be worked throughout by the engine of one Company. This arrangement remained in force until shortly after the outbreak of the first world war.

UNION PROPOSED

To such an extent did relations between the two companies improve that towards the end of 1904 the question of amalgamation was mooted. The idea took definite shape in the course of the following year, and it was finally proposed that the union should become effective on 1 January 1907. Opposition to the scheme came from certain Scottish and English railways, and from the town of Inverness, where it was feared, not without good reason, that the fusion would result in the removal of the cramped locomotive and carriage shops to the new works of the Great North of Scotland Railway at Inverurie. The step was rendered the more likely by the attitude of the town council over the question of petty customs.

By ancient right, the Burgh of Inverness levied petty customs dues on cattle and goods brought into the town. By the beginning of the present century these payments had reached an estimated total of £1,800 per annum, of which sum the Highland Railway paid a considerable proportion. The total abolition of the dues had been contemplated for some time, but definite action towards this end had been delayed. Prior to 1904, the Highland Railway had allowed the council's officers access to its books to determine the amounts due from traders and others, but in that year the Company refused to continue these facilities, and stated that henceforth it intended to give information only in respect of goods for which the railway itself was liable to pay. At the first half-yearly meeting in 1904 it was stated that unless the dues were soon abolished, it would be necessary to remove the locomotive works and the coal depot in order to escape the imposition.

At that time the council did not take this threat seriously and, pending a definite legal settlement, barriers were erected in the street at the Company's boundary to prevent goods from leaving the railway premises before the dues had been paid. Early in 1905 the Court of Session gave judgment in favour of the railway, but the council decided to carry the matter further, and the dispute was still unsettled when the announcement of the proposed amalgamation was made. Faced with the prospect of a serious loss of trade in the town, the council, on 2 October, unanimously decided to oppose the bill, while seeking a conciliation with the railway Company. One speaker even went so far as to say that 'although regrettable things had been done by the town council in connection with the petty customs, still the town had always had the best interests of the Highland Railway at heart'. One month later it was decided to make application for the postponement of the council's action against the railway Company in respect of the latter assisting to collect the dues. This decision was followed by action to secure the total abolition of the dues.

Meantime, the amalgamation scheme had gone ahead, and the question was put to a vote of the Highland shareholders on 7 March 1906. Although the result showed a majority in favour of the bill, not only was there a substantial opposition, but large numbers did not record a vote. In the report issued by the board it was stated that

> In consequence of the substantial opposition among the Shareholders towards the Bill for amalgamation with the Great North of Scotland Railway, and of the indifference shown by a large number of the Shareholders, who did not vote at all, and considering that in a matter of such importance they ought not to proceed except with the approval of such a majority as would amount practically to unanimity, they had resolved, after consultation with the representatives of the Great North of Scotland Railway, to withdraw the Bill.

Thus did a modicum of opposition, strengthened by an inordinate amount of apathy, rob northern Scotland of the benefits of amalgamating two relatively small railways into a combined system with a route mileage of slightly less than 850. The scheme was never revived, and the two companies which had been so long estranged, only to come within an ace of fusion, were finally sundered by the terms of the Railways Act of 1921.

CHAPTER 9

Growth of Train Services

The development of the train services of the Highland Railway falls naturally into three periods. The first represents the railway as a more or less local concern, dependent for its outlet to the south on the circuitous route of the Great North of Scotland Railway *via* Aberdeen; the second is ushered in by the opening of the direct line from Forres to Perth; and the final stage is reached in 1898, when the shortened route to Inverness, *via* Carr Bridge, was completed.

In November 1855 a service of five trains in each direction was provided on the Inverness & Nairn Railway. Most of the trains called at all stations, and required 45 to 50 m. for the journey of 15 miles. One, however, was faster, and carried the mails. It called at Fort George only, and completed its journey in 35 m.

The connection beyond Nairn was by coach to Huntly, whence the Great North of Scotland Railway continued to Aberdeen. Three trains in each direction had Aberdeen connections. The fastest time was made by the down mail, which left Aberdeen at 3 p.m. and reached Inverness at 11.31 p.m. The up mail was 17 m. slower, and left Inverness at the inconvenient time of 12.40 a.m. This hour of departure was necessary in order to connect with the train leaving Aberdeen for the south at 9.45 a.m. The journey by the other trains took about ten hours.

When the Great North was extended to Keith, and the coach journey became shorter, the times of the Inverness & Nairn Company's trains were slightly altered. The up mail began to leave at 1.30 a.m., and reached Aberdeen at 9.42 a.m., a gain of an hour. In the opposite direction the arrival time was 10.59 p.m., a gain of 30 m. In June 1857 only two connections in each direction were provided, but when the railway was opened to Keith, in 1858, four trains were provided in each direction. With the exception of the mails, which omitted a few stops, trains called at all stations. The up mail left Inverness at 3.50 a.m., and reached Aberdeen in less than six hours. The corresponding down train was slower.

By March 1859 the train service south of Aberdeen had been speeded up, and the Great North was able to start its down mail train at 1.17 p.m., Keith being reached at 3.57 p.m. The connection for Inverness left at 4.12 p.m., and calling at all stations reached its destination at 7.2 p.m. The up mail left at 6.40 a.m., and reached Keith at 9 a.m., and Aberdeen at 11.55 a.m. The other services had also improved slightly.

Four trains were run in each direction, calling at all stations, when the northern main line was opened to Dingwall in 1862, and extended to Invergordon in the following year. The average time was about 1 h. 40 m. for the journey of 31 miles. Three trains in each direction had connections to or from the Great North of Scotland Railway. Sunday services were limited to the main-line mail trains, which ran to their weekday schedules.

On the ill-fated Findhorn branch four trains were run in each direction until 1864. For a short time during that year the number was increased to five, but the additional service was soon withdrawn. The Burghead branch had three trains in each direction.

SECOND PERIOD: 1863—1898 (SOUTHERN MAIN LINE)

With the opening of the line from Forres to Perth, the train services underwent a complete change. Connections were given to the same up and down mail trains as before, but the shorter route permitted of greatly reduced over-all times. For some time there were two through trains in each direction between Perth and Inverness. The down mail train left Perth at 9.30 a.m., in connection with the train leaving London (Euston) at 8.40 p.m. on the previous evening. Inverness was reached at 4.20 p.m. after calls at all stations. The second train left at 1 p.m., and omitting some half-dozen stops reached Inverness at 7 p.m.

The up mail left Inverness at 8 a.m., and calling at all stations reached Perth at 3.30 p.m. Passengers arrived in London at 4.37 the next morning. The second up train left at 1.5 p.m. and reached Perth at 7. Like the midday down train, it passed about half-a-dozen stations.

In addition to the trains performing the complete journey, an early-morning train ran from Kingussie to Inverness, and a corresponding return train in the evening. There were also two trains in each direction between Perth and Blair Atholl. Most of these local trains were mixed and very slow.

By March 1865 the down mail had been speeded up by the omission of several stops, and reached Inverness at 2.45 p.m. The midday down train now called at all stations, and leaving Perth at 12.50 p.m. reached Inverness at 7.20 p.m. In the opposite direction the up mail left at 10.18 a.m. and reached Perth at 3.33 p.m. The second train was now slow, and required 6 h. 20 m. to reach Perth.

In the following year, two new down trains were put on. The first, running in connection with the 10 a.m. from Euston, left Perth at 1 a.m. as a mixed passenger and goods train. Inverness was reached at 9 a.m. after stops at nearly all stations. The second train, with no London connection, left Perth at 4.10 p.m., and omitting about six stops reached Inverness at 10.10 p.m. In the up direction a new train left Inverness at 6.30 a.m. and reached Perth at 1 p.m. after calling at all stations.

These services continued for some years with only a few detail alterations, but the 6.30 a.m. up and 4.10 p.m. down trains ran during the summer only. The midday down train also began to run about an hour earlier. In 1873 an extra down train was put on, leaving Perth at 10.10 a.m., and reaching Inverness at 5.55 p.m., after many stops. The service lasted five years, and ran during the early part of August only.

It was not until 1872 that a night train was run in the up direction. For some years it left Inverness at 7.30 p.m., and reached Perth at 5.5 a.m., but in 1878 it was altered to start at 10 p.m. and arrive at Perth at 7 a.m. A sleeping car was now run between Inverness and Perth. A connecting train reached London at 9.40 p.m.

By 1881 the night train from London had been speeded up, and the down mail left Perth at 9 a.m., reaching Inverness at 1.30 p.m., an improvement of 45 m. on the Highland Railway. The bulk of this saving was achieved by the train running non-stop from Perth to Blair Atholl in 55 m. at 38 m.p.h. The 9.30 now became a slow train, running as far as Blair Atholl only, but a few years later it began to run right through to Inverness in the summer only. The midday up train had also been improved. It now left at 1.30 p.m., but reached Perth at 7 p.m. as before. Two years later the early-morning up and the afternoon down trains began to run throughout the year.

In July 1883 there were four trains in each direction between Perth and Inverness. Most of them still stopped many times, and required 5¾ to 7 h. for the journey of 144 miles. The best time was made by the down mail which covered the distance in 4½ h. with 11 intermediate stops. The best up train (the 10.10 a.m. from

The Class of Trains refers to the respective Sections only

Miles from Perth	STATIONS	1 MIX. 1&Pl.	-.2 MIX. 1,2,Pl.	3 MIXD 1,2,Pl.	4 MIXD. 1,2,Pl.	5 MIXD 1&Pl.	6 LIMD. MAIL. 1,2,Pl.	7	8 PASS. 1,2,Pl.	9 PASS. 1,2,Pl.	10 EXC'N. 1&3	11 PASS. 1,2,Pl	12 MIXD. 1,2,Pl	SUNDY MAIL 1,2,Pl
	London, L. & N.W. dep			10 0A						10 0P			5 15A	8 50P
	Do. G.N. "		11 0	10 0			8 0P		8 50P	9 0			5 15	8 30
	Do. Midland ... "			10.35		8 0			8 30					
	Do. Midland "			10 55					8 25	9 15				8 25
	Glasgow, Buchanan St. "			9 25P			f3 5A		7 10A	9 0A		35P		f8 20A
	Edinbro', Stirl. "			9 10			5 3		6 10	8 30		2 0P	1 30 3 55	6 10
	Do. via Fife "			7 20					6 30				1 30 4 0	
	Dundee "			6 40					7 40	11 5		2 30P	3 30 6 40	
				A.M.	A.M.		A.M.		A.M.	A.M.	P.M.	P.M.	P.M.	A.M.
4¼	Perth ....depart			12 40	6 10		7 50		9 30	11 50	3 30	4 30	7 25	8 50
	Luncarty......... "				6 20								7 35	
7¼	Stanley......... "			1 0	6 35				9 45	12 10P	3 45	4 47	7 45	9 2
10¼	Murthly......... "			1 12	7 0				9 51	12 22	3 53	4 55	7 55	9 8
15¼	Dunkeld......... "			1 27	7 20				10 4	12 35	4 5	5 10	8 10	9 18
20¼	Dalguise ...... "				7 35					12 46	Stop	5 22	8 22	
21	Guay......... "				7 42					12 51		5 26	8 28	
23¾	Rallinluig .. "			1 50	7 50				10 22	1 1		5 32	8 40	9 34
32¼	Aberfeldy { depart				6 25				9 45	12 20		4 55	8 0	
	{ arrive			2 5	9 0				10 55	1 35		6 10	9 15	
28½	Pitlochry...... "			2 5	8 5				10 33	1 16		5 43	8 55	9 42
32¾	Killiecrankie... "				8 15					1 26		5 52	9 5	
35½	Blair-Athole... "			2 25	8 25		8 45		10 47	1 36		6 5	9 15	9 55
40	Struan .... "				Stop				10 56	1 50		6 14	Stop	10 3
51	Dalnaspidal ... "			3 15						2 15				
58¾	Dalwhinnie ... "			3 35					11 39	2 30		6 53		10 40
68¾	Newtonmore.... "					A.M.				2 50				
71¾	Kingussie...... "			4 10	8 0		9 50		12 6P	3 1		7 23		11 10
77¼	Kincraig ...... "				† 8 20					3 15		7 33		
83½	Aviemore...... "			4 40	8 40				12 28	3 27		7 45		11 31
88½	Boat of Garten . "			4 55	8 58				12 38	3 37		7 55		11 40
92¼	Broomhill...... "				9 10					3 44				
96	Grantown...... "			5 15	9 22		10 25		12 53	3 52		8 10		11 55
104½	Dava .... "				9 45					4 9				
110¾	Dunphail...... "			6 0	10 5				1 26	4 27		8 40		12 21¼
	Forres.........arrive			6 30	10 35		11 0		1 45	4 50		9 0		12 35
				Pass. 1,2,Pl					Mixed Pass.	Pass. 1,2,Pl		Pass. 1,2,Pl.		
	Forres & Keith Trains, see p 8													
119½	Forres.........depart			6 40A	8 50A		11 5A		11 25	1 50P		9 5		12 0
122½	Brodie......... "			6 48	8 57							9 13		
128¾	Nairn......... "			7 6	9 11		11 20		11 49	2 9		9 27		12 57
134½	Fort-George..... "			7 24	9 23				12 7	2 21		9 46		1 8
137½	Dalcross...... "			7 33	9 29				12 17			9 46		
140½	Culloden...... "			7 45	9 36				12 15			9 54		
144	Inverness.....arrive			8 0	9 45		11 50		12 25	2 45		10 5		1 30
				Mixd. 1,2,pl.	Pass. 1,2,Pl		Mail 1,2,Pl		Pass. 1,2,pl.	Pass. 1,2,Pl	Mixd. 1,2,pl	Pass. 1,2,Pl.		
144	Inverness ...depart			5 30A	9 0A		12 10P		3 15P	4 5P	7 25P			1 45P
145½	Clachnaharry .. "			5 35	9 5				3 19	4 9	7 30			1 48
147¼	Bunchrew...... "			5 45	9 11				3 25	4 19	7 35			1 52
149½	Lentran...... "			5 55	9 18				3 31	4 29	7 43			1 58
151¼	Clunes......... "				9 25				3 37	4 37	7 49			2 3
154	Beauly......... "			6 15	9 35				3 45	4 50	8 0			2 9
157	Muir of Ord..... "			6 30	9 46		12 29		3 55	4 55	8 9			2 17
160½	Conon .... "			6 45	9 57				4 5	5 20	8 19			2 25
162½	Dingwall..... "			7 7	10 9		12 47		4 12	5 45	8 28			2 35
166¾	Fowlis......... "				10 21				4 23	6 0	8 38			
169	Novar......... "			7 30	10 28				4 29	6 9	8 45			2 49
172½	Alness......... "			7 55	10 37				4 39	6 25	8 55			2 56
175½	Invergordon.. "			8 7	10 47				4 46	6 40	9 4			3 5
178½	Delny......... "			8 20	10 56				4 54	6 52	9 13			
180½	Kildary......... "			8 28	11 1		1 28		4 58	7 0	9 20			3 18
183½	Nigg .... "			8 37	11 7				5 4	7 10	9 25			
184½	Fearn......... "			8 55	11 12		1 38		5 10	7 20	9 31			3 28
188¼	Tain { arr.			9 5	11 20		1 44			7 35	9 45			
193½	{ dep.			9 15	11 22		1 46		5 20	Stop	Stop			3 36
	Edderton...... "			9 35	11 37		1 58		5 35					3 48
201½	Bonar-Bridge { arr.			10 0	11 58				5 55					
	{ dep.			10 10	12 8P		2 18		6 5					4 8
204½	Culrain Platform			10 25										
205½	Invershin ...... "			10 30	12 17		2 26		6 15					4 16
220¼	Lairg......... "			10 55	12 32		2 39		6 29					4 29
224½	Rogart......... "			11 26	12 59		3 14		6 55					4 54
228¼	The Mound..... "			11 40	1 9		3 14		7 6					5 4
230	Golspie......... "			9 0 11 55	1 18		3 24		7 13					5 14
234½	Dunrobin (Priv			9 4										
234½	Brora......... "			9 15	12 10P	1 35	3 37		7 28					5 27
239½	Loth......... "			9 25	12 37	1 50			7 40					
245½	Helmsdale..... "			9 40	12 55	2 10	4 1		7 55					5 51
254½	Kildonan...... "			10 4	Stop	2 35			stop					
257¼	Borrobol Plat.... "			*		*								
262	Kinbrace ...... "			10 19	2 55			†						
269½	Forsinard ...... "			10 34	3 15		4 49							6 39
277½	Altnabreac..... "			10 51	3 40									
287	Scotscalder .... "			11 10	4 5									
289½	Halkirk......... "			11 17	4 11									
291½	Georgemas Jun..arr			11 23	4 15		5 33							7 23
	Do. dep. for Thurso			11 28	4 20		5 40							
	Thurso......... dep						5 10							7 0
292½	Hoy .... "			11 33	4 25		5 25							7 15
298	Thurso......... arr			11 45	4 40		6 0A							7 50
294	Georgemas Jun...dep				4 25		5 35							7 25
297¾	Bower......... "				4 33		*							
300¼	Watten......... "				4 42		5 49							7 39
	Bilbster......... "				4 49		*							
305¼	Wick.........arr				5 0		6 10							8 0

a PULLMAN SLEEPING CARS

† Will stop at Kincraig by signal to pick up Passengers only.

P Will stop at Muir of Ord to pick up Passengers on Wednesdays and Thursdays of the monthly markets.

‡ Will stop to set down Passengers only, on their informing Guard at previous stopping Stations.

A page from the timetable of July 1885

Inverness) required 5 h. 23 m., but this was 8 m. slower than in 1880. The 1.30 p.m. from Inverness took 5½ hours.

Two years later there was a big change for the better. Previously, with the exception of the 9 a.m. from Perth which ran non-stop to Blair Atholl, and the 1.30 p.m. up train which called only at Dunkeld between Blair Atholl and Perth, no fast trains of any sort had been run. In that year, however, the Highland Railway began to run the connections to the London mail trains to much faster schedules. Improvements had been made south of Perth, and the Highland was able to start its train at 7.50 a.m. Inverness was reached at 11.50 a.m.[1] In the up direction the 1.30 began to leave at 3 p.m., and ran to a similar schedule. A year later, a new train running in advance of the express was put on. It left Inverness at noon, and reached Perth at 6.30 p.m. Subsequently this schedule was cut by 40 m. The timetables of the two expresses were:

Down Train				Up Train			
Perth	...	...	7.50 a.m.	Inverness	...	...	3.0 p.m.
Blair Atholl	...	...	8.45 a.m.	Nairn	...	...	3.25 p.m.
Kingussie	...	...	9.50 a.m.	Forres	...	...	⎰ 3.40 p.m.
Grantown	...	...	10.25 a.m.				⎱ 3.45 p.m.
Forres	...	... ⎰	11.0 a.m.	Grantown		...	4.23 p.m.
		⎱	11.5 a.m.	Kingussie	...	...	5.5 p.m.
Nairn	...	...	11.20 a.m.	Blair Atholl		...	6.5 p.m.
Inverness	...	...	11.50 a.m.	Perth	...	...	7.0 p.m.

When the heavy gradients and the long stretches of single line are taken into consideration, this represents no poor performance. Although the winter loads were light, those taken by the down train during the summer were frequently colossal.

Foxwell in *Express Trains English and Foreign* comments thus on this train:

> In July and August this 7.50 train is the unique railway phenomenon. Passenger carriages, saloons, horseboxes and vans, concentrated at Perth from all parts of England, and intermixed to make an irregular caravan. Engines are attached fore and aft, and the procession toils pluckily over the Grampians. Thus, on August 7th 1888, the train sailed out of Perth composed as follows:

L.B. & S.C.R. —Horsebox		L. & N.W.R. —Horsebox
L.B. & S.C.R. —Horsebox		N.E.R. —Horsebox
L.B. & S.C.R. —Carriage Van		L. & N.W.R. —Saloon
L.B. & S.C.R. —Horsebox		L. & N.W.R. —Luggage Van

[1] A four-hour schedule for the mail trains in each direction had been proposed by the Post Office in 1863, but the idea was abandoned on the grounds of expense.

Midland Rly.	—Saloon	W.C.J.S.	—Composite
Midland Rly.	—Luggage Van	L. & N.W.R.	—Horsebox
Midland Rly.	—Carriage Truck	L. & N.W.R.	—Meat Van
Midland Rly.	—Horsebox	Highland Rly.	—P.O. Van
L. & N.W.R.	—Horsebox	Highland Rly.	—Luggage Van
N.B.R.	—Luggage Van	Highland Rly.	—Third-Class Passenger
N.B.R.	—Horsebox	Highland Rly.	—First-Class Passenger
N.B.R.	—Horsebox	Highland Rly.	—Second-Class Passenger
N.B.R.	—Horsebox	Highland Rly.	—Third-Class Passenger
E.C.J.S.	—Sleeping Car	Highland Rly.	—Luggage Van
G.N.R.	—Saloon	Highland Rly.	—Third-Class Passenger
W.C.J.S.	—Composite	Highland Rly.	—First-Class Passenger
Midland Rly.	—Composite	Highland Rly.	—Third-Class Passenger
L. & N.W.R.	—Luggage Van	Highland Rly.	—Guard's Van
L. & N.W.R.	—Horsebox		

Nine Companies, 36 carriages, two engines in front, 1 put on behind at Blair Atholl. Left Perth 20 minutes late; left Kingussie 72 minutes late.[1]

With few possible exceptions the whole of the passenger stock was six-wheeled, and all the horseboxes and carriage trucks four-wheeled. Nevertheless it is an extraordinary load for any railway's best regular express, since the train was in no sense a special. Even if the train had been divided at Perth the second portion probably would have lost more time while waiting for the first train to clear the long stretches of single line and for up trains to pass.

By 1891 the down mail was leaving Perth at 7.5 a.m. The schedule was still 4 h., but the train called additionally at Boat of Garten. The down night train had been considerably speeded up. It left Perth at 12.15 a.m. and reached Inverness at 6.30 a.m., an improvement of 65 m. In the following year a further 20 m. were gained, when the arrival time became 6.10, and in 1895 there was a further improvement of 25 m. The 10 p.m. from Inverness was leaving at 10.30, and reaching Perth at 7.45 a.m., but in 1893 the arrival time of 7 a.m. was restored.

With the growth of the tourist traffic a special express was run in advance of the down mail. In 1890 this train left Perth at 7.10 a.m., and calling only at Blair Atholl and Forres, reached Inverness at 11.30. This was 20 m. slower than the mail. In the following year the departure time became 5.55 a.m., and extra stops were put in. The journey now occupied 4¾ h., but by 1893 it had been reduced to 4½ h.

[1] The above is a verbatim extract. The final note should read: 'Ten Companies, *thirty-seven* carriages . . .' Even this load was exceeded on at least one occasion by the afternoon down train, which reached Inverness (very late) with no less than 40 vehicles.

The summer services of 1896 showed a great advance. The 3 p.m. up train was now divided. The first portion ran to the original schedule, and reached Perth at 7 p.m., but the second ,which conveyed the through sleeping cars for London, left at 4.30 p.m. and reached Perth at 8.40, with six regular and two conditional stops. The down tourist express had been altered to leave Perth at 5.30 a.m. and reach Inverness at 9.40. The up night train had also been improved, and ran from Inverness to Perth in 6¼ h.

The summer services for 1898 are the last that can be considered in this second period. In August the down sleeping-car express was run in two portions. The first, which ran until the 12th only, left Perth at 5 a.m., and the second at 5.30. Both trains reached Inverness in 4 h. 10 m. The down mail now left Perth at 6.15 a.m. and arrived at Inverness at 10.15. The down midday train had been divided, the second portion leaving Perth at 12.10 p.m. as a slow train.

In the up direction the 10.10 a.m. from Inverness was relieved by a new train, leaving at 9.20, and reaching Perth at 3.15 p.m. The London sleeping-car express now left at 4.55 p.m., and retained its former schedule, but the midday train had been speeded by 25 m.

Until 1878 Sunday services were restricted to the mail trains in each direction, which observed their weekday times. In that year, however, the up night train began to run on Sundays; it had never run on Saturday—Sunday nights, nor did it ever do so. This extra service remained in operation until 1891. Subsequently, only the mail trains were run. In 1881 the down service was altered to leave Perth at 8.50 a.m. (instead of 9.30) and reach Inverness at 1.30 p.m.

SECOND PERIOD: 1863—1898 (NORTHERN MAIN LINE)

The railway was extended from Invergordon to Meikle Ferry on 1 June 1864, and to Bonar Bridge on 1 October following. For some years there were four trains in each direction between Inverness and Tain, and three to Bonar Bridge, but when the railway was extended into Sutherland two trains only ran north of Tain. The speed of all these trains was little more than 20 m.p.h., inclusive of stops at all stations.

At first, one train in each direction had a connection to or from Perth, but from 1866 to 1868 three down trains and two up made connection. Subsequently this number was reduced to two for stations north of Tain. Coach connections to and from the north were given to the mail trains in each direction.

LOCOMOTIVES

(22)   *The 'Small Ben' class 4—4—0 was Peter Drummond's first design, introduced in 1898. This view of the first of the twenty 'Small Bens', No 1 Ben-y-Gloe, shows the engine before the reversing lever and underslung reach rod were replaced by steam reversing gear. As the first inside-cylinder tender locomotives on the HR, they caused early misgivings amongst enginemen, but soon became popular.*

(23)   *Drummond's 'Castle' class 4—6—0s were a development of Jones's 'Big Goods', although much of the credit for the design work on both engines must go to David Hendrie who served under both locomotive superintendents. No 143 Gordon Castle is seen here shortly after delivery from Dübs in 1900.*

LOCOMOTIVES

(24)   *The tragedy of Frederick Smith's six 'River' class 4—6—0s has been a source of controversy. Their rejection by the Chief Engineer, Alexander Newlands, on account of their weight has been interpreted as due to a combination of personal antagonism and a desire on the part of the HR board to find a scapegoat for the parlous state of the Highland locomotive stock under the pressure of wartime traffic. The marginal discrepancy between their estimated and actual weights and the pressing need for extra motive power lend credence to this theory. The engine name on this works photograph of the first locomotive, No 70 River Ness, appears to have been doctored, though the smokebox and cabside numerals are almost certainly genuine.*

(25)   *No 55 Clan Mackinnon, built by Hawthorn Leslie in 1921, is seen here at Perth in Cumming's moss green livery.*

When the railway was completed to Wick in 1874 the services were altered. An early train left Inverness at 4 a.m. (subsequently 5 a.m.) for Helmsdale, calling at all stations. It had no connection from the south or east. This was followed by a connection with the night train from Perth, leaving at 9.15, and reaching Wick at 4.20 p.m. after stops at all stations, A year or so later this train was 40 m. slower, but by 1881 it was leaving Inverness at 9 a.m. and reaching Wick at 5 p.m. A similar train in connection with the down mail left Inverness at 3.10 p.m., reaching Wick at 10.35 p.m.

In the up direction a train left Wick at 4.45 and reached Inverness at 12.15 p.m., after calling at all stations. This train connected with the 12.40 for Perth. A second train left at 11.50 and reached Inverness at 7 p.m., whence the journey could be continued south by the night train. A train also left Bonar Bridge at 7.6 a.m., arriving in Inverness at 9.50 in time to connect with the 10.18 a.m. for Perth. There was also a train from Helmsdale at 9.44 a.m., which ran as far as Dingwall.

In the following year the 4.45 from Wick was altered to leave at 1 a.m., and reach Inverness at 9.50. North of Tain it was a mixed train. The second train now left at 11.30 a.m., but still reached Inverness at 7 p.m. There was now no connection north of Tain to the 12.40 p.m. from Inverness. The morning train from Helmsdale to Dingwall had been made earlier, and there was a corresponding return train from Dingwall to Tain. By 1880 the up train was leaving Helmsdale at 6.10 a.m. and running through to Inverness in 5 h. 50 m., to connect with the midday service to the south. There were also some local trips between Thurso and Wick.*

When the down mail was expedited in 1881 to reach Inverness at 1.30 p.m. the connection for the north was altered to leave at 2 p.m. and run to a faster schedule, certain small stations being omitted. Wick was reached at 8 p.m., a gain of 70 m. In the up direction the former 1 a.m. from Wick was altered to leave at 12.10 a.m,. and slowed by 40 m.

The speeding-up of the services on the southern main line in 1885

* During the months July to October inclusive, in 1878 to 1885, a morning train conveying first-class and parliamentary third-class passengers only, was run on certain days of the week (originally Saturdays, but latterly Tuesdays and Fridays and finally on Fridays only) between Golspie and varying destinations north thereof. At the outset Forsinard was the terminus, then Thurso, Wick and finally back to Thurso again. It returned in the late afternoon, reaching Golspie about 7 PM. As the working timetables show, these trains were worked by the Duke of Sutherland's private engine which, along with the coaches, was kept at Brora at this time.

caused several alterations north of Inverness. The 9 a.m. remained, but the 2 p.m. was altered to leave at 12.10. It retained its six-hour schedule. Its place in the afternoon was taken by a slow train leaving Inverness at 3.15, and running as far as Helmsdale, where it arrived at 7.55 p.m. This train connected in the summer only with the 9.30 a.m. from Perth. The 11.30 a.m. from Wick was made much earlier, leaving at 8 a.m. and reaching Inverness at 2.30 p.m., to connect with the 3 p.m. for the south. This was the last up train from Wick, but a new train was put on, leaving Helmsdale at 2.20 p.m. and reaching Inverness at 7.20, whence the journey could be continued to Perth by the night train.

Further changes were made in 1892 when the early train from Inverness was altered to leave at 6.30 a.m., thus affording a connection to the night train from Perth, which arrived at 6.10. It was also extended through to Wick, where it was due at 1.25 p.m. The 9 a.m. from Inverness now ran as far as Helmsdale only, by which time it was only 30 m. in advance of the mail, leaving Inverness at 11.25 a.m. The mail passed the slower train, which followed on to Wick some 50 m. later, serving some of the smaller stations omitted by the preceding train. This arrangement was only in force for a year or two, after which the 9 a.m. from Inverness did not run beyond Tain. This left certain stations north of Helmsdale with only one down train per day.

In the up direction, the afternoon train from Helmsdale was altered to start from Wick at 2.45, Inverness being reached at 9.25 p.m. This was a great improvement, as for some years the last through train had left Wick at the very early hour of 8 a.m. These alterations resulted in the uneven service of three up trains and two down. In 1895 the 12.10 a.m. from Wick was suspended, but the early train from Helmsdale was retimed to leave at 5.20 a.m., and reach Inverness at 9.45 a.m., to make connection with the 10.10 a.m. for the south.

In the following year the 5.20 from Helmsdale was started from Wick at 2.30 a.m., but this only lasted for a short while. However, for many years a peculiar arrangement was in force which gave additional facilities north of Helmsdale. First-class passengers were permitted, on signing an 'indemnity form' (absolving the railway Company from all liability for injury) to leave Wick at 1 a.m. by the night goods train. At Helmsdale they could transfer to the early morning train for Inverness. A similar arrangement was in force for the afternoon train from Inverness.[1] During the summer of 1896

[1] Passengers could also travel by goods train on certain other parts of the system.

the 3.10 p.m. down train ran as far as Tain only, being followed at 5.15 by a connection with the midday train from Perth. The new train ran non-stop from Inverness to Dingwall, and then called at all stations to Wick, which was reached at 11.20 p.m. This fore-runner of the 'Further North Express' only lasted a short while, however, after which the 3.10 p.m. was once more extended to Helmsdale.

In the remaining two years of the period the only important change was the alteration of the down mail. When the connection from Perth began to reach Inverness at 10.15 a.m. the train for Wick was automatically made to start at 10.35, and retaining its schedule of six hours reached Wick at 4.35 p.m. The gradual im-provement of the morning mail trains from Perth to Inverness had resulted in a retrograde step on the northern main line, as the last departure from Inverness for stations north of Helmsdale became progressively earlier.

The Sunday train services call for little comment. For some years the connections to the up and down mail trains ran to their weekday schedules. When the line was opened to Wick, the up Sunday train left the northern terminus at the inconvenient hour of 2.30 a.m. and arrived in Inverness at 9.50 a.m. This was over two hours faster than the 12.10 a.m. weekday train, but on Sundays no goods wagons were attached. The down train from Inverness ran to the same schedule on Sundays as on weekdays.

SECOND PERIOD: 1863—1898 (OTHER SERVICES)

As soon as the direct line from Forres to Perth was opened, the services on the Keith line became of secondary importance. The majority of the trains called at all stations and required about 2¾ h. for the journey of 55 miles. At Keith the Great North of Scotland Railway provided connections to about three trains in each direc-tion, and the over-all time between Inverness and Aberdeen varied from 5¼ h. (by the early morning up mail) to 7¾ h. The average time for the 108 miles was slightly less than 6 h. For a short time the mail trains ran on Sundays and weekdays, but by 1865 they had been withdrawn between Aberdeen and Keith, although the Highland Railway continued to provide one train in each direction between Keith and Forres.

By February 1872 the services were slightly better. The trains still called at nearly all stations, but the best time from Aberdeen to Inverness had been reduced to 4½ h. This train started at 10.15 a.m.

and ran semi-fast to Keith, where it arrived at 12.25 p.m. The connection on the Highland Railway left 10 m. later. On the other hand, the best train in the opposite direction still required 5½ h.

The sweeping changes that followed William Moffatt's appointment as general manager of the Great North began to be apparent in 1885. In November of that year the number of connections had been increased to four in each direction. The 10.10 a.m. from Aberdeen ran to Keith in 96 m., and Inverness was reached at 1.30 p.m. The remaining trains occupied 4½ to 5 h. on the journey. For some obscure reason the eastbound service was slower, the best train (4 p.m. from Inverness) requiring 5 h., but this included a wait of 45 m. at Keith, as against 4 m. in the opposite direction. This performance was very nearly equalled by two trains which took about 10 m. longer.

Prior to 1886, no attempt had been made to exchange traffic at Elgin, but following the completion of the railway from Keith to Elgin, *via* the coast, the Great North made certain alterations in services which gave passengers the option of changing at either station by one or two trains in each direction. A few years later at least one train was making connection at Elgin only.

A new early-morning train was put on, leaving Aberdeen at 3.35 a.m., and reaching Keith at 5.25. The Inverness connection left 10 m. later and arrived at 7.55. Subsequently this schedule was slightly eased. The 10.10 a.m. ex-Aberdeen still reached Keith at 11.46 a.m., but the Highland connection did not leave until 12.10 p.m. (instead of 11.50 a.m.) and made several extra stops. It arrived in Inverness at 2.15 p.m., a deceleration of 20 m.

These services continued for some years with only a few slight changes, save that the 10.10 a.m. from Aberdeen was altered to leave 40 m. earlier and run correspondingly earlier throughout. In 1894 a new train was put on, leaving Inverness at 8.45 a.m. and reaching Keith at 11.5, where it connected with an express reaching Aberdeen at 12.55 p.m.

When, as a result of the race of 1895, the competing night trains from London began to reach Aberdeen at about 6.30 a.m., the Great North put on a new train in connection, leaving at 6.45 a.m. For a short while the arrival time at Elgin was 9.15, but subsequently several stops were cut out and the train reached Elgin (*via* the coast) at 8.48. The Highland Railway had a slow train leaving Elgin for Inverness at 8.53 a.m., but the connection with the GNSR arrival at 8.48 was not guaranteed. To make certain of reaching Inverness at 10.15 a.m., passengers from Aberdeen by the 6.45 a.m.

had to travel in the back part of the train (detached at Huntly) and join the Highland train at Keith. This was a typical example of the lack of facilities in the days of the 'warfare', and one that led to many bitter complaints.

By May 1897 a great improvement had taken place. The Great North had inserted several stops in the schedule of the 6.45 a.m. from Aberdeen, which now reached Elgin at 9. The Highland ran a train in connection at 9.10, which joined the morning mail from Perth at Forres. The journey from Elgin to Forres was performed non-stop in 17 m. Several other trains in each direction ran to corresponding schedules between Elgin and Forres, to the general betterment of the service. The best time from Aberdeen to Inverness became 3½ h., by two trains leaving at 6.45 a.m. and p.m. respectively. Two others were only 10 m. slower.

In the opposite direction the best time was 3 h. 5 m. by the 3 p.m. from Inverness, which ran via Keith. The 55 miles from Inverness to Keith were covered in 90 m., with stops at Nairn, Forres and Elgin. There was no corresponding return service. The best trains via Elgin required 3½ to 4 h. for the whole journey. These services remained in force until the end of the period under review.

When the railway was opened to Strome Ferry in 1870, two trains in each direction were provided. These called at all stations and required about 3 h. for the journey of 53 miles from Dingwall. The down trains ran in connection with the night and morning mail trains from Perth. The up service was similarly arranged. The morning down and the afternoon up trains connected at Strome Ferry with the Hebridean steamers. These services continued for many years with only minor alterations.

For a considerable period the second down and the first up trains were suspended during the winter, but later on two trains in each direction were run throughout the year, and a third during the summer. By 1885 the morning mail train from Perth had been improved sufficiently to allow the steamer connection to be provided by the second train from Dingwall. A few years later it became the practice to work certain trains through to and from Inverness, instead of attaching the coaches to main-line trains, or making passengers change at Dingwall.

The Skye line never enjoyed Sunday services. In all probability, lightness of traffic was the determining factor. On the other hand, the people of Wester Ross were evidently strict sabbatarians in the early days of the railway. Pendleton, in *Our Railways*, records a serious disturbance which occurred at Strome Ferry in 1883, when it was desired to run a Sunday fish special:

A remarkable scene was witnessed at Strome Ferry—on (Sunday) June 3rd, 1883. The people were determined at all hazards that others besides themselves should keep the Sabbath. The Railway Company proposed to send a load of fish by special train, so that the provender might be taken on by the limited mail (from Inverness). When the fishing boats came inshore to unload, the villagers mustered, armed with clubs and sticks. They menaced the crews, and prevented the landing of the fish. Not only the police, but the railway officials interfered; but the combined forces were overcome by the indignant coast-dwellers, who took possession of the pier and the station.

The crowd prayed and sang in the railway station and—actually remembered the Directors in their supplications—until midnight, when traffic was resumed. Ten of the men, found guilty of mobbing and rioting, were sent to prison for four months each. The riot was the subject of questions in the House of Commons, and Sir William Harcourt, then Home Secretary, replied that if the men had really expressed sincere regret he would consult with the judge with a view to securing a remission of the sentence. He did consult with his lordship; and on September 23rd the men were liberated from Calton Jail, Edinburgh.

The minor branches call for little notice. In the majority of cases, four or five trains were run in each direction, on weekdays only. They called at all stations, and speeds were low. Mixed trains were run on certain services. From October 1863 to May 1867 a morning and afternoon service was provided in each direction on the Inverness harbour branch; possibly they connected with coastal steamers at the harbour.

THIRD PERIOD: 1898—1922 (SOUTHERN MAIN LINE)

The opening of the direct line to Inverness, *via* Carr Bridge, caused big alterations in the train services. Most of the trains were diverted to the new line, and the journey time between Perth and Inverness was reduced by about one hour. Connections for the older route were provided at Aviemore.

The morning mail still left Perth at 6.15 a.m., and reached Aviemore at 8.30. Leaving at 8.35, it arrived in Inverness at 9.30. To cover the 34½ miles of steeply-graded line at an average speed of 37.6 m.p.h. was a distinctly good performance. The special summer tourist express was similarly expedited. The down night train left Perth at 12.50 a.m., and Aviemore at 3.55, reaching Inverness at 5.10 (subsequently 4.56). The 9.25 a.m. from Perth was continued during the winter, and reached Inverness at 1.30 p.m. Later on, the arrival time became 1.50. The midday and afternoon

(E) *LMS Class 5 4—6—0 No 45361 at Achnasheen with a train for Inverness.*

trains called at all stations on the new line, but reached Inverness over an hour earlier than before.

In the up direction the early morning train left Inverness at 7.20. and reached Perth at 11.30. For the time being the 9.20 a.m. relief train was suspended north of Aviemore, but was later restored, in summer, to leave Inverness at 10.10, and run *via* Forres. The 10.10 a.m. from Inverness was altered to leave at 11.10, and run *via* the new line. It reached Perth at its old time of 3.33 p.m. The 3.5 p.m. left at 3.50, and was booked to Aviemore in 60 m., where it took up its old schedule. In summer a relief train was run *via* Forres. For some time it followed the main express from Aviemore, but later ran in advance right through to Perth. The original midday relief train survived as a slow train leaving Inverness at 2 p.m., and reaching Perth at 6.40, *via* Carr Bridge. In 1902, it was diverted *via* Forres, and considerably slowed. A year later it was curtailed to start from Grantown during the summer, and from Blair Atholl in the winter.

The summer sleeping-car express for London was altered to start at 5.45 p.m., and reach Perth at 9.25, a gain of 30 m. This schedule was soon eased, and by 1904 the train was leaving Inverness at 5 and reaching Perth at 9.5. The night train for Perth continued to run *via* Forres, and the schedule was slightly eased.

In the summer of 1900 a new evening express was put on, leaving Perth at 8.15. It included through coaches leaving London (King's Cross and Euston) at 10 a.m. Stops were made at Pitlochry, Blair Atholl and Kingussie, and the train reached Inverness at 11.30 p.m. A corresponding up train, calling additionally at Aviemore, left Inverness at 8.50 a.m., and reached Perth at noon, in time for the midday departures for London. The down service ran in the summer only, but the up train was continued throughout the year, and was expedited to reach Perth at 11.56 a.m., thus becoming the fastest train on the line. It ran from Blair Atholl to Perth in 46 m., at a speed of 46 m.p.h.

In the summer of 1902 the down train was diverted *via* Forres, and considerably slowed by the inclusion of several regular and conditional stops. It did not reach Inverness until 12.10 a.m. In 1904 it was altered to leave Perth at 7.5 p.m., and reach Inverness at 11.10. Good connections were provided from Edinburgh, Glasgow and the North of England, but London passengers had to leave Euston at 5.15 a.m. The train was withdrawn as usual during the following winter, and never reinstated. The primary reason for the failure of the northbound service to become a regular feature of

(F) *The only preserved Highland Railway engine, 'Jones Goods' 4—6—0 No 103, at St Rollox Works in 1946 in her first restoration livery*

the summer timetables appears to have been the refusal of the Highland Railway to maintain the connection at Perth when the trains from the south were running late (by no means uncommon in those days).

For several years the services continued almost unaltered. The 8.50 a.m. from Inverness was slowed by 10 m., and made to start at 8.40. During the winter it called at all stations between Inverness and Aviemore, but the schedule for the 34½ miles remained 63 m. The up night train still ran *via* Forres, but was slightly accelerated. In the opposite direction, during the summer, the first part of the midday train from Perth was shown as running non-stop to Newtonmore, but a stop was usually made at Blair Atholl for water and banking assistance. This train reached Inverness *via* Forres. After 1911 the 9.25 a.m. from Perth ceased once more to run to Inverness during the winter, and terminated at Blair Atholl.

The provision of sleeping cars from London to Inverness *via* the East Coast, West Coast and Midland routes did not prove an unmixed blessing to the Highland Railway. The cars were well patronized during the summer, but in the winter months the number of through passengers was small. The Highland Railway naturally objected to hauling this extra load over its mountainous road with but little prospect of an adequate return, and in 1903 suggested to the English companies that in subsequent winters each should run one car twice per week. This arrangement, together with interavailability of tickets, would have assured passengers of a through service every night in each direction.

The English companies agreed, but the Caledonian Railway objected, on the grounds that the North British Railway would haul four services between the Border and Perth, while it would work only the West Coast cars. It demanded to be allowed to haul one of the Midland services north of Carlisle. Over this trifling dispute negotiations broke down, and for the time being the sleeping cars terminated at Perth, because the Highland Railway refused to take more than one car per night through to Inverness. Subsequently agreement was reached, and the Highland Railway's suggestion put into force. A few years later the Midland Railway withdrew its cars in the winter, and the service was provided to and from Euston and King's Cross on alternate nights.

The outbreak of war in August 1914 brought a vast amount of extra traffic to the Highland Railway. Until the end of 1916 the timetables did not show many important alterations or curtailments although the service provided during the summers of 1915 and 1916 was little better than that of a normal winter. The relief train to the regular midday service from Perth was continued throughout the winter of 1914, on Fridays only, but it did not survive after the following summer. On the other hand, the up night service from Inverness, which had run during the summer only after 1911, was continued throughout the year from 1915.

In the winter of 1915 the 9.30 a.m. stopping train from Perth to Blair Atholl continued to Inverness with only one advertised stop, at Kingussie. The time allowed from Blair Atholl to Kingussie was 58 m., and the final 46½ miles to Inverness were scheduled in 99 m. This curious schedule remained in force until the end of 1916. The afternoon down train also worked to an unusual schedule. It ran non-stop to Dalnaspidal, but called at all stations thence to Inverness *via* Carr Bridge. This working was continued throughout the war period, although subsequently an additional stop, at Struan, was included.

In 1917 drastic alterations and curtailments were made. The night trains from London were considerably slowed, and the Highland Railway was unable to start the connection from Perth until 7.15 a.m. Inverness was reached at 11.10, a deceleration of 35 m. The through sleeping cars were suspended. The 9.30 a.m. from Perth was withdrawn north of Blair Atholl, and the schedules of many other trains were eased. In the up direction the 8.40 a.m. from Inverness was suspended, and the 11.10 was altered to leave at 9.30 a.m. It required 4½ h. to reach Perth, with many stops. The afternoon up train was also made slower.

The years following the war witnessed a gradual improvement. The summer sleeping-car expresses to and from London, and the relief trains, *via* Forres, to the mid-morning and afternoon departures from Inverness were restored in 1919. In the following year the 8.40 a.m. from Inverness was reinstated, but the arrival time in Perth (12.18 p.m.) did not allow of the journey to London being completed in the same day. This facility was restored in 1921, when the departure time from Inverness became 8.10 a.m., and the train reached Perth at 11.28. In the winter of the following year the train reverted to its pre-war schedule, but it had been suspended during the winters of 1920 and 1921. The early-morning slow train from Inverness to Perth was not reinstated. In 1920 the up night train was altered to start at 11.20 p.m., run *via* Carr Bridge, and reach Perth at 5.5 a.m.

By the winter of 1922 the down morning mail was leaving Perth at 6.40 a.m. and reaching Inverness at 10.15. Certain other trains also showed slight improvement, but on the whole the schedules fell far short of their pre-war levels. The summer of that year saw the introduction of restaurant-car facilities. A Pullman car from the Caledonian Railway ran with the midday train from Perth as far as Aviemore. It returned south with the afternoon train from Inverness. In the following autumn a restaurant car from the Great North of Scotland Railway worked through to Inverness on the 8.5 a.m. train from Aberdeen, and returned with the midday service. Previously passengers had been obliged to rely on the station refreshment rooms, and many of the trains waited for some minutes at Kingussie and Bonar Bridge for that purpose.

Sunday services were still restricted to one mail train in each direction. The schedules remained almost unaltered, and the trains travelled *via* Forres. From 1911 to 1914 a down relief train was run during the summer only, leaving Perth 20 m. in advance of the mail, but there was no corresponding up service. In 1916 the trains were diverted to the Carr Bridge route, and ran non-stop between Aviemore and Inverness. For the time being Nairn and Forres were served by connecting trains from Inverness, but these facilities were soon withdrawn.

In 1920 the Postmaster-General decided to suspend the Sunday deliveries of letters throughout the country. In consequence the Sunday train service between Perth and Inverness was withdrawn. The connecting trains on the northern main line shared a like fate, and at the grouping the passenger services on the Highland Railway were restricted to weekdays only.

THIRD PERIOD : 1898—1922 (NORTHERN MAIN LINE)

For several years after 1898 no radical changes were made in the train services north of Inverness. The earlier arrivals from the south enabled the connecting trains to leave correspondingly earlier, but the schedules remained almost unaltered. The connection to the down night train now left Inverness at 5.40 a.m. and reached Wick at 12.25 p.m. The down northern mail left at 9.50 a.m., but still required 6 h. for its journey of 161¼ miles. This was the last departure from Inverness for stations north of Helmsdale. In the opposite direction the early train started from Helmsdale at 6 a.m., and the morning departure from Wick was at 8.40 a.m. In each case, however, the journey times remained almost unaltered. The afternoon train from Wick ran to its former timing, as its connection for the south still travelled *via* Forres. Until the outbreak of the war these

Further North !

Further North !

FORTNIGHTLY PASSES

FOR

Visiting the Northern Highlands

From 1st JUNE UNTIL 30th SEPTEMBER, VISITORS from SOUTH and EAST of PERTH, holding RETURN TICKETS to NEWTONMORE or ANY STATION NORTH THEREOF, can obtain

FORTNIGHTLY PASSES

AVAILABLE BETWEEN

NEWTONMORE, FORRES, FORT-GEORGE, INVERNESS, FORTROSE, STRATHPEFFER, KYLE OF LOCHALSH, DORNOCH, THURSO, WICK, LYBSTER, and Intermediate Stations, at the undernoted Rates :—

FIRST CLASS.	THIRD CLASS.
£3.	**£2.**

The Passes will be available by any Ordinary Train during the Fortnight without limit as to the number of Journeys, provided they are used for Pleasure Excursions only.

They will not be available for Business Purposes.

Forms of Requisition can be obtained at any Station within the above-named area, or at the Traffic Manager's Office, Inverness, on presentation of the Return Half of Ticket from South or East of Perth.

Twenty-Four Hours' Notice will be necessary when the Passes are required at Stations outside Inverness.

An offer in the winter timetable of 1908

services suffered no more than minor alterations. Most of the changes tended towards easier schedules.

In the summer of 1906 the 'Further North Express' was put on. The train ran on Fridays only, leaving Inverness at 4.30 p.m., in connection with the 11.50 a.m. from Perth, and ran to Dornoch. It ran nominally non-stop to The Mound in 2 h. 35 m., and reached its destination at 7.33 p.m. This distinctly easy schedule included stops for water. There was no corresponding return service.

At the conclusion of the summer service the train was altered to leave Inverness on Fridays only at 2.20 p.m. (in connection with the 9.25 a.m. from Perth) and extended to Wick, where it was due at 7.25 p.m., after calling at Dingwall, Tain, Bonar Bridge, Golspie, Helmsdale, Forsinard and Georgemas. An up express, running on Thursdays only, left Wick at 10.35 a.m. and reached Inverness at 3.30 p.m., with six intermediate stops. The down train ran to this schedule for one winter only. In the following summer the original departure time (4.30 p.m.) was restored. Extra stops at The Mound and Brora were put in, and Wick was reached at 9.20 p.m. The up train remained unaltered. These expresses ran throughout the year until the autumn of 1912, when they were withdrawn for the winter. In 1908 the down train was accelerated to reach Wick at 9.5 p.m. It ran non-stop from Inverness to Tain in 65 m. (40.6 m.p.h.). In the winter it reverted to its slower schedule. During 1913 and 1914 the northbound train ran on Wednesdays and Fridays, and in the opposite direction the service was provided on Thursdays and Saturdays. Both services were withdrawn on the outbreak of the war and neither was restored until after the Highland Railway had become part of the LMSR in 1923.

A few years after the opening of the branch to Strathpeffer, a through train was run to the spa, on Saturdays only, starting from Inverness at 3 p.m., and making connection with the 9.25 a.m. from Perth. The train returned in the evening at 8.15 p.m. In each direction stops were made only at Beauly, Muir of Ord and Dingwall. The departure time and the schedule varied slightly from year to year, but the service remained in operation until 1914.

On 1 June 1911 the Highland Railway opened its hotel at Strathpeffer. To encourage traffic a through service from the south was provided on Tuesdays only. The new train started from Aviemore at 2.30 p.m., in connection with the 11.50 a.m. from Perth, which reached Inverness *via* Forres. It ran non-stop to Dingwall in 90 m., and thence to Strathpeffer, where it arrived at 4.15 p.m. Throughout the history of the Highland Railway this was the only regular train

that ran past Inverness without stopping.[1] There was no corresponding service in the up direction. The 'Strathpeffer Express' ran during
the summer only. It was finally withdrawn in the autumn of 1915,
on account of the war, and never reinstated. During its last summer
it started from Perth at 11.45 a.m. and called only at Kingussie
before running non-stop from Aviemore to Dingwall in 85 m. The
11.50 a.m. from Perth had been suspended, and passengers for
Inverness had to use the slower train leaving at midday.

In common with all other services the trains on the northern
main line were decelerated during the war period, although their
number was not seriously reduced. Slight improvements were made
shortly before the grouping, but in December 1922 the schedules
had not regained their 1914 standard.

THIRD PERIOD: 1898—1922 (OTHER SERVICES)

The opening of the shortened route to Inverness did not materially
affect the Aberdeen services. Most of the trains continued almost
unaltered, but the 6.45 a.m. from Aberdeen was altered to leave
45 m. earlier, and reach Elgin at 8.20. The connecting train on the
Highland Railway was due in Inverness at 9.35, in time for the
departure of the northern mail at 9.50. In summer the train ran
every day, but after 1902 the service was provided on Mondays
only during the winter, and the connection with the Highland
Railway was made at Keith. In the opposite direction the 3 p.m.
from Inverness was changed to leave at 3.55, because of the later
arrival of the train from Wick. It was considerably slowed by the
inclusion of several stops, and did not reach Aberdeen until 7.20
p.m. Some years later it was still further decelerated and required
4 h. 5 m. for the journey.

The services continued on these lines until the outbreak of the
1914 war. Such alterations as were made tended for the most part
towards somewhat easier timings. In 1917 the trains were slowed
and drastically reduced in number. Slight improvements were made
in the years following the war, but, as with most other services,
the recovery was by no means complete when the grouping came
into force.

No radical changes were made on the long cross-country line to
Kyle of Lochalsh in the autumn of 1898. The timetable was, of

---

[1] If the 11.50 a.m. from Perth was seriously delayed, the 'Further North
Express' was also started from Aviemore, but the train called at Inverness to
pick up passengers.

course, adjusted to suit the altered services on the southern main line, but the schedules remained almost unaltered. In summer four trains were run in each direction. For a few years three services each way were run in winter, but the timetable soon became unbalanced by the cancellation of one westbound train.

A fast train appeared in the summer of 1901. It left Dingwall at 10.36 (in connection with the 9.50 a.m. from Inverness) and called only at Garve, Achnasheen and Strathcarron. Kyle of Lochalsh was reached at 1 p.m. The ordinary mail train followed from Dingwall at 11.10 a.m. and continued to call at all stations. The new train ran during the summer only, and was finally withdrawn in the autumn of 1903. At no time was there a corresponding eastbound service, although for several summers the early-morning train from Kyle of Lochalsh connecting with the steamer from Stornoway only called conditionally at certain stations. It reached Inverness in time to allow passengers to catch the day train to London.

With the exception of the branch from Keith to Portessie, where services were completely suspended, no section of the Highland Railway suffered more drastic wartime reductions of services than the line from Dingwall to Kyle of Lochalsh. Such was the volume of special traffic arriving by sea at Kyle, and proceeding east by rail, that the service was ultimately reduced to one daily passenger train in each direction. Soon after the armistice, it was found possible to provide extra facilities, and by 1922 the service consisted of three eastbound and two westbound trains throughout the year. A third train ran from Dingwall to Kyle of Lochalsh on Wednesdays and Saturdays during the summer.

CHAPTER 10

Problems of Operation

SINGLE LINE AND ITS DIFFICULTIES

In one respect the Highland differed from most British railways: the greater proportion of it was single track. When the Company received its Act of Incorporation in 1865, out of a route mileage of 242 the only double-track section was the 6¾ miles from Inverness to Dalcross, widened on 1 October 1864. For many years this amount remained unaltered, because none of the extensions of the system was provided with a double line. The 7¼ miles from Perth to Stanley Junction were also double, but the Highland Railway only exercised running powers over this section.

So long as the railway extended only from Inverness to Keith, serious delays do not appear to have been common, but as soon as the line from Forres to Perth was opened, the Company began to experience difficulty in getting the trains through to time, and great inconvenience to passengers often resulted. As an instance of this, the following extract from a letter, written from Perth in September 1863 a few days after the line had been opened, is illuminating:

> Here we are safely landed, but by no means without adventure. While the Directors of the new line were complimenting each other, I wish they could have heard the other side of the question—the passengers' point of view of the new management. There was nothing but abuse of them on all sides, and regret that they should have opened the line before they could manage it properly and comfortably. Delay after delay occurred—want of water—waiting until this or that train should have passed—or dawdling from no visible cause whatever, until we were six hours too long on the road. The last train had left Perth for the south when we were only dragging through Dunkeld.
>
> But the worst of it was that Perth was not equal to such an enormous influx of strangers, and we were all flying hither and thither in quest of beds of any sort. In our case the labour was in vain. We tried The British, The George, The Salutation, The Commercial, The Temperance, etc., besides lodging and private houses, but all were full. At last, thoroughly tired out, we came back to the station, and made up what sleeping places we could on the sofas and chairs in the Waiting Room. There were several other persons, with children,

reduced to the same extremity, so you may be sure that there was but little quiet for rest and sleep. Morning, however, came at last. In the midst of our troubles, we were amused with a jolly Englishman in the train, who was making fun of the whole affair. He had left Inverness the day before, and had only got to Dalwhinnie at two o'clock in the morning. He betook himself, vexed and fatigued, to the hotel, and at four o'clock in the afternoon the train was still there. Here he was, getting into Perth on the second night by our train, and chaffing the guards with speeches such as: 'Extraordinary dispatch, Inverness to Perth in two days! Great cheapness, only two hotel bills besides the train fare!'

In fairness, it must be admitted that the unfinished state of the line and the steep gradients were largely responsible for this exceptional delay, although the long stretches of single line evidently played their part.

Punctuality on the Highland Railway was always adversely affected by two important factors: the long and steep gradients over the mountains, and the possibility of the connecting trains from the south reaching Perth much behind their scheduled times. As traffic developed, and trains increased in weight and frequency, serious delays became the rule. At periods of high pressure, much time was lost at stations waiting for other trains to pass, and chaos ensued. Towards the end of the century, with the approaching completion of the direct line from Aviemore to Inverness, the problem was taken seriously in hand. On the new line, the 11 miles from Inverness to Daviot, covering the major portion of the formidable bank of 1 in 60, which begins almost as soon as the terminus is left, were constructed as a double road.

Meanwhile, steps had been taken to improve arrangements for single-line working. Until the early 1890s, the old-fashioned system of telegraphing passing orders for trains along the line had been in vogue, but the whole of the main lines and the more important branches were subsequently equipped with train staff or tablet instruments. At a later date, automatic token exchange apparatus was introduced on the main lines, and many of the crossing loops were re-aligned to give the straighter road to the direction in which the faster running might be expected.

In 1897 parliamentary powers were obtained for doubling the line throughout between Stanley and Aviemore, including abolition of the 310-yard Murthly Tunnel, but only the portion over the Grampians was widened. The opening dates appear in Appendix V. Likewise, an ambitious scheme to double the line between Aviemore and Inverness was not proceeded with, but some relief was afforded by provision of extra crossing places between sta-

ROLLING STOCK

(26) *Five-compartment third No 145 was one of twenty third-class carriages built in 1873 by the Metropolitan Carriage & Wagon Co for the extension of the North line to Wick and Thurso. They were expected to seat fifty.*

(27) *Six-wheel third No 29 adjacent to one of David Jones's coupé-ended first-class carriages.*

INVERNESS

(28) 'Clan' class 4—6—0 No 14769 (HR No 57) Clan Cameron *leaves Inverness in 1928.*

(29) 'Castle' class 4—6—0 No 146 Skibo Castle *waits to leave Inverness with what appears to be a mixed train; it was common practice for the HR to include fitted goods vehicles in passenger trains. Behind the locomotive may be seen a typical HR brake van with 'dovecot window' as the raised central section was termed on the Highland. The HR and GNSR both used 'Engine Following' boards to advise that a special train would follow or that the regular train would follow the special carrying the board.*

tions and a crossing loop at certain additional roadside stations; locations and opening dates are shown in Appendix II.

So successful was the widening that it was soon decided to continue from Druimuachdar to Dalwhinnie, a distance of 5½ miles. The first section, to Balsporran (signalbox), was brought into use on 1 June 1908, and the work was completed on 17 May 1909.

A further section of widening was put in hand a few years later, in much easier country immediately north of Inverness. The first 1¼ miles, from the terminus to Clachnaharry, were not included, because the doubling of this length would have necessitated the widening of the bridges over the River Ness and the Caledonian Canal. Beyond Clachnaharry station, however, a double line was provided as far as Clunes, a distance of six miles. When completed in 1914, the double-line mileage on the Highland Railway was:

Section			Opening Date	Distance
Inverness to Dalcross	...	...	1864	6¾ miles
Inverness to Daviot	...	...	1898	11 ,,
Blair Atholl to Dalwhinnie	...	1900-1909	23¼ ,,
Clachnaharry to Clunes	...	1913-1914	6 ,,
Total	...	47 miles	

Similar provision was made north of Clunes, reducing the single-line sections on the northern main line to about five miles, but the loop at The Mound could only be used for goods trains, or for one passenger and one goods train, as the station had only one platform on the main line; the side platform served the Dornoch branch.

For about three miles north of Boat of Garten, the main line of the Highland Railway and the Strathspey branch of the Great North of Scotland Railway were laid side by side. This section was worked as two single lines, and the only physical connection was imme-

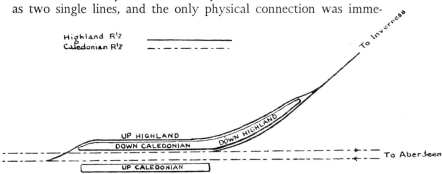

The Track Layout at Stanley Junction.

diately south of the station. The arrangement was adopted to save a signalbox at the point of divergence.

Another curious layout was at Stanley Junction. Down trains for the Highland Railway were accommodated at an extension of the down platform, clear of the line to Aberdeen, while up trains used the outer face of the same platform, joining the Caledonian Railway south of the station. This arrangement enabled a Highland up train to clear the single line, and yet wait before proceeding towards Perth. In the same way, a Highland down train could stand at the platform until an up train had arrived, leaving both Caledonian roads clear.

At one time it was proposed to continue the widening of the mountain section from Dalwhinnie to Newtonmore, or possibly as far as Aviemore, but none of this work was ever started. Nor did any part of a far more ambitious scheme for doubling the line right through to Inverness ever get beyond the proposal stage. Some relief was, however, afforded by the provision of extra crossing places between stations and a crossing loop at certain additional roadside stations.

The following table gives details of the additional crossing facilities, with the dates of opening:

SOUTHERN MAIN LINE (Perth to Inverness)

EXTRA LOOPS (Between Stations)

Name of Loop	Between	Opening Date
Inchmagranachan	Dunkeld and Dalguise	9 July 1897
Moulinearn	Ballinluig and Pitlochry	8 July 1897
Inchlea	Dalwhinnie and Newtonmore	8 July 1897
Dalraddy	Kincraig and Aviemore	28 June 1903
Kingswood	Murthly and Dunkeld	3 June 1908
Etteridge	Dalwhinnie and Newtonmore	25 June 1911

EXTRA LOOPS (At Stations)

Station		Opening Date
Killiecrankie	...	9 July 1896
[1]Gollanfield Junction	...	1 July 1899
[2]Auldearn	...	3 July 1905

These works reduced the length of the single-line sections on the southern main line to an average of approximately three miles.

[1] The station was re-modelled as the junction for the Fort George branch, opened on the same day.

[2] This station had only been opened in 1895.

NORTHERN MAIN LINE (Inverness to Wick)

EXTRA LOOPS (Between Stations)

Name of Loop	Between	Opening Date
[1]Bruichnain	Clachnaharry and Bunchrew	15 Mar. 1902
Acheilidh	Lairg and Rogart	1 July 1909

EXTRA LOOPS (At Stations)

Station			Opening Date
Culrain	...	...	2 June 1902
[2]Clunes	...	...	13 June 1904
Fearn	...	...	30 July 1910
Conon	...	...	29 June 1911
[3]Fowlis	...	...	4 Oct. 1916

These works reduced the length of the single-line sections on the northern main line to about five miles, but the loop at The Mound could only be used for goods trains, or for one passenger and one goods train, as the station had only one platform on the main line; the side platform served the Dornoch branch.

EASTERN SECTION (Forres to Keith)

EXTRA LOOPS (Between Stations)
None was provided.

EXTRA LOOPS (At Stations)

Station			Opening Date
Mosstowie	...	...	1 July 1902
Kinloss	...	...	30 May 1904

These works reduced the length of the single-line sections between Forres and Keith to about 3¾ miles.

[1] This loop subsequently became part of the double-line section from Clachnaharry to Clunes.

[2] This loop subsequently formed the end of the widening from Clachnaharry to Clunes.

[3] The loop was constructed immediately to the south of the station, clear of the platform.

WESTERN SECTION (Dingwall to Kyle of Lochalsh)

EXTRA LOOPS (Between Stations)

Name of Loop	Between	Opening Date
[1]Luib Summit	Achnasheen and Glencarron Platform	1 Feb. 1918

EXTRA LOOPS (At Stations)

Station	Opening Date
Achnashellach	1 June 1900

While the crossing loop at Luib Summit was in use, the average length of the single-line sections was reduced from seven miles (approx.) to $6\frac{1}{4}$ miles (approx.).

THE HIGHLAND RAILWAY IN WARTIME

Immediately after the outbreak of war in 1914 the North of Scotland became of extreme strategical importance. The Fleet was already at Scapa Flow, in the Orkneys, and a permanent naval base was established there. The nearest point of embarkation on the mainland was Scrabster Harbour, situated two miles from Thurso.

Further south, at Invergordon, on the Cromarty Firth, a huge repair base for ships of war was established. The works included a new pier (carrying railway sidings, water mains, and oil-pipe lines), well-equipped engineering shops, stores and housing accommodation for about 4,000 workers. Situated 31 miles from Inverness, on the northern main line of the Highland Railway, Invergordon in pre-war days was little more than a village. It began to assume importance when the Admiralty adopted the Cromarty Firth as a practice base, and an oil-fuel depot was established there. The number of tanks was greatly increased in the early days of the war. Three large military camps, accommodating some 7,000 men, were also established in the vicinity. While these new works were in progress, every siding north of Perth was choked with wagons consigned to Invergordon which the main line of the Highland Railway was unable to accommodate.

The building of the defence works at Scapa Flow and the entrance to the Cromarty Firth brought a huge timber traffic to the Highland Railway. Whole trainloads of heavy baulks were sent to Scapa for

[1] This loop was provided to accommodate heavy war-time traffic, and was removed after conditions had returned to normal. It was situated four miles west of Achnasheen.

(G) *'Jones Goods' 4—6—0 No 103 was used on many special trains between 1959–65 and is seen here at the Thurso branch platform at Georgemas Junction with an RCTS/SLS railtour on 15 June 1962*

this purpose. Simultaneously came an urgent and ever-increasing demand for pit-timber to be sent southwards, and large areas in the North of Scotland were completely denuded of trees. This work was performed largely by the Canadian Forestry Battalion, but, in certain cases, German prisoners were employed. By 1918 this class of traffic had increased to ten times its normal amount.

Prior to the war, coal for the North of Scotland was carried almost exclusively by coaling steamers. The bulk of this traffic was subsequently transferred to the railway, and there were occasions when the sidings of nearly all the stations between Inverness and Wick were blocked with coal wagons which could not be moved because of the congested state of the lines. The Highland Railway, on whose system there were no coalfields, had to obtain from collieries south of Perth the greatly-increased quantities of locomotive coal required for working the heavy additional traffic. Fortunately the Company was not called upon to handle the huge supplies of Admiralty coal required at Scapa. These were taken by rail to Grangemouth Docks, on the Firth of Forth, and shipped thence by sea.

Inverness became a centre for the distribution of ammunition to the Grand Fleet, and for this purpose a new branch from the station to the harbour was constructed under rather exceptional circumstances. The line was proposed early in 1915, and the Highland Railway undertook to complete it in six weeks. No more was heard of the scheme until in the middle of May a message was received that the work must be started at once, as trains carrying ammunition had already been despatched from the south! The chief engineer undertook to carry out the task in a fortnight and, assisted by 100 men from the Royal Engineers, he kept his promise. The new line was so far completed in ten days that the first of the waiting trains was able to use it.

Letters and parcels to and from the Grand Fleet were also concentrated at Inverness. To accommodate this heavy traffic, a special shed was built on the station premises, and additional accommodation was subsequently provided in part of the laundry belonging to the Station Hotel. The mails were first sorted on the train between Perth and Inverness, and placed in bags bearing the names of the ships to which they were to go. Subsequently the sorting carriage was put on at Edinburgh. On arrival at Inverness, fresh bags for the Post Offices at the various naval bases were made up. From the bases the bags were sent to the ships concerned.

The huge influx of goods traffic did not by any means represent

(H) *Birmingham RCW Type 2 D5337 alongside Loch Carron with an Inverness to Kyle of Lochalsh train; this stretch of line has few rivals for scenic beauty*

the whole of the extra burden thrown upon the Highland Railway. Following the adoption of the North of Scotland and the Orkneys as naval bases, large and increasing numbers of officers and men had to be carried to and from London and elsewhere. This traffic was naturally irregular, and depended on fleet movements, leave, or other conditions. For some time attempts were made to spread it over a number of trains, but this arrangement was not a success, and the whole position threatened to become chaotic.

At length, it was decided to run a special naval train every weekday in each direction, between London (Euston) and Thurso. The train made its first journey on 15 February 1917, and continued to run until 30 April 1919. Until 20 May 1917 it ran from Carlisle to Perth non-stop, *via* the Caledonian Railway, but after that date it was diverted over the Waverley route of the North British Railway to Edinburgh, and reached Perth *via* the Forth Bridge. This alteration enabled men for Rosyth Dockyard to reach their destination without changing. The journey of 717 miles from London to Thurso was covered in 21½ hours. In the reverse direction the time was 22 h. 20 m. The train ran 272 miles over the Highland Railway in 10½ hours (approx.), including a wait of 30 m. at Inverness for meals. North of Inverness stops were made at Alness and Invergordon for passengers, and at Helmsdale and Forsinard for locomotive purposes. The up train left Thurso at 11.45 a.m. throughout the year. In the opposite direction London was left at 6 p.m. in the summer and 3 p.m. in the winter. The earlier departure during the winter months enabled embarkation at Thurso to be completed during daylight.

The special usually consisted of 14 vehicles, although on occasions it was run in two or three parts. Sleeping accommodation was provided for officers. The train was made up entirely of corridor stock, and the travelling master-at-arms thus had easy access to all coaches. Certain compartments were converted into prison cells for naval prisoners who had outstayed their leave, or who were guilty of other offences. The number of prisoners on the train might be anything up to 35.

When the length of the journey is taken into consideration, the record of punctuality is high. On Sunday 13 January 1918 the northbound special became stuck in a deep snowdrift near Scotscalder and there was no early prospect of getting it free again. Next morning the 300 passengers abandoned the train and tramped across the snow to Thurso, a distance of eight miles. So deep were the drifts, and so severe the weather, that a week elapsed before the line had been sufficiently cleared for normal traffic to be resumed. Meantime, the specials terminated at Invergordon, whence the men proceeded by sea to Scapa Flow.

In addition to the regular naval special, many extra troop and naval specials were required. At Invergordon alone, between August 1914 and August 1919, no less than 1,020 special trains, in addition to naval ambulance trains, were dealt with.

Quite early in the war the North of Scotland received the unwelcome attentions of enemy spies. Two of them, a man and a woman, were arrested in the Station Hotel at Inverness, thanks to the vigilance of the staff. They were taken to London for trial and convicted. It was no doubt owing to experiences such as these that in August 1916, Inverness and the whole of the country to the west and north were declared a special military area. Railway passengers who arrived at Inverness without a permit were not allowed to leave the station or continue their journeys to places beyond. In the same way, naval ratings or civilians proceeding to the Grand Fleet had to be identified by the senior naval officer's staff before they were allowed to go further.

The entry of the United States of America into the war brought a heavy extra traffic to the Highland Railway. It was decided to lay a huge minefield, known as the Northern Barrage, from the Orkneys to the Norwegian coast, a distance of over 230 miles. The United States were to supply the materials, which were to be shipped to the North of Scotland in parts, and assembled there ready for use. The work of assembling and laying the mines was to be carried out by American naval ratings, and two bases were set up, one at Inverness, and the other at Dalmore, near Invergordon.

The two bases were known as 'U.S. Naval Base 18' and 'U.S. Naval Base 17' respectively. The former was situated near the Muirtown Basin of the Caledonian Canal, about a mile from Inverness. Stores and workshops were erected nearby, and the Highland Railway's canal branch was commandeered by the Admiralty, and greatly extended. The American staff was housed in the adjacent Glen Albyn Distillery. Material for this base was brought across the Atlantic to the western end of the canal, at Corpach, where it was transhipped into lighters and conveyed through the canal to Muirtown.

At Dalmore, another distillery was requisitioned. In this case it was converted into workshops and stores, the staff being accommodated in hutments close by. Work on the new base was started in January 1918, and the first mines arrived in the following May.

INVERNESS.

The Highland Railway Company's
STATION HOTEL.

Patronised by their Royal Highnesses the Prince and Princess of Wales,
the Duke of Cambridge Prince and Princess Christian,
and other Members of the Royal Family, and by most of the Nobility of Europe.

This Large and Handsome Hotel, adjoining the Station, with all the modern Improvements, and elegantly Furnished, is acknowledged to be one of the best appointed in the Kingdom. Has recently undergone extensive Additions and Alterations, and contains numerous Suites of comfortable and lofty Apartments. A new elegant Coffee-room, Drawing-room **Smoking** and Billiard-rooms, Lavatories, and Bath rooms.

Pianos are at the free disposal of the occupants in every Private Sitting-room.

Parties leaving in the morning can go over the grand Scenery along the Skye Railway, or visit either Loch-Maree, Gairloch, Dunrobin, or Golspie, and return the same day to the Hotel.

Table d'Hôte at 6.30 and 7.30; on Sundays at 5 p.m. only.

AN OMNIBUS ATTENDS THE STEAMERS.
HOTEL PORTERS ATTEND AT THE STATION.
POSTING

TARIFF:

SITTING-ROOMS—Ground Floor, per Day 5s	LUNCHEONS and SUPPERS—Cold Meat 1s 6d
Do. —1st Floor . 7s 6d to 10s	Soup . . . . . . 1s and 1s 6d
BEDROOMS—1st „ . . 3s 6d	DINNERS—From the Joints . 2s 6d
Do. —2nd „ . . 3s 0d	Soups, Fish, Entrées, &c., &c., as per daily bill
Do. —3rd „ . . 2s 6d	of fare, at proportionally moderate charges.
If two Persons occupy one Bed, 1s extra.	TABLE D'HÔTE 4s 6d
BOARD—Plain BREAKFASTS & TEAS. 1s 6d	SPECIAL DINNERS in Private Sitting-
Do., with Cold Meat or Broiled	Rooms from 5s
Ham 2s	
Do., with Chops or White Fish, 2s 6d	A large assortment of choice WINES as per
Do., with Salmon, Steak, or	List.
Ham and Eggs, or Chicken	
with Ham and Tongue 3s	FIRES—Sitting-room, 1s 6d ; Bedroom, 1s.
TABLE D'HÔTE BREAKFAST . . 3s	BATHS—Hot, 1s 6d ; Cold, 1s ; Hip or
	Sponge, 6d.

SERVICE—A charge of 1s 6d per day will be made to Visitors occupying **Rooms**. In other cases, 3d per Meal.

A Large Comfortable Room is provided for Commercial Gentlemen.

EDWARD CESARI, Manager.

Gracious living as advertised in the timetable of July 1885

There was at first no pier available, and the mines had to be sent by rail to Invergordon, four miles distant, largely by means of an extra line, laid beside a public road. The construction of a pier was begun in July 1918, but it was not finished until after the Armistice had been signed. In 1919 it proved exceedingly useful when the Northern Barrage was being dismantled.

Material for Dalmore was landed at Kyle of Lochalsh, and sent thence by train. Ships from America arrived about once per fortnight, and three or four special trains were then worked daily for about a week. Because of the heavy gradients and sharp curves between Dingwall and Kyle, loads were restricted to 11 wagons each. The whole railway west of Dingwall, together with the pier at Kyle, was commandeered by the Admiralty. The Highland Railway was allowed to run one train each way for passengers and mails, but all goods traffic for the Isle of Skye and the Outer Hebrides by this route was stopped. Whatever was sent had to be worked by sea from Glasgow.

The Company's hotels also played their part in the struggle. At the Station Hotel in Inverness scenes of great activity were witnessed. Prior to the provision of naval barracks, many ratings who had arrived in Inverness too late to complete their journey the same day were accommodated on hastily-made-up shakedowns on the floor. Later on, officers and men travelling by the Euston—Thurso naval special were provided with a meal during the short time that the train waited at the station. There were occasions when the numbers catered for approached 1,000 in a single day.

At Kyle of Lochalsh the hotel was taken over and used for officers and quarters in connection with the work of the senior naval officer for the district. The hotel at Dornoch was used first by the Gordon Highlanders, while they were in training in the district, and later by the Canadian Forestry Corps. To provide hospital accommodation for the American naval ratings on service in this country, the Strathpeffer Hotel was commandeered.

The Highland was a comparatively small railway, and the task of those responsible for its operation was beset with peculiar difficulties. Of the 272 miles of main line between Perth and Thurso, only about 47 were double track (including the 7¼ miles from Perth to Stanley Junction), although there was the alternative route from Aviemore to Inverness, via Forres. Nor was the system well provided with sidings. On the outbreak of the war the Company possessed only 75 miles. Between Perth and Inverness, both of which are practically at sea level, the trains have to surmount one summit of 1,484 ft, and another of 1,315 ft, by means of long and severe gradients. On the northern main line, the railway reaches a height of 484 ft above sea level, near Lairg, and of 708 ft, near Forsinard.

Under pre-war conditions the traffic was only heavy during the summer. The bulk of the necessary repairs to the track and rolling stock were carried out during the rest of the year. The Company's stock of locomotives, carriages and wagons was limited, although it sufficed for all normal needs.

Such, in brief, was the system that was suddenly called upon to handle a vastly increased traffic, and it is not surprising that the Company soon found itself in serious difficulties. The continuous heavy work since August 1914 rendered it impossible to carry out the usual programme of locomotive repairs during the winter. By the summer of 1915, partly for this reason, and partly on account of the excessive strain to which they were subjected, locomotives were constantly breaking down. In August of that year, out of 152 engines owned by the Company, 50 had had to be withdrawn from service, and 50 others were in urgent need of repairs. Nor was it possible to remedy these deficiencies. Many of the Company's engine-fitters had been called up for service, and there were not enough left to carry out repairs. Engines sent to repairing firms in the south were detained for long periods for like reasons. Not only was important Government traffic seriously delayed, but there was every prospect of a complete failure.

An appeal was made to the Railway Executive Committee, and a meeting took place, at Perth, between the locomotive superintendent and the chief engineer of the Highland Railway, and the mechanical engineers of certain other railways. As a result, it was decided that 20 locomotives should be loaned to the Highland by other companies; that any fitters that could be spared from other railways should be released for temporary employment at Inverness; and that representations should be made to the War Office with a view to securing the return of certain Highland fitters then serving with the Forces. The efforts to obtain extra skilled labour failed completely, but the additional engine power proved invaluable.

A year later the situation again became acute. Three crossing loops, between Perth and Inverness, had been closed for lack of signalmen. The main line was badly congested with special traffic, while many of the regular trains had to be run in duplicate, or even triplicate. Nineteen engines were still on loan, but 42 of the Company's own locomotives were undergoing repairs. To these difficulties was added another, in the form of a serious shortage of wagons. Ordinary and special goods traffic had greatly increased, and the various forestry camps in the Highlands were responsible for a large and growing timber traffic.

An appreciable measure of relief was afforded by diverting a large amount of goods traffic for the south over the Great North of Scotland Railway, *via* Keith and Aberdeen, but this arrangement by no means solved the problem, and a number of wagons were hired from certain Scottish and English companies. In February 1918, 150 additional 12-ton coal wagons were secured from the South Eastern & Chatham Railway for carrying the American mines from Kyle of Lochalsh. These trains were hauled by engines supplied by the London & South Western Railway.

By the summer of 1918 the Highland Railway had 850 wagons on loan, but notice had been given that 700 of these would be required by their owners in the early autumn. As the result of further appeals to the Railway Executive Committee, it was arranged that 1,150 wagons should be loaned to the Company (in addition to those specially reserved for the Kyle of Lochalsh traffic).

Nor did the advent of peace at once relieve the Highland of its difficulties. There was a progressive decline in naval and military traffic, but the timber traffic continued to be exceptionally heavy. The position was also complicated by the resumption of holiday traffic in the summer of 1919.

Had it not been for the Government control, and the existence of the powerful Railway Executive Committee, the Highland Railway would have been faced with an impossible task during the war years. Fortunately, as part of a temporarily unified national railway system, it was able to rely for help on its larger partners. It was this fact alone that enabled the Company to avoid the complete breakdown that would have been little short of a national disaster.

Out of a staff of approximately 3,000 in August 1914, no less than 756 served with the fighting forces in the course of the next four years, and 87 made the supreme sacrifice. A memorial to the fallen was placed on the wall of the head offices in the Station Square at Inverness, and unveiled on 6 August 1921 by General Lord Horne.

SOME NOTABLE ACCIDENTS

Throughout its history, the Highland Railway enjoyed an exceptional freedom from serious accidents. Minor mishaps there were in plenty, but until the year 1894 it stood to the Company's credit that no accident had been fatal to a passenger. In that year there was a collision, resulting in one death. Many years passed by, and then, in 1914, came a second disaster in which several passengers lost their lives. But it must be admitted that the circumstances were exceptional, and could not have been foreseen.

The opening ceremony of the Inverness & Nairn Railway, in November 1855, was marred by an alarming incident. A young man riding in one of the open trucks of the special train incautiously leaned over the side of the vehicle and struck his head against the abutment of a bridge. Fortunately his injuries, although serious, did not prove fatal.

As an instance of the rather slipshod methods of early railway working, on 6 May 1856, as a passenger train from Nairn to Inverness was approaching the terminus, it was diverted, without warning, on to the harbour branch and came into collision with some loaded wagons. Several passengers were bruised and shaken. It transpired that after the passage of the wagons on to the branch, the points had not been reset for the main line, to allow the train to enter the station.

Shortly after the opening of the line to Keith, the unfinished state of the Spey viaduct at Orton (see Chapter 2), together with unauthorized procedure, gave rise to an accident at Mulben. On 4 September 1858 the last train of the day (the 4.45 p.m. from Inverness) had been hauled over the bridge by means of ropes, and was waiting, on the east side, for the engine to take it on to Keith. The driver backed on to his train somewhat too hard, with the result that the special brake van, attached at the rear of all trains between Elgin and Keith, because of the steep gradients on either side of the Spey viaduct, was derailed. Efforts to re-rail the van failed, and it was finally decided to let the train proceed to Keith, on the understanding that the driver should return with the engine to pick up the vehicle. The stationmaster at Mulben, unaware of this arrangement, closed his station for the night after the train had passed and, in accordance with his instructions, set the points for a safety siding, at the head of the gradient leading down to the river.

On arrival at Keith, the driver shunted the coaches into a siding, and set out to pick up the derailed van. With him, on the engine, were his fireman, the guard of the train, and three engine cleaners, who wished to return to their homes. The engine was diverted, without warning, into the siding at Mulben, and derailed at the buffer stops. The three cleaners were killed, and the guard and fireman seriously injured. The primary responsibility was found to rest with the driver and guard, who had returned along the main line without seeking authority, or without warning the station-master at Mulben.

Failure to take adequate precautions with a heavy train led to a collision at Pitlochry on 21 October 1865. The 12.40 p.m. passenger train from Inverness to Perth was approaching the station, when the brakes proved insufficient, and the train ran past the platform, and came into sidelong collision with a down train, which was just arriving. The latter sustained considerable damage, and nine passengers were injured. The inspecting officer drew attention to the necessity for an adequate reserve of brake power on a line abounding in steep gradients, and suggested that at stations where trains were booked to cross, one should be brought to rest before the other was allowed to approach the crossing loop.

It would appear, however, that some six years later the traffic arrangements were still far from perfect. On 9 November 1871 a collision occurred at Dava, in which five persons were injured. A heavy passenger train required assistance in the rear up the long bank to the summit, but the pilot engine was not attached while the coaches were at rest. Instead it was sent in pursuit, after the train had left, with the result that it came into violent collision with the rear vehicle. At the enquiry, the Board of Trade inspector stressed the undesirability of pilot engines following moving trains.[1]

Nor were the regulations governing single-line working always strictly observed. On 11 November 1872 an up goods train from Tain to Inverness arrived at Novar, where it was booked to cross the down mail train. In defiance of the regulations the stationmaster allowed the goods train to draw forward to pick up some sacks of potatoes, which had been stacked beside the line. Before it could return to the crossing loop, the passenger train arrived, and a collision took place in which eight persons were injured.

Within a few days of the opening of the railway to Wick and Thurso, a rather curious mishap occurred near Altnabreac, on 6 August 1874. Torrential rain had fallen for some hours, and the sides of a shallow cutting were badly washed away. As the early-morning train from Wick to the south was approaching, a mass of rock, about 1½ tons in weight, fell across the track. The engine and the first two vehicles were completely derailed, but the passengers escaped with a shaking.

An accident that might have had very serious results occurred on 26 November 1885, at The Mound, where the line runs for some

[1] This practice was not confined to the Highland. It was allowed for some years on other railways.

distance close to the seashore. An up mixed train, made up of 11 wagons and seven passenger vehicles, was approaching the station, when an axle on one of the leading wagons broke, and the whole train was derailed. The engine and several wagons ploughed along the track for about 500 yd before coming to rest, but the remainder of the train, including the passenger coaches, ran down the embankment and fell in the sea. There were several passengers on the train, but all escaped with a shaking and a wetting.

The year 1886 was remarkable for a series of mishaps to mixed trains. In each case the goods wagons were marshalled in front of the passenger coaches, a practice contrary to the recommendations of the Board of Trade. On 24 May a train consisting of 40 wagons and two passenger coaches was descending the incline between Dava and Forres when one of the rear vehicles ran off the road. The engine and the leading wagons continued in safety, but the remainder of the train was derailed. A few days later, on 1 June, another derailment, due to a broken axle, took place between Golspie and Brora. In this case, the train consisted of 34 goods wagons and two passenger coaches marshalled in the rear. The third mishap occurred on 28 September between Mulben and Keith, with a short train. None of these accidents resulted in more than slight injuries to passengers.[1]

In his report, the Board of Trade inspecting officer drew attention to the undesirability of placing wagons in front of passenger coaches on mixed trains. Not only did it deprive the driver of his continuous brake, but in each of the above cases the derailment was due to a wagon running off the road. The passengers would have suffered no ill-effects had the marshalling been reversed.

The railway Company replied that it was unable to adopt the Board's recommendations, as this would necessitate the removal of the passenger coaches before shunting operations could be carried out, and the trains would suffer considerable delay.

An unusual accident occurred on 14 October 1892, at Achnashellach, on the Dingwall & Skye Railway. When the afternoon mixed train from Dingwall arrived, the engine was detached to do some shunting, the weight of the coaches overcame the resistance of the brake in the rear van, which was out of order, and the whole train ran back down a steep gradient. It came to rest some distance up the succeeding rise, whence it moved forward once more towards the station.

[1] The Company was not always so fortunate. In a similar mishap between Kingussie and Kincraig, on 2 August 1888, six persons were injured.

Although darkness had fallen, the engine was sent back to pick up the train. It had proceeded some distance when it met the runaways moving in the opposite direction, and a violent collision ensued in which eight passengers were seriously injured. The primary responsibility for the accident was found to rest with the guard and driver, who should not have allowed the engine to be uncoupled until the train was adequately braked. The stationmaster was also severely censured for sending the engine in pursuit of the runaways, before he had ascertained their exact whereabouts.

The Regulation of Railways Act of 1889 brought the question of mixed trains to a head. Under the Act, the Board of Trade issued an order to the Highland Railway on 16 February 1891, requiring all passenger vehicles on mixed trains to be marshalled next to the engine, so that the continuous brake might work on them. On more than one occasion the time given to the railway Company in which to comply with the order was extended, and it was not until 1 January 1896 that it came into force. It would appear, however, that some 18 months later the regulations were not always observed, and correspondence passed between the Board of Trade and the Company.

On 20 September 1897, the general manager stated that in future trains would comply with the order. Five days later, however, a mixed train was allowed to leave Dingwall for Strome Ferry with four passenger coaches attached in the rear. Near Raven Rock Summit a coupling broke between two goods wagons, and the ten rear vehicles began to run back down the steep incline. Gathering speed, they overcame the brake in the guard's van, and it was not until they had covered nearly six miles, and crashed through the gates of a level crossing, that they could be brought to rest, some 200 yd from the junction with the main line. Fortunately, there was no derailment, and the passengers escaped unhurt. The mishap was due to the failure of a faulty coupling on another company's wagon, and could not have been prevented, but the inspecting officer pointed out that the passenger coaches need not have been involved had the marshalling been reversed. The Company's representative stated that following the occurrence the Board of Trade order had been enforced.

On 2 August 1894 a collision occurred at Newtonmore in which one passenger was killed and eight other persons seriously injured. The 11.50 a.m. passenger train from Perth to Inverness was booked to cross an up goods train at Kingussie, but on that day it was running late, and the goods train was allowed to proceed to

Newtonmore. For some reason which was never satisfactorily explained, the points at the south end of the station were left set for the up crossing loop, but the down home signal was, of course, locked in the 'on' position. Unfortunately, the down distant signal was defective, and had remained at 'all clear' after the passing of the previous train. The driver of the passenger train observed this signal and, expecting a clear road, approached the station at the usual speed. The train overran the home signal, and collided head-on with the engine of the goods train.

Amongst the passengers was Professor Dobbie, of Edinburgh, who was taking one of his horses by train to Inverness. From Perth to Blair Atholl, the professor had travelled in an ordinary compartment, in the centre of the train, but wishing to feed the animal, he alighted at that station, and travelled thence in the horsebox, marshalled next to the engine. This change cost him his life, because the leading vehicle bore the brunt of the collision.

By a curious coincidence, this same train was involved in the most serious accident that ever occurred on the Highland Railway. Soon after noon on 18 June 1914, a terrific thunderstorm broke in the hills near Carr Bridge, on the direct line to Inverness. Swollen by torrential rain, the waters of the Baddengorm Burn, which passes under the railway close to the station, rose to an abnormal height. The arch of the bridge became blocked with tree trunks and other debris, with the result that the water became 20 ft deep and 170 ft wide on the upstream side, and the foundations of the bridge were undermined.

When the train reached the bridge, the structure had partially collapsed, but the damage was not apparent from the footplate. The subsidence of the track threw the tender of the engine off the road, and the train came to rest on the bridge. The extra weight of the coaches caused the complete collapse of the arch, and the train was thrown down the bank. The middle passenger coach fell into the raging torrent, and was submerged. Five passengers were drowned, and nine others injured.

It was stated at the enquiry that the bridge had been solidly built and well maintained. Every reasonable allowance had been made for sudden floods, but the storm was exceptionally severe. The flood had even demolished the century-old road bridge a short distance upstream and had swept away many tons of soil from the adjacent farm lands. The disaster was due to the scouring effect of the water seeking an outlet, after the arch had become blocked. A new bridge, with an even more generous allowance for flood water,

KYLE OF LOCHALSH

(30)   *The pier at Kyle with David MacBrayne's vessel* Lovedale, *built in 1867 and formerly owned by the Great Western Railway. The ship was usually employed on the Stornoway mail service.*

(31)   *Kyle of Lochalsh engine shed on 18 June 1937 with two 'Superheated Goods' 4—6—0s, better known as 'Clan Goods', and a 'Small Ben'. The numbers are indecipherable but in November 1935 the allocation was 4—6—0s Nos 17950 and 17951 (HR Nos 75 and 76) and 4—4—0 No 14416 (HR No 47) Ben a' Bhuird. By May 1957, the only engine permanently stationed at the shed was Caledonian 0—4—4T No 55216. Lattice post signals, like the fine example on the embankment, were most common on the Kyle line, wooden posts being the norm.*

THE FAR NORTH

(32) *The most northerly station in Britain: Thurso c1890 with rebuilt 'Glenbarry' class 2—4—0 No 55 Invergordon with coupé-bodied coach next to the engine. It is surprising to see the door to the leading compartment open, as these were generally locked when next to the engine, which was probably a precaution against the possibility of coal becoming dislodged and breaking the glass.*

(33) *Wick shed in 1935 with 'Castle' class 4—6—0 No 14676 (HR No 141) Ballindalloch Castle, a 'Small Ben' and 'Big Goods'.*

was erected in the remarkably short space of three weeks. Meanwhile, all traffic had to be sent *via* Forres.[1]

THE SNOW FIEND

Although the North of Scotland enjoys the advantages of an insular climate, and its extremes of cold are still further tempered by the genial influence of the Gulf Stream, the advent of winter frequently brings heavy falls of snow. It seldom happens, however, that the weather is uniformly severe throughout the country, and a raging blizzard may sweep Sutherland and Caithness, while on the Grampians the snow is comparatively light. In the same way the moors of Ross-shire may escape lightly, when deep drifts are accumulating in the uplands of Moray. As a general rule, storms are more severe in the east than in the west.

Fortunately, avalanches are rare in the Highlands, and in no case are conditions near a railway suitable for their occurrence. On the other hand, serious difficulties frequently arise through deep drifting.

A snowfall of quite moderate depth, if accompanied by a high wind, can pile up in drifts several feet thick. And the wind frequently blows the already deposited snow across open country until it encounters some obstacle—such as the side of a railway cutting—against which it can accumulate.

The Inverness & Nairn and Inverness & Aberdeen Junction Railways passed through comparatively low-lying country, where the risk of serious drifting was reduced to a minimum, but it was otherwise with the direct line to Perth, which crossed high mountains, and bleak, open moorlands, affording little, if any, protection from the fury of the storm. In the spring of 1864, after the railway had been open for seven months, the engineer reported that, although there had been several sharp storms, no serious trouble had arisen. In February 1865, however, snow fell heavily throughout the North of Scotland, and communication between Perth and Inverness was only restored with difficulty after the line had been closed for five days. It was realised that special precautions were necessary to guard against deep drifting.

It was decided to erect artificial barriers, known as 'snow fences', beside the railway at the most vulnerable points. The fences were

[1] A similar cloudburst occurred on 8 July 1923, at almost the same point. In this case, the material damage was far greater, and the line was closed for some weeks. Fortunately no train was involved.

built up from old sleepers, set upright in the ground, like a palisade.[1]
A careful study of local conditions determined the direction from
which the worst drifting usually occurred, and for that reason the
fences were not always parallel to the track. The snow accumulated
on the weather side of the fence, leaving the lee side more or less
clear. Experience showed that one line of fencing was not always
sufficient, and a second, or even a third, line was provided in certain
cases. Sometimes fences were needed on both sides of the line.

North of Inverness, on the borders of Sutherland and Caithness,
a special type of fencing, known as a 'blower', the invention of a
Lancashire man named Howie, was tried with some success. Close-
boarded fences, very similar to long wooden tables, were erected on
both sides of the track, much closer to the rails than the ordinary
snow fences. The inner edges of the blowers almost touched the
ground, but the outer edges were raised some eight or ten feet.
These artificial troughs deflected the wind currents away from the
railway, causing the snow to be swept up and deposited on the far
side, out of harm's way.[2]

To preserve the lines of communication intact during severe
storms, telegraph poles were placed in the most sheltered positions
possible. Point rods were encased with wood, and signal wires were
carried on high posts.

Although the snow fences afforded a large measure of protection,
deep drifts calling for the use of snowploughs were common. The
earliest ploughs were designed by William Stroudley, and were of
three types, to suit varying conditions. So successful did they prove
that those built subsequently were generally similar. At the beginning of the winter many engines were fitted with a small or nose
plough, similar to a cowcatcher, attached to the front buffer beam.
The running of the engine was not impeded in any way, and if
necessary two engines could be coupled together. Engines so fitted
were used for hauling trains, and were capable of overcoming drifts
up to 2 ft in depth. If the depth of snow was between 2 and 5 ft,
a pilot engine fitted with a somewhat larger plough was attached to
the train. The third and largest type of plough extended to the top
of the smokebox of the engine, and was used for clearing the line
of drifts of 10 or 12 ft. Three or four engines were coupled together,
and the plough charged at full speed into the snow from a distance
of about half a mile.

[1] At some points, mounds of earth were made to serve the same purpose.
[2] On the Burghead branch, where the line ran some miles beside the
shore of the Moray Firth, blowers were used to clear the line of drifted sand.

If the engines were unable to force their way through the drift, they had to be dug out, and the line cleared by manual labour, a task rendered the harder if the line was in a deep cutting, as the snow had first to be thrown part of the way up the slope, whence a second, or even a third, gang of men lifted it clear over the top. Often an accumulation of ice in the flange-ways threw the snow-plough engines off the road, and it was no easy matter to get them re-railed.

Whenever a heavy fall of snow was expected, the stationmasters along the line were instructed to wire reports of local weather conditions to Inverness. These telegrams were remarkable for their brevity, and, although they might vary considerably, usually mentioned the state of the wind (a matter of the utmost importance). A typical selection would read as follows:

'Fair and calm.'

'High wind, but little snow.'

'Snowing heavily, but little wind.'

'Heavy snow, wind rising.'

'Bad drifts. Trains should be piloted and loads reduced where possible.'

'Blizzard raging. No trains should be run unless preceded by snowplough engines.'

Long experience had shown the staff at headquarters exactly how to act on the receipt of such information. But the telegraph wires were liable to break under the weight of the snow, and outlying stations were isolated.

A close watch was kept on certain well-known danger-spots, and none gave rise to greater anxiety than Dava Moor, where the drifts frequently defied the efforts of the ploughs, with the result that the train service was temporarily suspended. On more than one occasion trains were completely buried, after being abandoned. Scarcely less notorious were the windswept heights on either side of Druimuachdar Summit, where a cutting some three miles north of Struan, known as the Black Tank, earned an evil reputation. The doubling of the railway over the mountains effected a marked improvement on this section, as the wider space between the banks gave the snow less chance to accumulate.

The bleak, exposed moors on the borders of Sutherland and Caithness have been aptly termed 'The Country of the Snow Drifts'. Between Helmsdale and Georgemas, the railway ran through the heart of this district, and serious blocks were common. One particularly bad spot, near Altnabreac, was known as the Fairy

Hillocks, a name suggestive of anything rather than trouble of this kind. As was the case at Dava, trains were buried on more than one occasion.

Fortunately it was not every winter that was memorable for its severe storms, although it was but seldom that the ploughs were idle throughout the season. During six consecutive winters, from 1866 to 1871, and again from January to March 1875, heavy snowfalls were experienced throughout the Highlands. The snowplough engines kept the line open with great difficulty, and many trains were seriously delayed. In January 1868 a sudden thaw caused extensive flooding, and the railway was severely damaged in several places. By way of contrast, the winters of 1876 and 1877 were remarkable for their mild weather and absence of snow.

The arctic conditions which prevailed throughout the winter of 1880-81 were long remembered. On 17 December a train became snowbound some distance south of Dava station, and had to be abandoned. The passengers managed to reach the shelter of the station before the storm increased to an intensity that would have rendered escape impossible. The train was completely buried, and when at last it was located, the snow had accumulated to a height of 60 ft above the coaches. An up train, carrying passengers and five trucks of cattle, shared a like fate on the other side of the station. The passengers made good their escape, but the cattle were not so fortunate. Despite desperate efforts to liberate them, the animals refused to leave the shelter of the trucks, and perished by suffocation. In after years, the men who laboured so heroically yet unavailingly to avert this catastrophe, recalled with reluctance the frenzied bellowings of the stricken beasts, who seemed conscious of the disaster that was overtaking them. A relief train, hurriedly despatched to the scene of the block, was itself lost for some time.

One month later, on 17 January, the whole country was swept by a terrific blizzard, which paralysed communications far and wide. By the 21st, two trains were buried in the snow, north of Helmsdale, and the southern main line was blocked at Dava and Druimuachdar. Telegraphic communication was completely interrupted, and on the following day a slight collision occurred, near Forres, between a snowplough engine and a passenger train. Traffic was resumed between Inverness and Perth on the 23rd, but the north line was not cleared until the 24th. For some days the service was very uncertain, and many trains were delayed.

Traffic on the Caithness line was again brought to a standstill on 7 February, although the ploughs succeeded in forcing a passage through the drifts within 24 hours. But the respite was of short duration, for on the 13th a blizzard swept over the Highlands which disorganised the whole system for three days. Thurso and Wick were isolated, and some of the drifts on the Perth line were upwards of 200 yd in length and 25 ft deep.

Further storms occurred early in March, and deep drifts accumulated at several points. Between Grantown and Forres a long length of telegraph wires collapsed under the weight of the snow, and the greater portion of the southern main line was completely cut off from headquarters. On the morning of the 3rd, Thomas Robertson, the superintendent, and a telegraph clerk, John Menmuir, travelled by train from Inverness to Grantown, *via* Elgin and the Speyside branch of the Great North of Scotland Railway, whence they made their way on horseback to a snowed-up train at Huntly's Cave, two miles south of Dava. There a wire was tapped, an instrument was placed in circuit, and for the time being crossing orders and instructions were issued from a carriage of the train.

Even more severe and long-continued were the snow blocks of 1894-1895. A severe blizzard on 29 December was followed by a succession of heavy storms in January and February, and the last of the drifts on the Highland Railway was not cleared away until 4 March. During some of this period all sections of the main line from Perth to Wick were snowbound, except the 100 miles from Inverness to Helmsdale. A regular service, suffering no more than slight delays, was worked between these points, although on more than one occasion the snowploughs had difficulty in keeping the line clear near Lairg. The Dingwall & Skye Railway was abandoned completely, while every effort was made to reopen the main lines.

The winter herring season was in full swing, and serious delays were experienced in getting the fish through from Wick to the south. One of the first trains to be snowed up was a fish special, which was completely buried near the Fairy Hillocks, after being hastily abandoned. When it was relieved, ten days later, the contents were delivered to their destinations in perfect condition. The snow had acted as a gigantic refrigerator.

Gangs of men laboured unceasingly to clear the line, and when the drift had been reduced to about a mile in length, an attempt was made to get the mails through by carrying them over the blocked section to a train waiting at the south side. Some gentlemen, who had been held up in Thurso, asked leave to accompany the party and, at length, received permission to do so 'at their own risk'. That the journey was of unusual interest, although somewhat hazardous, may be judged by the following extract from a letter written by one of them some days later:

> In the cold grey of the early morning we travelled in the van, getting various tips from the platelayers and Post Office men as to the best way of getting through the deep snow. The chief of these was to tie your trousers tightly round your boots with stout string, which you brought round under your boots, like a stirrup. Thus equipped, a line of men, each with a mail-bag over his shoulder, followed by six passengers, struggled through the deep snow. If you did not break through the crust, it was all right; if you did, you went down three or four feet, and had to drag your legs up as best you could. It was very picturesque to come upon one hundred men working in the snow in that lonely spot, looking like silhouettes against the white. The men were in triple tier, and each spadeful had to be handled three times before it reached the top.

Towards the end of January the line was cleared, and several fish specials were worked through to the south. Two days later a gale, accompanied by heavy snow, sprang up in the opposite direction and reblocked the cuttings in a single night! The position was now much worse. The passage of the ploughs had made deep artificial cuttings in open places, and the height of the natural cuttings had been increased by the snow thrown out over the sides. The arduous task of digging had to be begun all over again, rendered the harder by the height through which the snow had to be lifted before it could be thrown clear, and by further falls of snow. Meanwhile, deep drifting had occurred further south, at Dava and Druimuachdar. The ploughs had been constantly at work, and on more than one occasion traffic had been brought to a complete standstill.

Twelve years later came the Christmas blizzard of 1906. On 28 December conditions were exceptionally severe. The north mail was snowed up at Ardullie, near Foulis, and great difficulty was experienced in getting it dug out. Deep drifts accumulated on the Skye line at Achterneed, and traffic was suspended for three days.

Exceptionally deep drifts were again experienced in January 1918, on the moors of Caithness. On the 13th a snowplough engine, sent to clear the line for the Euston—Thurso naval special, became completely stuck in a drift near Scotscalder, and the special itself was snowed up a few hours later a short distance to the south. A relief train, carrying a party of 100 men, including 50 naval ratings and men taken from urgent Government work at Kyle of Lochalsh, was hastily despatched to the scene of the block, but so severe was the weather that a week elapsed before the line had been sufficiently cleared for the full service to be resumed.

CHAPTER 11

Locomotives and Rolling Stock

WILLIAM BARCLAY: 1855—1865

In readiness for the opening of the Inverness & Nairn Railway, William Barclay was appointed locomotive superintendent. He continued in this position after the Company had been amalgamated with the Inverness & Aberdeen Junction Railway. A native of Montrose, Barclay was a nephew of Alexander Allan, formerly of the London & North Western Railway, and well known as the inventor of the straight link valve motion. His engines were similar in design to those built at Crewe under the supervision of his uncle.

The locomotive works were established beside the passenger station at Inverness, on a site formerly occupied by a small sheet of water known as Loch Gorm. The buildings were surrounded by a triangle of lines formed by the approaches to the two parts of the passenger station, and the connecting spur, or Rose Street curve. Subsequently, separate carriage and wagon shops were erected on a piece of land known as Needlefield, lying to the north of the through line.

The first locomotive class introduced by Barclay consisted of four 2—2—2 tender engines which were built by Hawthorns, of Leith, between 1855 and 1857. As the Inverness & Nairn Railway was isolated from all other railways, the engines were taken by sea from Leith to Inverness. They bore numbers 1 to 4, and were named after residences of directors: No. 1, *Raigmore*; No. 2, *Aldourie*; No. 3, *St. Martin's*; No. 4, *Ardross*.

They had outside cylinders, 15 in. diameter by 20 in. stroke, 6 ft driving wheels, and 3ft 6 in. carrying wheels. The boiler carried two safety valves, and was domeless. Originally the only protection for the engine men was a small, plain weatherboard. The tenders ran on four wheels. Nos. 1 and 2 were the only two engines delivered to the Inverness & Nairn Railway, the remaining pair being built for the Inverness & Aberdeen Junction Railway. For some time they worked the whole of the passenger and goods traffic.

Nos. 1 and 2 were rebuilt as 2—4—0s by William Stroudley about the year 1869. The additional pairs of wheels were removed from Nos. 3 and 4 which were scrapped. At the same time No. 2 was provided with a large boiler, and the cylinders were enlarged to 15½ in. diameter by 22 in. stroke. As rebuilt the engines weighed 27½ tons, but details of their weights when new have not survived. No. 1 was scrapped a few years later, but No. 2 worked until 1899.

Two more singles, Nos. 12 and 13 (named *Belladrum* and *Lovat* respectively), were built by Hawthorns in 1862 for working the Inverness & Ross-shire Railway. They were generally similar to those already described, but they had 16-in. by 22-in. cylinders, and were fitted with cabs. No. 12 was rebuilt as a 2—2—2 tank engine in 1871, and put to work on the Aberfeldy branch, where it remained until 1879, named *Breadalbane*. It was reconditioned, fitted with a dome, and renamed *Strathpeffer* in 1885, and worked the branch from Dingwall to the spa for some time, being finally withdrawn in 1898. No. 13 was not converted. In 1874 it was renamed *Thurso* and sent to work the branch from that town to Georgemas Junction. It was scrapped in 1890.

In 1863 and 1864 a further series of 2—2—2 passenger locomotives appeared, the first two being built by Hawthorns, and the remainder by Neilson & Co. They had 17-in. by 22-in. cylinders, and 6-ft 1½-in. driving wheels. Except for a few minor differences they were similar to the earlier series of engines, but had generally increased dimensions. The weight in working order was 31 tons. The tenders ran on six wheels and weighed 24 tons. The names and numbers were:

BUILT BY HAWTHORNS OF LEITH

No.	Name		Renamed
28	*Glenbarry*	...	*Grantown*
29	*Highlander*	...	*Forres*

BUILT BY NEILSON & CO.

No.	Name		Renamed
30	*Prince*[1]	...	—
31	*Princess*[1]	...	—
32	*Sutherland*	...	*Cluny*
33	*Atholl*	...	*Birnam*
34	*Seafield*	...	*Perthshire*
35	*Kingsmills*	...	*Isla Bank*

[1] These names were bestowed in honour of the Prince and Princess of Wales (afterwards King Edward and Queen Alexandra), who were married in 1863.

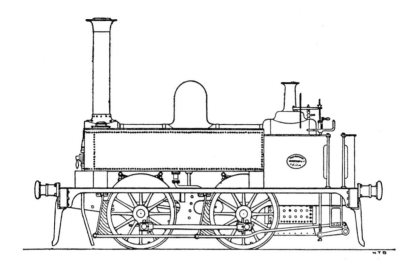

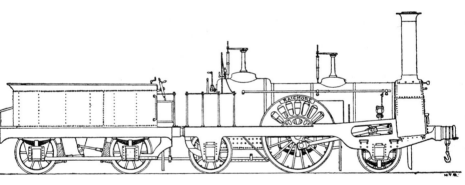

(*Top*) Tank engine No. 17 as originally built

(*Bottom*) Inverness & Nairn Railway locomotive No. 1, *Raigmore*,
as built in 1855

46	Clachnacuddin	...	Kingussie
47	Bruce	...	(1) Lovat; (2) Beauly
48	Cadboll	...	Dingwall
49	Belladrum	...	Helmsdale
50	Aultnaskiah	...	Badenoch
51	Caithness	...	Blair Atholl
52	Dunphail	...	—
53	Stafford	...	Golspie
54	Macduff	...	—
55	Cluny	...	(1) Sutherland; (2) Invergordon

All except No. 32 of this class were converted into 2—4—0s by David Jones between 1872 and 1892. Their cylinders were enlarged (not in all cases at the time of their conversion) to 18 in. diameter by 24 in. stroke, and the weight in working order increased to 36 tons. Seven of them were reboilered between 1881 and 1896, and at the same time were fitted with tyres which increased the diameter of the driving wheels to 6 ft 3 in. After this last alteration they weighed 37½ tons in working order. The remainder of this class, which did not receive new boilers, were scrapped between 1897 and 1900. The others survived for some years longer, and No. 35 lasted until the grouping as No. 35A.

The first locomotives designed solely for goods traffic were a series of seven 2—4—0s, built by Hawthorns in 1858 and 1859. Their chief dimensions were: cylinders 16 in. by 22 in., coupled wheels 5ft diameter, boilers 10 ft 9 in. long by 4 ft diameter, and weight in working order 28 tons. The tenders ran on four wheels and weighed 16 tons. As there was still no through railway to the south, these engines were delivered by sea to Lossiemouth, and reached the Inverness & Aberdeen Junction Railway via the Morayshire Railway. The names and numbers of this class were:

No.	Name		Renamed
5	Seafield	...	Tain
6	Bruce	...	Helmsdale
7	Fife	...	Dingwall
8	Altyre	...	Beauly
9	Aultnaskiah	...	Golspie
10	Westhall	...	Duncraig
11	Stafford	...	Skibo

Between 1873 and 1875, Nos. 7 and 10 were fitted with bogies for working on the Dingwall & Skye Railway. Their cylinders were enlarged to 17 in. by 24 in., and the weight increased to 32½ tons. At the same time they were provided with Jones's standard chimney and cab. Renaming took place at the time of these alterations, but the names were removed later. The remainder of the class were fitted with standard chimneys and cabs between 1875 and 1880, and had their cylinder stroke increased to 24 in. The whole series was scrapped between 1893 and 1899.

Two more 2—4—0s, Nos. 14 and 15, were built by Hawthorns in 1862. They were slightly larger than the earlier goods engines, and were fitted with cabs. They weighed 30½ tons in working order. Subsequently they were fitted with 5 ft 2½ in. wheels and 17 in. by 24 in. cylinders. No. 15 was scrapped in 1893, and at the same time No. 14 was renumbered 6. It was withdrawn from service (after being renumbered 49) in 1901. Originally these locomotives were named *Loch* and *Sutherland* respectively. No. 14 was renamed *Evanton*, and No. 15 became successively *Dunkeld* and *Foulis*.

Two further series of ten 2—4—0 goods engines were built by Sharp, Stewart & Co. in 1863 and 1864 respectively. The two sets were generally similar, both having cylinders 17 in. diameter by 22 in. stroke, 5 ft 1½ in. coupled wheels, and boilers 4 ft 1 in. in diameter. The second set differed from the first in having longer boilers, larger fireboxes, and a greater wheelbase. The weights in working order were 32 and 33 tons respectively. The first set were numbered 18 to 27, and the second 36 to 45.

The numbers and names of the two series were as follows:

No.	Name		Renamed
18	Inverness	...	—
19	Dingwall	...	Golspie
20	Birnam	...	—
21	Forres	...	—
22	Aviemore	...	—
23	Murthly	...	Dalcross
24	Invergordon	...	Lairg
25	Novar	...	—
26	Beauly	...	—
27	Conon	...	—
36	Nairn	...	—
37	Struan	...	—
38	Kincraig	...	—
39	Aviemore	...	—
40	Keith	...	—
41	Kingussie	...	—
42	Lentran	...	—
43	Dava	...	—
44	Brodie	...	—
45	Dalcross	...	—

With the exception of No. 24, which retained its second name (*Lairg*) until the end, all these locomotives had their names removed before they were withdrawn from service. It appears that both

No. 22 of the earlier series and No. 39 of the later entered service with the name *Aviemore*. Unless confusion has arisen in following the vagaries of Highland Railway renaming, the most probable explanation is that No. 22 became nameless a few months after it was built.

Both series were rebuilt by Jones between 1874 and 1893, with domed boilers and flush-topped fireboxes. The cylinders were enlarged to 18 in. diameter by 26 in. stroke, and the diameter of the driving wheels was increased to 5 ft 3 in. by means of thicker tyres. Standard cabs were fitted and the weights were increased by 1 ton. No. 22 was withdrawn from service in 1896, and most of the others shared a like fate within the next few years, but three veterans (Nos. 27, 37 and 42) survived until the grouping.

In 1862 the Inverness & Aberdeen Junction Railway took over the Findhorn Railway, and with it a small 0—4—0 tank engine which had been purchased by that Company from Neilson & Co. It had a square saddle tank extending to the front of the smokebox, 12 in. by 16 in. cylinders, and cast-iron wheels 3 ft 6 in. in diameter. A peculiarity of the design was that the valves were operated by means of gab motion, rendering the engine incapable of working expansively. Later, Stroudley discarded this motion in favour of standard Stephenson link motion. While in the service of the Findhorn Railway the engine was not designated by either name or number, but it became No. 16 on the books of its new owners. In 1872 it was sold to Hector Mackenzie, of Wick, and used on the construction of the northern section of the Sutherland & Caithness Railway. Subsequently it performed similar work in the south of Scotland.

For working the Burghead branch a small 0—4—0 tank engine, with 4ft wheels, was purchased from Hawthorns in 1863, numbered 17, and named *Hopeman*. It had inside cylinders, 13 in. diameter by 18 in. stroke, and was the first inside-cylinder engine possessed by the Company. The boiler had a raised firebox, and a plain weatherboard was the only protection afforded to the enginemen. The side-tanks were raised above the footplate, and extended to the front of the smokebox. Owing to the considerable overhang at the trailing end, the engine proved unsteady, and a pair of wheels, 3 ft 1 in. in diameter, was added by Stroudley. The weight in working order then became 20 tons.

In 1879 it was replaced on the branch by a more powerful engine, and became successively goods yard pilot at Forres, and carriage works shunter at Inverness. After this second change of duty, the number was removed, and the engine was named *Needlefield*. A cab was fitted, and the original chimney replaced by one of Jones's standard design. Subsequently it was converted into a stationary engine for driving the saw-mill at Lochgorm works, but in 1898 it was renovated, numbered 1A, and set to work again as a shunting engine. It remained on this duty until it was sold in 1902.

On 31 May 1865 Barclay resigned his position of locomotive superintendent at Inverness, and took over the management of an hotel in Liverpool. Some time later he returned to railway work, under Samuel Johnson, at the Stratford works of the Great Eastern Railway. After that he became locomotive superintendent to the Thetford & Watton Railway, but relinquished that position in 1878 to re-enter the service of Johnson, who had joined the Midland Railway. He died a few years later.

While Barclay was at Inverness, the engines were painted dark green, with black borders and bands, without any lining. The numbers were painted on the buffer beam.

WILLIAM STROUDLEY : 1865—1869

Barclay's resignation coincided with the formation of the Highland Railway, and his successor thus became that Company's first locomotive superintendent. The choice of the directors fell on William Stroudley, works manager at the Cowlairs shops of the Edinburgh & Glasgow Railway. Born in 1833, in Oxfordshire, Stroudley had secured wide experience with railway companies and private firms before taking up his duties at Inverness.

The only locomotives built for the Highland Railway to Stroudley's designs were three small 0—6—0 saddle-tank engines, which were turned out from Lochgorm works in 1869, 1873 and 1874. They had 14 in. by 20 in. inside cylinders, 120 lb. per sq. in. boiler pressure, and 3 ft 7 in. wheels. The boilers were 7 ft 9¼ in. long and 3 ft 7 in. in diameter. The weight in working order was 23½ tons. The class is interesting historically both on account of being the first constructed at the Company's works, and as the prototype of the well-known 'Terriers', introduced by Stroudley on the London, Brighton & South Coast Railway. The engines were numbered and named as follows:

No.		Name
56	...	*Balnain*
57	...	*Lochgorm*
16	...	*St. Martin's*

No. 56 was the only one completed while Stroudley was at Inverness. The remaining two were built after Jones had become locomotive superintendent. No. 16 replaced the Findhorn engine after the latter had been sold.

No. 56 was rebuilt by Jones in 1895, and Nos. 16 and 57 by Peter Drummond two years later. The alterations consisted of sub-stituting larger boilers, fitting thicker tyres to increase the diameter of the wheels to 3 ft 8 in., and providing a bunker of increased capacity. These changes brought the weight up to 26 tons.

In 1899, No. 16 was named *Fort George*, and sent to work on the branch to that place when first opened. Two years later it was renumbered 49. No. 56 was named *Dornoch* in 1902, and was the first engine to work on the Dornoch Light Railway. The three engines were still in service when the Highland became part of the LMSR in 1923.

Stroudley resigned at the end of 1869 in order to take up a similar appointment on the London Brighton & South Coast Railway. He remained at Brighton until his untimely death in December 1889. He introduced on the Highland Railway the style of painting which was afterwards so well known on the south coast. Passenger engines were yellow, with crimson framing and elaborate lining. For goods engines a dark green livery was adopted. The names were painted in gilt letters on the driving splashers or side-tanks, and the number plates were oval, with raised brass figures on a ver-milion ground.

DAVID JONES : 1870—1896

Stroudley was succeeded by David Jones, his chief assistant. Born in Manchester in 1834, Jones had served his apprenticeship under John Ramsbottom, at the Longsight shops of the London & North Western Railway. In November 1855 he entered the service of the Inverness & Nairn Railway, and was appointed assistant locomotive superintendent three years later. For a short time after Barclay's resignation, Jones was in charge at Lochgorm, but on the appointment of Stroudley he reverted to his former position for another four years.

The first locomotive to be built to the designs of Jones was a 4—4—0, which appeared in 1874. It was named *Bruce*, and was intended for working main-line passenger services. It had outside cylinders, 18 in. diameter by 24 in. stroke, 140 lb. per sq. in. boiler pressure, and 6 ft 3 in. coupled wheels. The boiler was 10 ft 8½ in.

long and 4 ft 2 in. in diameter. The engine weighed 42 tons in working order, of which 27 tons rested on the driving wheels. The design embodied several features which afterwards became standard on the Highland. These included the curious double chimney, its outer casing fitted with louvres which, by inducing a strong upward current of air, were intended to assist in forcing the draught, and to lift the exhaust well clear of the cab windows. The safety valves were placed transversely on the firebox casing, and the cabs were of unusual design, with rounded corners and square fronts. The tenders weighed 30 tons, and were of rather small capacity. They ran on six wheels. Ten engines of this class were built by Dübs & Co., of Glasgow, in 1874. Numbers and names were:

No.	Name		Renamed
60	*Bruce*	...	*Sutherland*
61	*Sutherlandshire*	...	*Duke*
62	*Perthshire*	...	(1) *Stemster*; (2) *Huntingtower*; (3) *Ault Wharrie*
63	*Inverness-shire*	...	*Inverness*
64	*Morayshire*	...	*Seafield*
65	*Nairnshire*	...	*Dalraddy*
66	*Ross-shire*	...	*Ardvuela*
67	*The Duke*	...	*Cromartie*
68	*Caithness-shire*	...	(1) *Caithness*; (2) *Muirtown*
69	*The Lord Provost*	...	(1) *Sir James*; (2) *Aldourie*

Between 1876 and 1888 seven more engines of this class were constructed at Inverness:

No.	Date New	Name		Renamed
4	1876	*Ardross*	...	*Auchtertyre*
71	1883	*Clachnacuddin*	...	—
72	1884	*Bruce*	...	*Grange*
73	1885	*Thurlow*	...	*Rosehaugh*
74	1885	*Beaufort*	...	—
75	1886	*Breadalbane*	...	—
84	1888	*Dochfour*	...	—

No. 4 was renumbered 31 in 1899, and 31A in 1911. Between 1897 and 1900 Drummond rebuilt Nos. 60, 61, 62, 66, 67, 68 and 69 with new boilers having a pressure of 150 lb. per sq. in.

Although somewhat handicapped by their small tenders, these engines performed a vast amount of useful work. They all remained in service until 1907, but at the end of 1922 only Nos. 67, 72, 74, 75 and 84 survived. By that time they had all passed on to the 'A' list.

In 1877 two 2—4—0 passenger engines were built at Lochgorm

works. They had 16 in. by 22 in. outside cylinders, and 6 ft 3 in. coupled wheels. The boilers were 9 ft 5½ in. long and 4 ft 1 in. in diameter. The working pressure was 140 lb. per sq. in. They weighed 35 tons, of which 23 tons was available for adhesion. The tenders weighed 27 tons.

These engines were numbered 1 and 3, and replaced the older locomotives similarly designated. They were named *Raigmore* and *Ballindalloch* respectively. These names were retained throughout their existence, but the numbers were changed to 29 and 30 respectively in 1898. The latter was scrapped in 1910, but No. 29 (renumbered 29A) lasted until 1912. They were never rebuilt.

Jones's next class consisted of three 2—4—0 tank engines, built in 1878 and 1879 for branch line services and shunting. Their cylinders and fireboxes were the same size as those of the 2—4—0 tender engines, built in 1877, but the boilers were slightly shorter. They had 4 ft 9 in. coupled wheels, and weighed 36 tons in working order. The whole of this class were built in the Company's works, and received the following numbers and names:

No.		Name
17	...	Breadalbane
58	...	Burghead
59	...	Highlander

Soon after they appeared they were rebuilt with a leading bogie, because trouble was experienced with the single leading axle. No. 17 was renamed *Aberfeldy* in 1886, and renumbered 50 in 1901. All three survived (on the 'B' list) until the grouping, and were latterly used for shunting.

The satisfactory results obtained with the two converted 2—4—0 engines on the Dingwall & Skye Railway induced Jones to build the well-known 'Skye Bogie' class for working that section of the Highland Railway. They were generally similar to the 4—4—0 main-line engines, but differed in certain details. They had 5 ft 3 in. driving wheels, and 150 lb. per sq. in. boiler pressure. The weight in working order was 43 tons, of which 28 tons was available for adhesion. The tenders weighed 30 tons. Nine of this class were built at Lochgorm works:

No.		Date New
70	...	1882
85	...	1892
86	...	1893
87	...	1893
88	...	1895

KYLE LINE DIESELS

(34)   *A westbound train hauled by Birmingham RC&W Type 2 D5114 calls at Garve on 2 September 1967. The signal boxes were closed and the signals removed in 1984.*

(35)   *The Howard Doris sidings at Strome Ferry with Birmingham RC&W Type 2 on 17 October 1975. Built to supply the construction site at Loch Kishorn, the yard closed at the end of September 1977.*

PRESERVATION

(36)   LMS Class 5 4—6—0 No 5025, built by Vulcan Foundry in 1934, was bought by the late W. E. C. Watkinson for use on the Strathspey Railway. A special train is seen here on the way back to Aviemore on 18 September 1976.

(37)   Austerity 0—6—0ST No 48, built at Hunslet in 1943, was purchased from the NCB colliery at Backworth in Northumberland and is seen here shunting on the Strathspey Railway at Boat of Garten. The restoration of the station buildings here has won a Civic Trust award.

5	...	1897
6	...	1897
7	...	1898
48	...	1901

Contrary to usual Highland Railway practice, none of them received names. The last four were not completed until after Jones had resigned. In consequence they were fitted with Drummond's standard type of chimney.

In 1899, Nos. 5, 6 and 7 became Nos. 32, 33 and 34 respectively. Between 1903 and 1907, No. 48 worked on the Invergarry & Fort Augustus Railway. The whole of the class was still in active service at the end of 1922.

A further series of 4—4—0 tender engines for main-line services was constructed during 1886 by the Clyde Locomotive Co. Ltd., of Glasgow. They were the first engines to be built by this firm, which was later taken over by Sharp, Stewart & Co., and renamed the Atlas works. They differed from the previous series in having shorter boilers, 9 ft 9½ in. long, and longer fireboxes. The boiler pressure was 160 lb. per sq. in., and the weight in working order 43 tons. They were provided with tenders of increased capacity, weighing 31½ tons. Eight of this class were constructed:

No.	Name		Renamed
76	Bruce	...	—
77	Lovat	...	—
78	Lochalsh	...	—
79	Atholl	...	—
80	Stafford	...	—
81	Colville	...	—
82	Fife	...	Durn (this name was removed in 1916)
83	Cadboll	...	Monkland

No. 76 was sent to the Edinburgh Exhibition of 1886 before being placed in service. None of these engines had been withdrawn when the Highland lost its separate identity in 1923, although all had passed on to the 'A' list.

To replace the old single-wheeled tank engine, No. 12, on the Strathpeffer branch, Jones designed a small 0—4—4 saddle-tank engine specially for this service, which was built at Inverness in 1890. It was numbered 13 and named Strathpeffer. It had inside cylinders, 14 in. diameter by 20 in. stroke, and 4 ft 3 in. coupled wheels. The boiler was 3 ft 6½ in. in diameter, and the weight in working order was 32 tons.

In 1901 this locomotive was rebuilt at Inverness with side tanks

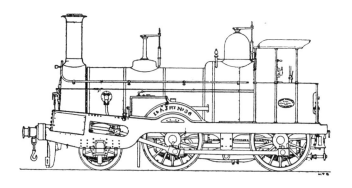

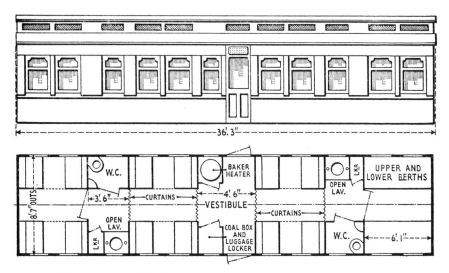

(*Top*) Inverness & Aberdeen Junction Railway 2—4—0 goods engine
No. 36, built in 1864

(*Bottom*) Side elevation and plan of Pullman sleeping car

and a new boiler of Drummond's design. The adhesion weight was slightly reduced, although the total weight was increased to 34 tons. It had previously been renumbered 53. Two years later it was renamed *Lybster*, and sent to work on the Wick & Lybster Light Railway, where it remained until the grouping.

The next addition to the stock was a series of 4—4—0 tender engines for main-line passenger services, constructed in 1892 by Neilson & Co. They were merely an enlargement of Jones's standard designs, having similar cylinders, wheels and motion, but larger boilers, 9 ft 9½ in. long by 4 ft 6 in. diameter, and carrying a steam pressure of 160 lb. per sq. in. The weight, in working order, was 45 tons, of which 29½ tons rested on the coupled wheels. This series was known as the 'Strath' class, and consisted of 12 engines, all in service in December 1922:

No.	Name		Renamed
89	*Sir George*	...	—
90	*Tweeddale*	...	*Grandtully*
91	*Strathspey*	...	—
92	*Strathdearn*	...	*Glendean*
93	*Strathnairn*	...	—
94	*Strathtay*	...	—
95	*Strathcarron*	...	—
96	*Glentilt*	...	—
97	*Glenmore*	...	—
98	*Glentruim*	...	—
99	*Glentromie*	...	—
100	*Glenbruar*	...	—

In 1892 the Highland Railway purchased from Dübs & Co. two 4—4—0 outside-cylinder side-tank engines, which had been built for the Uruguay Eastern Railway, but which had not been delivered owing to some financial hitch. They became Nos. 101 and 102 on the books of the Highland Railway. With the exception that the cow-catchers and the American pattern head-lights were removed, the engines were delivered practically as built. They had 16 in. by 22 in. outside cylinders, 5 ft 3 in. driving wheels, and carried 140 lb. per sq. in. working pressure. The weight in working order was 41 tons 12 cwt. It was thought that the covers over the side bars would prove useful on the Burghead branch, where heavy sand drifts occur, but they were soon dispensed with because it was impossible to get at the cross heads without removing the covers.

In the following year three more 4—4—0 tank engines were built by Dübs & Co. They were slightly heavier than the two previous engines, and had standard Highland Railway fittings, but were otherwise similar. They were numbered 11, 14 and 15. In 1899, No. 11 was renumbered 51, and in 1900, Nos. 14 and 15 became 50 and 52 respectively. In the following year No. 50 was again altered to 54. In 1906, No. 102 was rebuilt by Drummond with his standard chimney and boiler mountings.

These engines proved exceedingly useful on branch lines. For many years they ran to Burghead, Fortrose, Portessie and Aberfeldy. No. 52 worked on the Invergarry & Fort Augustus Railway while that line was under the management of the Highland Railway. The whole of the class survived until the grouping.

The year 1894 witnessed the introduction of Jones's famous bogie goods engines, the first 4—6—0s to work on a British railway. The design was a radical departure from existing practice, and every credit is due to Jones for the bold way in which he broke with long-established tradition by introducing an entirely new wheel arrangement. The class comprised 15 engines, all built by Sharp, Stewart & Co. They were numbered 103 to 117 inclusive.

At the time of their construction, they were undoubtedly the most powerful main-line engines in the country. They had 20 in. by 26 in. outside cylinders, 5 ft 3 in. coupled wheels, and 175 lb. per sq. in. boiler pressure. The boilers were 13 ft 9in. long by 4 ft 7⅞ in. diameter. The weight in working order was 56 tons, of which 42 tons were available for adhesion. The tenders had six wheels and weighed 38 tons 7 cwt. Although intended for hauling goods trains, they also did good work with passenger services. The whole of the class passed into the hands of the LMSR in 1923.

The last series of engines designed by Jones were 15 large 4—4—0s, which appeared from the works of Dübs & Co. in 1896. Considerably more powerful than any which had hitherto worked on the Highland Railway, they were among the foremost in the country as regards tractive effort at the time of their construction. They had 19 in. by 24 in. outside cylinders, 6 ft 3½ in. coupled wheels, and 175 lb. per sq. in. boiler pressure. The boilers were 10 ft 6⅜ in. long by 4 ft 4⅞ in. diameter. The weight in working order was 47 tons, of which 29 tons 19 cwt. rested on the coupled wheels. The tenders were identical with those of the 4—6—0 goods engines. These engines were known as the 'Loch' class:

No.		Name
119	...	*Loch Insh*
120	...	*Loch Ness*
121	...	*Loch Ericht*
122	...	*Loch Moy*
123	...	*Loch an Dorb*

124	...	Loch *Laggan*
125	...	Loch *Tay*
126	...	Loch *Tummel*
127	...	Loch *Garry*
128	...	Loch *Luichart*
129	...	Loch *Maree*
130	...	Loch *Fannich*
131	...	Loch *Shin*
132	...	Loch *Naver*
133	...	Loch *Laoghal*

Mention must be made of the engines owned by the Duke of Sutherland. When the railway was extended from Golspie to Helmsdale, the third Duke purchased a small 2—4—0 tank engine from Kitson & Co., of Leeds. For the time being it worked a passenger service from Dunrobin to the temporary station at Gartymor, near Helmsdale, but as soon as the extension was linked up with the main line from Inverness it was reserved for hauling the Duke's private coach, and kept at Brora. As delivered to the Duke, it was named *Dunrobin*, and had outside cylinders 10 in. diameter by 18 in. stroke, and coupled wheels 4 ft diameter. The weight in working order was 21 tons.

On the death of the Duke in 1892, his son decided to have a more powerful engine for his own use. Three years later Jones designed, and Sharp, Stewart & Co. built, an 0—4—4 side-tank engine, with 13 in. by 18 in. inside cylinders, and 4 ft 6 in. coupled wheels. Like its predecessor, it was named *Dunrobin*, and was painted dark green, with black bands and yellow lines. For the accommodation of the Duke and his friends while riding on the footplate, a seat with leather cushions, extending the full width of the cab, was provided over the bunker. On the front weatherboard were inscribed the names of several illustrious travellers who inspected the engine while guests of the Duke. In 1896 a new shed was built for the engine at Golspie.

The original *Dunrobin* passed to the Highland Railway, who sent it to Sharp, Stewart & Co. for rebuilding in 1896. A new and larger boiler was provided, the cylinders were increased to 12 in. diameter by 18 in. stroke, and the side tanks were extended halfway along the boiler barrel. The weight in working order was increased to 24 tons. On its return it was numbered 118, named *Gordon Castle*, and sent to work the branch from Orbliston Junction to Fochabers. Subsequently it was renamed *Invergordon* and used for shunting at Invergordon Harbour. During the war it was lent to the Great North of Scotland Railway, but it was still on the books of the

Highland Railway at the end of 1922. It was sold to a contractor shortly after the grouping.

On 31 October 1896, as the result of an accident while testing a new engine, David Jones was forced to resign his position, after 48 years of railway life, 41 of which had been spent at Lochgorm works. Some time later he left the north of Scotland for London, where he died in 1906 in his 73rd year.

Jones continued Stroudley's style of painting for some years, but afterwards adopted black, lined with red and white, for goods engines. In 1885 radical changes were made in the livery, which became standard for all locomotives. Save for the framing, which was dark crimson with a black border and yellow and red lines, the engines were painted a pea green with a border of a darker shade, black bands, and red and white lines. The buffer beams were painted like the framing, but had a vermilion panel in the centre. The Stroudley pattern number plates were retained.

PETER DRUMMOND: 1896—1912

To fill the vacancy occasioned by the retirement of David Jones, the directors chose Peter Drummond. A native of Ayrshire, Drummond had served his apprenticeship with Forrest & Moor, of Glasgow. In 1870 he joined the London Brighton & South Coast Railway under Stroudley, but returned to Scotland some years later to enter the service of the North British Railway. Eventually he joined his elder brother, Dugald, on the Caledonian Railway, and became works manager at St Rollox, the position he was holding at the time of his appointment to the Highland in November 1896.

The first locomotive class designed by Drummond was a series of 20 4—4—0 passenger engines, known as the 'Small Bens', which were named after mountains in the Highlands. Eight were built by Dübs & Co. in 1898 and 1899. These were followed between 1899 and 1901 by nine others, constructed at Lochgorm works, and the remaining three came from the North British Locomotive Co. of Glasgow in 1906[1] :

No.	Name	Date New		Makers
1	Ben-y-Gloe	1898	...	Dübs & Co.
2	Ben Alder	1898	...	,,
3	Ben Wyvis	1898	...	,,
4	Ben More	1899	...	,,

[1] The North British Locomotive Co. was formed in 1903 by an amalgamation of Sharp Stewart & Co., Dübs & Co., and Neilson Reid & Co.

5	*Ben Vrackie*	1899	...	Dübs & Co.
6	*Ben Armin*	1899	...	„
7	*Ben Attow*	1899	...	„
8	*Ben Clebrig*	1899	...	„
9	*Ben Rinnes*	1899	...	Highland Railway
10	*Ben Slioch*	1899	...	„
11	*Ben Macdhui*	1899	...	„
12	*Ben Hope*	1900	...	„
13	*Ben Alisky*	1900	...	„
14	*Ben Dearg*	1900	...	„
15	*Ben Loyal*	1901	...	„
16	*Ben Avon*	1901	...	„
17	*Ben Alligan*	1901	...	„
38	*Ben Udlaman*	1906	...	North British Loco. Co.
41	*Ben Bhach Ard*	1906	...	„ „
47	*Ben a' Bhuird*	1906	...	„ „

The design of these engines represented a complete departure from previous Highland Railway standards, and resembled very closely Dugald Drummond's practice on the North British and Caledonian Railways. They had 18¼ in. by 26 in. inside cylinders, and 6 ft coupled wheels. The boilers were 10 ft 6 in. long by 4 ft 6¼ in. diameter, and carried a steam pressure of 175 lb. per sq. in. Drummond further adhered to his brother's standards by mounting the safety valves on the dome. In 1920 they were moved to a separate mounting above the firebox. The weight of the engine in working order was 46 tons, of which 31 tons 4 cwt rested on the driving wheels. The tenders also embodied the usual Drummond characteristics. They ran on six wheels, and weighed 37½ tons. Subsequently, four of the class were fitted with eight-wheel tenders.

These engines were slightly smaller than the 'Loch' class, and were seldom called upon to undertake the heaviest duties on the southern main line. They usually worked north of Inverness, and to Keith. During the time that Highland engines were working through to Aberdeen the trains were frequently hauled by an engine of this class.

In 1900 six goods engines of entirely new design were introduced. They were of the 0—6—0 type with inside cylinders, and were built by Dübs & Co. They had 5-ft wheels, and their boilers and cylinders were interchangeable with the 'Small Bens'. The weight in working order was 43 tons. As delivered by the makers, they were provided with eight-wheeled tenders, weighing 40 tons, but these were subsequently exchanged for four six-wheel tenders belonging to the 'Small Ben' class, and two similar ones, originally supplied to the 'Big Bens', which appeared in 1908.

In 1902 four more 0—6—0 engines were built by Dübs & Co. They differed from the previous series in having water-tube fireboxes. The class was completed five years later by the addition of two further engines, with normal fireboxes, built by the North British Locomotive Co. The whole of these engines built after 1900 were supplied with six-wheeled tenders when new. The 12 engines of this class were built:

No.	Makers		Date New
134	Dübs & Co.	...	1900
135	,,	...	1900
136	,,	...	1900
137	,,	...	1900
138	,,	...	1900
139	..	...	1900
18	,,	...	1902
19	,,	...	1902
20	,,	...	1902
21	,,	...	1902
36	North British Loco. Co.	...	1907
55	,, ,,	...	1907

A series of six 4—6—0 passenger engines which were considerably more powerful than the existing 4—4—0 classes were built by Dübs & Co. in 1900. Four others followed from the same firm in 1902; and the North British Locomotive Co. added two more in 1910 and 1911. They had 19½ in. by 26 in. outside cylinders, and 5 ft 9 in. coupled wheels. The boilers were 14 ft 4½ in. long by 4 ft 9¾ in. diameter, and carried 180 lb. per sq. in. steam pressure. The safety valves were mounted over the firebox. The weight in working order was 58 tons 17 cwt, of which 43 tons 17 cwt rested on the coupled wheels. They were provided with large tenders, weighing 38 tons 2 cwt, running on two four-wheeled bogies. These engines were known as the 'Castle' class; their numbers and names were:

No.	Name		Date New
140	*Taymouth Castle*	...	1900
141	*Ballindalloch Castle*	...	1900
142	*Dunrobin Castle*	...	1900
143	*Gordon Castle*	...	1900
144	*Blair Castle*	...	1900
145	*Murthly Castle*	...	1900
146	*Skibo Castle*	...	1902
147	*Beaufort Castle*	...	1902
148	*Cawdor Castle*	...	1902
149	*Duncraig Castle*	...	1902
30	*Dunvegan Castle*	...	1910
35	*Urquhart Castle*	...	1911

They were primarily intended for working heavy traffic between Perth and Inverness, a task that they accomplished with conspicuous success. It was not until May 1913 that one of them worked through to Wick.

In 1910, No. 146 took part in some comparative trials with a North British Railway 4—4—0, No. 867, each engine hauling a train of eight bogie coaches, a saloon and a brake van. On the Highland Railway the trials took place between Blair Atholl and Dalwhinnie, and on the North British Railway over the steeply-graded section

THE HIGHLAND RAILWAY

LOCOMOTIVE DEPARTMENT

The Special

PASS TO RIDE ON LOCOMOTIVE ENGINE

INVERNESS, _18th Sept_ 1907.

Issued to _Mer Gauns_

Available _Inverness & Kyle of Lochalsh_

Drummond Loco. Sup.

N.B.—Before this Pass can be used the Holder must sign the declaration on back.

between Perth and Kinross. In 1912, No. 141 was fitted with a Phoenix superheater, but the experiment did not prove successful, and the apparatus was removed.

Following the introduction of the 'Castle' class, Drummond turned his attention to tank engines, of which the Highland Railway stood in need. In 1903 and 1904, three 0—6—0 shunting tank engines were built at Lochgorm works. They had 18 in. by 24 in. outside cylinders, and 5 ft $2\frac{1}{2}$ in. wheels. Their boilers were 10 ft 4 in. long by 4 ft diameter, and the working pressure was 160 lb. per sq. in. The weight in working order was $47\frac{1}{2}$ tons. The wheels and boilers had previously been used on older engines which had been withdrawn from service. This class was numbered 22, 23 and 24. These engines were followed by some small 0—4—4 tanks for branch-line services. Built at Inverness in 1905 and 1906, they had 14 in. by 20 in. outside cylinders and 4 ft 6 in. coupled wheels. The boilers were 8 ft 2 in. long by 3 ft 10¼ in. diameter, and the safety valves were mounted on the dome. The weight in working order was 35¾ tons. The class consisted of four engines:

No.	Name		Date New
25	Strathpeffer	...	1905
40	Gordon Lennox	...	1905
45	—	...	1905
46	—	...	1906

Six 4—4—0 tender engines, known as the 'Big Bens', were built by the North British Locomotive Co. in 1908 and 1909. They were generally similar to the 'Small Bens' differing only in having larger boilers, 5 ft 3 in. diameter, a steam pressure of 180 lb. per sq. in., and separate mountings for the dome and safety valves. The weight in working order was 52 tons 6 cwt, of which 35 tons 4 cwt rested on the coupled wheels.

The tenders of the first four were originally of the standard six-wheel pattern, weighing 38 tons 7 cwt, but two of them were subsequently supplied with eight-wheel tenders weighing 41 tons 14 cwt at the time of their construction:

No.	Name		Date New
61	Ben na Caillich	...	1908
63	Ben Mheadhouin	...	1908
66	Ben Mholach	...	1908
68	Ben a' Chait	...	1908
60	Ben Bhreac Mhor	...	1909
62	Ben a Chaoruinn	...	1909

In 1909, Nos. 66 and 68 were renumbered 64 and 65 respectively. Two of the class were fitted with Smith's feed water heater in 1914, but the upkeep of this complicated apparatus proved too costly, and it was soon removed.

The last locomotive design to be introduced to the Highland Railway by Drummond was a powerful 0—6—4 tank engine, with 18¼ in. by 26 in. inside cylinders and 5 ft coupled wheels. The boiler was 10 ft 6in. long and 4 ft 6¼ in. diameter, and the working pressure was 180 lb. per sq. in. The weight in working order was 69½ tons. Eight of this class were built by the North British Locomotive Co., four in 1909, and four in 1911. The first batch were numbered 39, 64, 65 and 69, and the second 29, 31, 42 and 44. Very soon after their arrival, Nos. 64 and 65 were altered to 66 and 68 respectively, to provide for consecutive numbering of the 'Big Ben' class. Although primarily intended for banking purposes, they were also used for local passenger and goods trains.

In January 1912 the position of locomotive superintendent on the Glasgow & South Western Railway became vacant on the retirement of James Manson. Peter Drummond obtained the appointment and remained at Kilmarnock until his death in June 1918.

During his 15 years at Inverness, he placed more than 60 new engines in service, and almost entirely changed the character of the locomotive stock. This extended to the external appearance of the engines, all of which exhibited unmistakeable Drummond features. He modified the painting of the engines soon after taking charge, the red lining being abolished, and the black boiler and panel bands being edged with white, whilst the initials HR appeared for the first time on the tender sides or tanks, and also on the front buffer beams, together with the number. When the 'Castle' class appeared, the lettering on the tender became 'Highland Railway', but in 1903 this was altered to 'The Highland Railway'. The same year also witnessed the introduction of a new livery. The engines, including the buffer beams, were painted a plain green of darker shade, with no lining whatever. The initials and the engine number on the buffer beam were retained.

The whole of the locomotives designed for the Highland Railway by Drummond passed into the hands of the LMSR in 1923.

FREDRICK SMITH : 1912—1915

Drummond was succeeded by Fredrick Smith. Born in 1872, Smith had served his apprenticeship in the Gateshead shops of the North Eastern Railway, and had been works manager at Inverness since 1903.

The first locomotives to be constructed under him were four 4—6—0s of the 'Castle' class which were built by the North British Locomotive Co. in 1913. They differed from the previous engines of the class in having extended smokeboxes and deflector chimneys :

No.		Name
26	...	*Brahan Castle*
27	...	*Thurso Castle*
28	..	*Cluny Castle*
43	...	*Dalcross Castle*

Shortly after it appeared, No. 43 became No. 29, exchanging numbers with one of the 0—6—4 tank engines.

To cope successfully with the heavy and increasing traffic between Perth and Inverness, Smith designed a large 4—6—0 tender engine, with 21 in. by 28 in. outside cylinders, and 6 ft coupled wheels. Steam distribution was effected by means of Walschærts valve gear, and the boiler, working at 170 lb. per sq. in., was provided with a Belpaire firebox, Robinson superheater, and Ross 'pop' safety valves. Wakefield mechanical lubricators and Smith's feed water apparatus were fitted. The weight of the engine in working order was 72 tons 6 cwt, and the six-wheel tender weighed 47 tons 7 cwt.

Six of the class were ordered from the shops of R. & W. Hawthorn, Leslie & Co., of Newcastle-on-Tyne. The first two, numbered 70 and 71, and named *River Ness* and *River Spey* respectively, were delivered in September 1915. By some extraordinary oversight the final designs had never been submitted to the chief engineer, and it was soon found that the locomotives were too heavy for the track and bridges on the Highland Railway. Their use was therefore vetoed, and a few weeks later they were sold, together with the remainder of the class, still under construction, to the Caledonian Railway. They were numbered 938 to 943 on that Company's books, and worked between Glasgow and Aberdeen. By this time the Highland Railway was experiencing considerable difficulty in handling the heavy wartime traffic owing to a serious shortage of locomotive power, and the sudden withdrawal of the eagerly-awaited new engines made the position even worse.[1]

Following the refusal of the chief engineer to sanction the use of his new engines, Smith resigned and, leaving Inverness, set up in practice as a consulting engineer in Newcastle-on-Tyne. During his short period of office, the external appearance of the engines underwent a further change. The number plates were removed from the cab sides, and the number was painted in large gilt figures higher up, while a small aluminium number plate with raised figures was fixed to the smokebox door. A somewhat lighter green was adopted, still without any lining, and except in the case of some of the more recent express engines, which were green all over, the boilers were plain black.

---

[1] The bridges and track on the Highland Railway were strengthened after the grouping, and the former 'River' class engines were able to work between Perth and Inverness.

CHRISTOPHER CUMMING : 1915—1922

The directors chose Christopher Cumming to replace Smith. Cumming had served an apprenticeship in the shops and drawing office of the North British Railway, and had subsequently gained experience at various locomotive depots on that system. At the time of his appointment to the Highland, he held the position of district locomotive superintendent at Burntisland. The outbreak of the war had thrown a great strain on the locomotive department at Inverness, and Cumming's first years of office were rendered exceedingly difficult on that account.

Additional locomotive power was urgently required, and the new superintendent decided, for the time being, to revert to the designs of David Jones. In 1916 an order was placed with the North British Locomotive Co. for three engines of the 'Loch' class. It is a great tribute to the designer that this type should have been considered suitable for new engines after the lapse of 20 years. Save for a few minor alterations, the new engines were similar to the series built in 1896. They were delivered in 1917 and were numbered 70 (*Loch Ashie*), 71 (*Loch Garve*), and 72 (*Loch Ruthven*).

The North British Locomotive Co. also received an order for three additional engines of the 'Castle' class. They appeared in 1917 :

No.		Name
50	...	*Brodie Castle*
58	...	*Darnaway Castle*
59	...	*Foulis Castle*

Although generally similar to Drummond's engines, they had larger boilers, and the diameter of the driving wheels was increased to 6 ft. The weight in working order was 60 tons 13 cwt. The tenders were also of increased capacity. They weighed 40 tons, and ran on six wheels.

The first locomotives built wholly to the designs of Cumming also appeared in 1917. They were two large 4—4—0 tender engines with 20 in. by 26 in. outside cylinders, fitted with Walschærts valve gear, and 6 ft 3 in. coupled wheels. The boilers were 11 ft 4⅝ in. long, and were provided with Belpaire fireboxes, Robinson superheaters, and Ross safety valves, working to a pressure of 160 lb. per sq. in. Lubrication was effected by means of a Wakefield mechanical lubricator. The weight of the engine in working order was 54 tons 19½ cwt. The tenders ran on six wheels and weighed 43 tons 3¼ cwt.

Both engines were constructed by R. & W. Hawthorn, Leslie & Co. and were numbered and named 73 (*Snaigow*) and 74 (*Durn*) respectively. They were sent to work on the northern line from Inverness to Wick.

In the following year Cumming designed, and Hawthorn, Leslie & Co. built, a series of four large 4—6—0 goods engines, numbered 75 to 78. They had 20½ in. by 26 in. outside cylinders, fitted with Walschærts valve gear, and 5 ft 3 in. coupled wheels. The boilers were 13 ft 9 in. long and tapered from 4 ft 7 11/16 in. to 4 ft 6⅝ in. diameter. They were fitted with Ross safety valves, arranged for a pressure of 160 lb. per sq. in. The firebox was of the Belpaire type, and Robinson superheaters were provided. The weight of the engine in working order was 65¼ tons. The tenders ran on six wheels, and weighed 39 tons 1½ cwt. Four more engines of this class were built by Hawthorn, Leslie & Co. in 1919, and numbered 79 to 82.

For handling the increasing traffic between Perth and Inverness, Cumming designed a new class of 4—6—0 engine, embodying his standard details of outside cylinders, fitted with Walschærts valve gear, Robinson superheaters, Belpaire fireboxes, and Ross safety valves, working to a pressure of 170 lb. per sq. in. The cylinders were 21 in. by 26 in. and the coupled wheels 6 ft diameter. The boilers were 14 ft 6 in. long, and the diameter tapered from 4 ft 9 11/16 in. to 4 ft 8 9/16 in. The weight of the engine and tender in working order was 104 tons 6½ cwt. The tenders ran on six wheels.

These engines were known as the 'Clan' class, and were built by Hawthorn, Leslie & Co. Four were delivered in 1919 and four in 1921:

No.	Name		Date New
49	Clan Campbell	...	1919
51	Clan Fraser	...	1919
52	Clan Munro	...	1919
53	Clan Stewart	...	1919
54	Clan Chattan	...	1921
55	Clan Mackinnon	...	1921
56	Clan Mackenzie	...	1921
57	Clan Cameron	...	1921

Early in 1921, No. 53 was adapted for burning oil fuel on the Scarab system. Although fairly successful results were obtained, the apparatus was later removed.

The 'Clan' class have an added interest in the light of after events. They proved to be not only the last engines designed by Cumming, but also for the Highland Railway. Early in 1922,

Cumming's health suffered a complete breakdown, and he was forced to resign on 1 March of that year. He died in 1924.

Cumming modified the style of painting by returning to the all-green livery standard in Drummond's time. The buffer beams were painted red. The oval number plates on the cab sides were restored, and the initials HR reappeared on the tenders.

Cumming's resignation had been unexpected, and two months elapsed before his successor could be appointed. The choice of the directors fell on David Chalmers Urie. The son of the chief mechanical engineer on the London & South Western Railway, Urie had served his apprenticeship under his father. In 1913 he was appointed assistant works manager at Eastleigh. Two years later he became assistant locomotive superintendent to the Midland Great Western Railway of Ireland, the position he was holding at the time of his appointment to Inverness in 1922.

The Railways Act had been passed in the previous summer, and in the course of the remaining months before the grouping became effective Urie was not called upon to design any locomotives for the Highland Railway. Early in 1923 he became assistant mechanical engineer to the Northern Division of the LMSR. On 31 December 1922 the Highland possessed 173 locomotives. All these passed to the LMSR, but 23 were soon withdrawn from service, and were not included in the complete renumbering scheme instituted by the new Company.

ROLLING STOCK

The rolling stock of the Inverness & Nairn and Inverness & Aberdeen Junction Railways adhered closely to the usual designs of the period, with few outstanding features. It ran on four wheels, and was of light construction, and of rather cramped dimensions, with flat roofs, and straight sides. A fair measure of comfort was provided in the first-class carriages, but third-class passengers had to be content with bare wooden benches.

Of particular interest were some mail vans, built by Brown, Marshall & Co. in 1858, for the Inverness—Keith trains. They were 20 ft 10 in. long, and weighed 9 tons. Passengers' luggage was carried on the roof, protected from the weather only by a tarpaulin, an iron railing being provided to keep it in position. Immediately in front of the luggage space was a seat for the guard, protected by a handrail and a footboard. At a later date, when the guard no longer rode outside, side wings were added to improve his view of the line. Dogs were carried in a boot, similar to that used on stage-coaches, at one end of the van. The vehicle was fitted with Newall's chain brake, and wood-covered spring buffers.

At least one of these vans survived for many years after being withdrawn from regular passenger services. It was latterly used as a spare tool van for the locomotive department at Perth, and was broken up in 1903. The luggage rails on the roof remained until the end.

For the time being it was decided to follow the example of the Great North of Scotland Railway and provide only two classes of carriage, first and third. However, as soon as the direct line to Perth was opened, in 1863, second-class bookings were introduced throughout the system. The standard of comfort was very little superior to that afforded to the third-class passenger, and at no time did the intermediate class become extensively patronized. It was abolished completely on 1 May 1893.

Between 1860 and 1870 several passenger coaches and vans were added to the Company's stock. They were generally similar to those already in use, but the outside seat for the guard and the baggage space on the roof were soon dispensed with.

In readiness for the opening of the railway to Wick a large order for extra rolling stock was placed with the Metropolitan Carriage & Wagon Co. The new coaches differed but little from those already described, save that they were slightly larger and heavier. They were 27 ft 6 in. long by 7 ft 4 in. wide, and weighed 9½ tons. The third-class coaches accommodated 50 passengers in five narrow compartments, with very small windows. The second and first-class compartments were wider and offered proportionately better accommodation. A curious feature of the design was that the doors were hung with the handles on the left and the hinges on the right of a person standing facing the coach, a reversal of usual practice. Several of these coaches continued in service for more than 30 years. Latterly they were relegated to minor branches and special trains for fish workers.

A year or two later a great advance in comfort was achieved when a number of six-wheel coaches, weighing about 15 tons, appeared. The first-class coaches seated 16 passengers in four com-partments, the two inner ones being provided with lavatories, while those at the ends were of the coupé type, with a seat on one side only. The latter did not prove popular, especially with summer tourists. Although they afforded an ample prospect of the end of the coach in front, the side view was no better than, if as good as, that from an ordinary compartment because of their extreme narrowness. The third-class coaches were far more economical from the railway Company's point of view. They carried 50 passengers in five compartments, and were not provided with lavatories. Oil lamps were used for lighting in both classes, and steam heating was still a dream of the future.

The first eight-wheel coaches appeared in 1878, in the form of three first-class sleeping cars. Each car accommodated nine passengers, and was divided into two single-berth coupés, at either end, and two larger compartments, one reserved for gentlemen, containing two upper and two lower berths, and the other reserved for ladies, containing three berths, all on the same level. A side corridor ran the full length of the coach.[1]

The cars were placed in service on 1 May and worked between Inverness and Perth in both directions, and between Wick and Inverness, in the up direction only. There was no down night train on the northern line. No special attendant was provided, and the guard was responsible for the comfort of the passengers. The supplementary charge was 5s per berth. South of Inverness the facility proved popular, but the Wick car was withdrawn after a few months. For many years goods vehicles were attached to the night trains, and a unique example was afforded of a mixed train conveying sleeping cars.

In 1885 it was decided to place the sleeping car arrangements in the hands of the Pullman Car Company, and two specially-designed vehicles, each accommodating 16 first-class passengers in upper and lower berths, were constructed at the Derby works of the Midland Railway, from parts manufactured in the United States of America and sent to Scotland. They were 33 ft 3 in. long, and weighed 16½ tons. Latterly they were fitted with four-wheel bogies, but it has been stated that originally they ran on six wheels. Oil lamps were used for lighting, and a Baker heater, burning coke fuel, was provided. As was usual with Pullman stock at that time, the external finish was dark brown, with gilt lining and lettering. The cars were named *Balmoral* and *Dunrobin*, and were the first Pullman vehicles supplied to a Scottish railway. The owners provided a travelling attendant, at the expense of the railway Company. The supplementary charge remained unaltered. The older vehicles were withdrawn and converted into ordinary first-class carriages.

---

[1] Exact details of the arrangement of the berths do not appear to have survived.

The principal trains on the southern main line frequently included stock from other railways. Both the North British and the Caledonian companies provided coaches for the through services between Inverness and Edinburgh and Glasgow, and the leading English railways with routes to Scotland sent their own, or jointly owned, sleeping cars and coaches through to Inverness. This cosmopolitan effect was to be seen at its best in August, shortly before the start of the grouse-shooting season. Foxwell, in *Express Trains, English and Foreign*, drew attention to the 7.50 a.m. express from Perth to Inverness, on 7 August 1888. The train was of extraordinary length and weight, and included stock from no less than nine foreign railways, in addition to Highland vehicles. It has been said, with a fair measure of truth, that many of the Company's regular patrons never saw the inside of a Highland coach. North and east of Inverness, foreign stock was the exception, although certain trains on the Keith line included vehicles from the Great North of Scotland Railway.

Bogie stock became general in the years following the appointment of Peter Drummond at Inverness. Soon after taking charge he designed a number of third-class and composite coaches for main-line services. The former were 48 ft long, divided into seven compartments. The composite coaches were slightly shorter, and had two first and four third-class compartments. In certain cases one of the latter had a seat on one side only. Lavatory accommodation was provided in both classes.

By this time gas had superseded oil for lighting, and the old-fashioned alarm bell on the tender of the engine, worked by a cord running along the eaves of the carriages, was discarded in favour of the improved system of chain communication. The new stock was steam heated and the familiar foot-warmer gradually became a thing of the past.

In 1902 a special family saloon, with clerestory roof, made its appearance. It was 48 ft 8 in. long by 8 ft 6 in. wide, and was divided into a main saloon, 22 ft long, furnished with couches and easy chairs upholstered in velvet, and a smoking compartment 8 ft long, provided with leather-covered revolving armchairs. An attendant's compartment, a lavatory and a luggage locker adjoined the main saloon.

Drummond broke with long-established practice by altering the style of painting. Previously the standard livery for passenger stock had been green, with yellow lining and lettering, but the new coaches were turned out with the upper panels painted white. The lower parts and the under frames were still green. For the time being, these colours became standard, but in 1903 it was decided to revert to an all-green livery, similar to that used for the locomotives. Some ten years later Smith abolished all lining. This alteration gave the trains a distinctly plain although not unpleasing appearance.

The Pullman sleeping cars were withdrawn from service in 1907, when the Highland Railway decided to provide its own vehicles. The new coaches were built by Hurst, Nelson & Co., of Motherwell, to Drummond's designs. They were 50 ft long by 9 ft wide, and ran on four-wheel bogies. Oil gas was used for lighting. Contrary to usual Highland Railway practice, the external finish was varnished teak.

The number of passengers requiring sleeping accommodation had fallen off considerably, and it was no longer necessary to devote a special car to their exclusive use. Each coach had four single-berth first-class sleeping compartments, connected in pairs by inner communicating doors. The remainder of the vehicle was divided into four third-class compartments, each seating eight passengers, and one, with a seat on one side only, seating four. An attendant's compartment adjoined the sleeping berths, and lavatories were provided at each end of the coach. Although a side corridor was provided, the ends of the vehicle were not vestibuled. These composite cars were found to be exceedingly useful and economical, especially in cases where balance working necessitated their use on day trains. They remained in use until the grouping.

The sleeping cars were followed by some new third-class coaches for main-line excursion trains. They were 46 ft 4 in. long, and seated 50 passengers in two saloons, connected by a short corridor. Varnished teak was adopted for the external finish, but the innovation was not further extended. During the first world war it was completely abandoned, and both the sleeping cars and the saloons were painted in the Company's standard livery.

The designs adopted by Drummond became more or less standard and subsequent additions to the passenger rolling stock differed but little from that already in service. Latterly, a number of vestibuled coaches appeared, and gas lighting gradually made way for electricity. In 1916 some new Travelling Post Office vans were built for the main-line services, running in connection with the postal trains on the Caledonian Railway. They were 46 ft 8 in. long by 9 ft wide, and weighed 26 tons.

Goods vehicles call for little notice, as they present comparatively few points of interest. In addition to open and covered wagons, and cattle trucks, there were some unusual double-decked covered wagons used for the conveyance of sheep, an item that figured largely in the Company's receipts. The animals were securely penned by the iron bars forming the sides of the vehicle. Of equal importance was the fish traffic from the northern ports to the markets in the south, and a large stock of wagons was reserved for this purpose.

On 31 December 1922 the Highland Railway possessed 797 coaching vehicles, 2,718 goods wagons, and 112 service vehicles. These figures, although small by comparison with many other companies, stand out in sharp contrast to the five passenger coaches and 26 goods wagons that formed the complete stock of the Inverness & Nairn Railway in November 1855.

HIGHLAND RAILWAY COMPANY.

——◆●◆——

STAFF NOTICE.

——◆●◆——

General Manager and Secretary's Office,
INVERNESS, 14th April 1884.

——◆●◆——

FACING POINTS.

In future the speed of Trains at Stations, where they are not required by the Time Bill to stop, must be reduced to 15 miles an hour when passing over Facing Points.

By order.

AND. DOUGALL,
General Manager

CHAPTER 12

The Highland Railway's Steamships

FIRST SERVICES

The opening of the Dingwall & Skye Railway in August 1870 marked the beginning of a new era in the Outer Hebrides and the Isle of Skye. Previously no railway had touched the west coast north of the Firth of Clyde, and the islands were isolated and difficult of access. The easiest, if not the most direct, route was by ship from Glasgow.

A regular fortnightly, and later weekly, service of steamers had been established in 1851 by David Hutcheson & Co., of Glasgow, between the Clyde and Stornoway, in the island of Lewis, calling in at several of the islands, in addition to places on the mainland. In 1879 the Company's interests were acquired by the late David MacBrayne, whose name has since become a household word in the Western Highlands. Under his management the number of services was greatly increased.

The directors of the Dingwall & Skye Railway had obtained powers to operate their own boats from Strome Ferry, and two steamers, the *Jura* and the *Oscar*, were purchased in readiness for the opening of the line.

The *Jura* was an iron-screw steamer (330 tons gross), built in 1857 by Wingate & Co., of Glasgow, for the West Hartlepool Screw Steam Shipping Co., and named *Admiral Cator*. Sold in 1869 to Sloan & Co., of Glasgow, and renamed *Jura*, the vessel passed into the hands of the railway Company in the following year.

The *Oscar* was an iron-screw steamer of 341 tons gross, built in 1850 by Denny Bros., of Dumbarton. After passing through the hands of several owners, she was purchased by Sloan & Co. in 1869, and sold to the Dingwall & Skye Railway with the *Jura*.

At first the two ships maintained a daily passenger service in connection with the trains between Strome Ferry and Portree, in Skye, and a weekly service to Stornoway. But traffic returns were unsatisfactory, and in the winter of 1870 the Portree service was reduced, and sailings to Stornoway suspended. The latter were restored in 1871, but were maintained during the summer only. It was possible to reach Stornoway on certain days by changing into Hutcheson's ship at Portree.

On 9 November 1870, less than three months after the opening of the railway, the *Oscar* ran aground off Applecross, and became a total loss, fortunately without loss of life. She was replaced in 1871 by the *Carham*, a small iron paddle steamer, of 159 tons gross. Built in 1864 by A. & J. Inglis, of Glasgow, this vessel had previously been employed on coastal services from Leith, and on the Clyde. At the same time the Company placed an order with J. & G. Thompson, of Glasgow, for an iron-screw steamer of 347 tons gross. The new ship was completed in 1872 and named the *Ferret*.

As soon as the *Ferret* was delivered, the *Jura* was withdrawn from service and sold. Purchased by J. Bell, of Ayr, she traded between Scotland and the Mediterranean for some years, but eventually passed into the hands of a Hull firm. On 15 February 1879 she left the Humber for Smyrna with a general cargo. Nothing more was heard of her, but a medicine chest and a boat were eventually picked up. It was assumed that she came to grief on the Cross Sand, off Great Yarmouth, on the day after leaving Hull, but her fate was never definitely ascertained.

The service from Strome Ferry to Portree continued to be worked by the *Carham*, relieved occasionally by the *Ferret*. The latter ran to Stornoway once a week, in addition to making trips up and down the coast. Subsequently it was found that the traffic did not require two ships, and the *Ferret* was taken out of service, overhauled on the Clyde, and advertised for charter.

THEFT OF A SHIP

In October 1880[1] enquiries were made by a London firm of shipbrokers, Henderson & Co., who stated that they were acting for a Mr Smith, a relative of the First Lord of the Admiralty, who wished to take his invalid wife for a health cruise in the Mediterranean. All references proving satisfactory, a contract was signed and the first three months' charter money (£270) paid over. The ship's new purser, Mr Walker, purchased large quantities of stores in Glasgow, and the *Ferret* left the Clyde for Cardiff, where she took in coal

---

[1] By this time, the Dingwall & Skye Railway had been amalgamated with the Highland Railway.

before sailing for the Mediterranean with her passengers and new crew on 25 October.

Heavy weather was encountered in the Bristol Channel, and the ship was forced to put into Milford Haven, where she remained weatherbound for a week. As soon as the weather moderated, the *Ferret* sailed for Marseilles, and was officially reported from Gibraltar on 11 November. After that nothing was heard, and at the expiration of three months the railway Company applied for a renewal of the charter money, but without result. Enquiries revealed that the firm of Henderson & Co. was non-existent, and that the rich gentleman and his invalid wife were unknown. It soon became evident that false references had been used, and that the ship had been stolen. Nor did the firms in Glasgow and Cardiff from whom stores had been obtained fare any better, as the bills given in settlement of the accounts were dishonoured when they became due three months later. To make matters worse came the startling news that some wreckage bearing the name *Ferret* had been washed up on the Spanish coast. It was assumed that the vessel had foundered in a sudden storm.

Some months passed and then came strange tidings from the Antipodes, which cleared up the mystery. A small steamer, the *India*, arrived in Melbourne, where an attempt was at once made to sell her. The suspicions of the port authorities were aroused by the fact that although the ship was offered for sale, steam was always kept up, ready for immediate departure, and that neither the captain nor the crew ever went on shore. An investigation of Lloyds Register of Shipping showed that there was no ship named the *India* answering to the description of the vessel. On 27 April 1881 the port authorities seized the ship, and it was soon discovered that the *India* was none other than the long-lost *Ferret*. Meanwhile, Mr and Mrs Smith and the captain made good their escape, taking with them a very considerable sum of money, which was never recovered. Smith was arrested a few days later, but for the moment Captain Wright eluded the police. He was eventually brought into court under an assumed name, on a charge of drunkenness and assault. There his identity was discovered, and he was at once re-arrested.

At the subsequent court proceedings, the whole story came to light. Smith was a notorious swindler, well known to the English police. Captain Wright and Walker, the purser, were his confederates. To gain possession of the *Ferret*, Smith opened an account in his own name at one of the leading London banks, and founded the fictitious firm of Henderson & Co., shipbrokers. The balance at the bank was withdrawn a day or so before the ship sailed from Cardiff. The remainder of the ship's company were honest, and completely ignorant of the enterprise. Once at sea, they were intimidated by threats, and promises of large rewards, from disclosing the real state of affairs. At the ports of call, only Smith and Walker went on shore. Captain Wright never left the ship.

After the ship had passed Gibraltar in the previous November, her appearance was altered, and the name changed to *Bentan*. Some wreckage was jettisoned to give the impression of total loss, and the captain set out for the Atlantic, passing Gibraltar unnoticed, under cover of darkness. After calling at the Cape Verde Islands for water and stores, the ship reached the Brazilian port of Santos early in January, 1881. By means of forged documents, a valuable cargo of coffee was secured, and the *Bentan* put to sea once more, ostensibly bound for Marseilles. Once out of sight of land she headed south, and in due course reached Cape Town. On the voyage the name was again changed, to *India*. The stolen cargo was disposed of at a handsome figure, but an attempt to sell the ship failed. When the negotiations fell through, the *India* hurriedly left port, and headed towards the Southern Ocean. On arrival in Melbourne, the whole plot was discovered.

By no means the least remarkable part of the whole affair was the verdict of the Australian court. No account was taken of the series of frauds in English and foreign ports, and Smith, Walker and Wright were found not guilty on the charge of attempting to steal the *Ferret*. On the other hand, they were convicted of conspiracy to defraud the intending purchasers of the vessel in Melbourne, and of conspiracy to deceive the Customs and Trade Commissioner by changing the name of the ship. Smith and Walker were sentenced to seven years' penal servitude, and Wright to three and a half years. The rest of the crew were discharged.

At the conclusion of the trial the ship was restored to her rightful owners. The Highland Railway's agent in Australia was authorized to sell her, and the *Ferret* passed to the Adelaide Steam Ship Co. She was eventually wrecked on the Yorke Peninsula, South Australia, in November 1920.

END OF MARITIME ACTIVITIES

The *Carham* remained at Strome Ferry for a short time after the withdrawal of the *Ferret*, but the railway Company withdrew in favour of MacBrayne in 1880. The daily service to Portree was continued, but for some time the Stornoway ship ran on certain days of the week only. Later on, however, regular daily sailings were introduced. In 1897 the steamers were transferred from Strome Ferry to Kyle of Lochalsh.

After lying idle for some time, the *Carham* was sold in 1883 to the Ramsgate Steam Ship Company and renamed *Queen of Thanet*. For three seasons she worked a regular service between Ramsgate and the holiday resorts on the French coast. These trips were popularly known as 'Shilling Emetics'. In 1886 the ship was again sold, to a Liverpool owner, and broken up two years later.

The steamer services from Strome Ferry do not represent the whole of the Highland Railway's maritime activities. On 24 April 1877 the Company was empowered to own and work its own ships, and an order was placed with Gourlay Brothers & Co., of Dundee, for an iron-screw steamer (384 tons gross), the *John o' Groat*. On 27 July following the ship was placed in service between Scrabster Harbour (Thurso) and Kirkwall and Stromness, in Orkney.

Regular sailings continued until the summer of 1882. By that time the Company had given up its west coast steamers, and was anxious to relinquish remaining shipping interests. At the same time it was unwilling to withdraw the ship until assured that the service would be maintained by some independent concern.

The sailings between Thurso and Orkney were continued by the North of Scotland & Orkney & Shetland Steam Navigation Co. The Highland Railway provided the trains in connection, but, as at Strome Ferry, made no further attempt to run its own ships.

The *John o' Groat* was sold to foreign owners, and in the course of the next ten years passed through several hands. On 19 December 1892, while sailing in the Adriatic under the Austrian flag, and renamed *Agathé*, the vessel struck a rock off Ancona, and became a total loss.

CHAPTER 13

Grouping and Nationalisation

THE PASSING OF THE HIGHLAND

It was realised that it would be impossible for the railways to revert to their former condition after the cessation of hostilities, and various schemes were produced for complete unification or amalgamations on a large scale. Meanwhile, Government control was maintained. At one stage it was proposed that the Scottish railways should form a single group, independent of any of the English lines. But this scheme was found to be unworkable, because of the relatively weaker financial position of the Scottish companies as compared to the larger English ones. At length, the Railway Companies' Association introduced an alternative scheme, which, with minor amendments, was embodied in the Railways Act of 19 August 1921.

The Act provided for the formation of four large groups, the Highland Railway being included in the largest of them to become part of the London, Midland & Scottish Railway. The LMSR had a route mileage of 7,500, of which total the Highland Railway's contribution was little more than 500 miles. But the Highland's importance as a constituent company of the amalgamated system was none the less on that account. Highland Railway debentures and stocks were exchanged for equivalent holdings in the new Company, but the shareholders of the Dornoch and Wick & Lybster Light Railways were bought out for cash at valuation. One Highland director, A. E. Pullar, deputy chairman since 1916, was appointed to the new Board. The LMSR came into being on 1 January 1923.

Although the disappearance of much that was characteristic of the Highland Railway was an inevitable sequel of the grouping, there were few sudden breaks with the past. That the changes should have been gradual is not surprising, in view of the highly individualistic nature of the system, and the strong local patriotism of the staff. Most of the innovations were made possible by the greater resources of the new and larger Company. Two particularly welcome improvements were the extended use of corridor coaches, and an increase in the number of trains with a refreshment car for at least part of the journey. Among the first services to benefit were those on the northern main line, to which refreshment cars were introduced in the summer of 1923. These cars worked daily return trips from Inverness to The Mound or Helmsdale and at times to Wick. After 14 June 1965 the two cars worked between Inverness and Thurso. In 1984–5 buffet facilities were available between Inverness and Rogart on all three trains over the Farther North line. Working of refreshment cars over the Kyle line after the grouping was sometimes throughout and at others to Achnasheen, where the car was transferred to the up train at the crossing loop. A buffet-observation car ran until 2 October 1967. The revival of this facility is described in Chapter 14.

A problem which had not been solved when the Highland Railway lost its separate identity was the future of the branch from Keith to Portessie. Goods traffic was working over the 2½ miles from Keith to the distillery at Aultmore, and fish traffic was using the 1½ miles between the Highland station at Buckie and the junction with the Great North of Scotland Railway at Portessie, but the track had been removed from the intervening ten miles after passenger trains and through goods services had been withdrawn in August 1915.

Some twelve months after the grouping, the dismantled section was relaid, and preparations for re-opening even went so far as changing the name of Drybridge station to Letterfourie. However, a final appraisal of the amount of traffic likely to be carried appears to have been unfavourable, because through working was not resumed. Eventually, fish traffic at the Bannffshire ports declined to such an extent that the Highland station at Buckie was no longer required, and the track was removed throughout the line from Aultmore to the junction at Portessie.

Halts at Balnaguard on the Aberfeldy branch and at Parkside, Roster Road and Welsh's Crossing on the Lybster branch were the only *additions* during the twenty-five years of grouping. During this period no stations were closed apart from those on branches listed in Appendix III.

As was frequently the case elsewhere, traffic on secondary routes in northern Scotland declined seriously with the development of bus services. The first of the former Highland Railway lines to be affected were the branches from Alves to Burghead and Hopeman, and from Orbliston Junction to Fochabers, from which passenger services were withdrawn on 14 September 1931. The latter was particularly vulnerable to road competition, because its terminus had been placed some distance from the town, to avoid a costly bridge over the Spey.

On the former Caledonian main line between Perth and Stanley, the two intermediate stations at which certain Highland trains called have not survived; Strathord was closed to passengers on 13 April 1931, and Luncarty on 18 June 1951, though the goods depots at both stations continued in use for many years.

Two more branches succumbed during the second world war. All passenger traffic, except special military trains, ceased on the branch to Fort George on 5 April 1943, and the Wick & Lybster Light Railway was closed completely on 1 April 1944, and subsequently dismantled. The improvement of the steeply-graded road over the Ord of Caithness had placed the Lybster line at a serious disadvantage. The distance by road between Lybster and Helmsdale is little more than 20 miles; by rail *via* Wick it was 74 miles. Less than twelve months after hostilities had ended, the Strathpeffer branch, on which services had been drastically reduced, ceased to carry passengers on 23 February 1946.

After the railways had been nationalised in 1948, competition from road transport, assisted by the peculiar topography of the coast north of Inverness, resulted in the closure of two other lines which afforded only a circuitous route to the south. Passenger services were withdrawn from the Black Isle branch on 1 October 1951 but the line remained open for goods traffic until 13 June 1960. The latter date also saw the complete closure of the Dornoch Light Railway, which had retained a meagre passenger service, despite its geographical handicap.

TRAIN SERVICE DEVELOPMENTS

The general pattern of the train services remained unchanged after the grouping. Such alterations as did occur generally tended towards improvement and acceleration. Sunday services were restored in the summer of 1929, when one train in each direction began to run between Perth and Inverness, *via* Forres, in connection with the night trains to and from the south. From the summer of 1934, a relief train ran from Inverness to Perth, *via* Carr Bridge, but there was no corresponding service in the opposite direction. In May of that year, Sunday services were resumed on the northern main line with a train from Lairg, reaching Inverness in time to connect with the afternoon departure for Perth. This service was balanced by a morning train from Inverness to Lairg, which connected with a night newspaper train from the south and did not carry passengers.

An outstanding development in 1936 was a new weekday evening train, leaving Perth at 6.5 and reaching Inverness at 9.40. It ran during the summer only, and had through coaches from Glasgow and a connection from Edinburgh. By leaving Kings Cross at 7.25 a.m. it was possible to travel from London to Inverness by day, with changes at Edinburgh and Perth.

On the northern main line, the 'Further North Express' was restored in the summer of 1923, in the northbound direction, and on Fridays only. The train started from Aviemore, in connection with the midday service from Perth, and ran non-stop to Dingwall in 95 m. Passengers from Inverness had to travel by the afternoon stopping train to Helmsdale, and change into the express. This arrangement lasted for one season only; when the train was restored in 1924, it ran to and from Inverness, and once a week in each direction. By the summer of 1933 it was running three days a week. It was then renamed the 'John o'Groat', and became a daily train a year later.

The early-morning train from Inverness to the north, and the afternoon return service, which connected with the ship plying between Scrabster Harbour (Thurso) and Orkney, were named the 'Orcadian' in 1936. Three years earlier, the trains to and from Kyle of Lochalsh in connection with MacBrayne's ships had been named the 'Hebridean' and the 'Lewisman' respectively. The practice of naming trains on the lines north of Inverness was not generally resumed after the war, but in 1962 the name 'Orcadian' was again used for the fastest summer train.

On the southern main line the only named service was the night train between London (Euston) and Inverness, which became the 'Royal Highlander' in 1928. September of that year saw the introduction of much-needed third-class sleeping berths on the principal Anglo-Scottish services, including the 'Royal Highlander' and the portion of the train which then ran to and from Kings Cross by the East Coast route. The sleeping cars run between Glasgow and Inverness remained first class only until new composite vehicles were placed in service in the summer of 1932.

During the second world war, the railways were again called upon to handle a vast amount of additional traffic. The state of emergency lasted for nearly six years, but, thanks to the relatively greater resources of the LMSR, the strain of the burden in the north of Scotland tended to be less severe than it was on the smaller Highland Railway in the earlier conflict. Train services were reduced and schedules were eased; restaurant cars and some through coaches were suspended, but inconvenience to passengers was reduced to a minimum. The sleeping-car services were maintained between London and Inverness by the West Coast route, and between Glasgow and Inverness, but the through coaches and sleeping cars between London and the Highlands by the East Coast route were withdrawn, and were not restored.

Recovery after the war was slow, and was by no means complete when the railways were nationalised on 1 January 1948. With the collective name of British Railways, the system was divided into six regions on a geographical basis, and the railways of Scotland were separated from the lines south of the Border, and placed in the Scottish Region. At the time of its formation the region had a route mileage of rather more than 3,700, to which the surviving lines of the Highland Railway contributed some 480 miles.

FROM STEAM TO DIESEL

Of the 150 Highland Railway locomotives which received LMSR numbers after the grouping, only 29 were still at work in January 1948. All the others had passed to the scrapheap, with the exception of the first of the 'Jones Goods' 4—6—0s, No. 103 (LMSR No. 17916), which had been partly restored to its original condition and livery, and preserved at the former Caledonian Railway works at St Rollox, Glasgow, after it was withdrawn from service in 1934. It is now at the Glasgow Museum of Transport. The survivors comprised eight 4—6—0s (two of the 'Clan' class, and six of the mixed traffic class); twelve 4—4—0s (two of the 'Loch' class, and ten of the 'Small Ben' class); seven of Drummond's 0—6—0s; and two 0—4—4 tanks, also designed by Drummond.

Withdrawals continued steadily after nationalisation, and at the end of 1952 only 4—4—0 No. 2 (BR No. 54398), *Ben Alder*, and the two 0—4—4 tank engines Nos. 25 and 45 (BR Nos. 55051 and 55053) remained in service. *Ben Alder* was withdrawn in 1953, and was stored, at first at Inverness and then at Boat of Garten, pending a decision as to its fate. Eventually it was decided to preserve it, and

HR No.	LMSR No.	BR No.	Name	Built	Withdrawn
'Clan' class 4—6—0s					
52	14764	—	Clan Munro	1919	1948
55	14767	54767	Clan Mackinnon	1921	1950
Mixed traffic 4—6—0s					
75	17950	57950	—	1918	1950
76	17951	57951	—	1918	1951
78	17953	57953	—	1918	1948
79	17954	57954	—	1919	1952
80	17955	—	—	1919	1952
81	17956	57956	—	1919	1952
'Loch' class 4—4—0s					
119	14379	54379	Loch Insh	1896	1948
125	14385	54385	Loch Tay	1896	1950
'Small Ben' class 4—4—0s					
1	14397	—	Ben-y-Gloe	1898	1949
2	14398	54398	Ben Alder	1898	1953[1]
3	14399	54399	Ben Wyvis	1898	1952
5	14401	—	Ben Vrackie	1899	1948
7	14403	—	Ben Attow	1899	1949
8	14404	54404	Ben Clebrig	1899	1950
13	14409	54409	Ben Alisky	1900	1950
14	14410	54410	Ben Dearg	1900	1949
41	14415	54415	Ben Bhac Ard	1906	1948
47	14416	54416	Ben a' Bhuird	1906	1948
0—6—0 goods					
134	17693	—	—	1900	1949
135	17694	—	—	1900	1950
136	17695	57695	—	1900	1952
138	17697	57697	—	1900	1951
139	17698	57698	—	1900	1951
18	17699	—	—	1902	1949
21	17702	—	—	1902	1949
0—4—4 tanks					
25	15051	55051	Strathpeffer[2]	1905	1956
45	15053	55053	—	1905	1957

in 1961 it was removed to a shed in the Glasgow area. The difficulty of restoring *Ben Alder* to original condition regrettably caused a reversal of this decision and the engine was sent for scrap in April 1966.

[1] Stored with a view to preservation until 1966.

[2] Name removed in 1920.

The two small tank engines continued at work, and took alternate turns of duty on the Dornoch branch, a line for which their light axle weights made them particularly suitable. No. 55051 was withdrawn in the summer of 1956, but No. 55053 was overhauled and repainted soon afterwards, and appeared to have been granted an extended lease of life. However, the end came suddenly and ingloriously, early in 1957, when the axle of the leading pair of driving wheels broke while the engine was hauling a mixed train on the branch. One of the wheels became detached, and careered along the track until it came into violent contact with a lineside gatepost. Fortunately, the train was not derailed and nobody was injured. No. 55053 was replaced on the Dornoch line by an 0—6—0 pannier tank engine from the Western Region.

The accompanying table shows the Highland Railway locomotives that passed to the Scottish Region. Nine of these veterans were withdrawn from service before they had been renumbered into British Railways stock.

As the Highland locomotives were withdrawn from service they were replaced by motive power from other constituents of the LMSR, and later by post-grouping types. Many locomotives of the former Caledonian Railway were transferred to the north of Scotland, and these were followed by the ubiquitous class '5' 4—6—0s, and after nationalisation by standard British Railways designs. Then came the decision that diesel traction was to replace steam as part of the railway modernisation plans, announced in 1955. Diesel locomotives began to appear in the Highlands in the spring of 1958, at first on trial trips, and then on regular passenger and freight duties. By June 1961 steam traction had almost disappeared from northern Scotland.

Two-car multiple-unit diesel trains began to work regularly on the local services between Perth and Blair Atholl in June 1959, and multiple-unit sets of the 'inter-city' type were used for the accelerated service between Inverness and Aberdeen inaugurated in July 1960. The trains ran *via* Mulben, and were allowed 2½ h. for the 108-mile journey, with four intermediate stops. So encouraging were the results that a year later the service was increased from two to four trains in each direction.

NATIONALISATION

Few changes of great consequence were made in the north of

Scotland during the first 12 years of nationalisation. Competition from road transport, assisted by the peculiar topography of the coast north of Inverness, resulted in withdrawal of the Black Isle branch passenger service on 1 October 1951. Goods traffic ceased from 13 June 1960, and lifting of the track was completed during January 1963. The Dornoch Light Railway was also closed (entirely) from 13 June; dismantling was completed on 25 June 1963. The only stations closed to passengers on lines that remained open for traffic, were Mosstowie on 7 March 1955, and Guay on 3 August 1959. Per contra, two formerly unadvertised platforms, Tauchers (near Keith) and Duncraig (on the Kyle of Lochalsh line) were inserted in the public timetables from 23 May 1949.

The station at Stanley remained in use for passengers until 11 June 1956. The platforms were subsequently demolished, and the peculiar layout, by which trains on the Highland line observed right-hand running through the station, was simplified, and restored to the form adopted in 1856 for the opening of the Perth & Dunkeld Railway. Trains from Inverness joined the northbound track at the junction, and almost immediately diverged through a crossover to reach the southbound line. A further change took place on 4 September 1967 when the former Caledonian main line to Forfar was converted to single track and the Highland officially became the 'main line'.

By far the greatest changes since nationalisation have occurred on the main line between Inverness and Wick. Including the private station at Dunrobin, this circuitous route had no less than 40 intermediate stations or platforms, some of which were inconveniently situated, and served only small and scattered communities. The main road from Inverness to the north runs roughly parallel with the railway, and in recent years these small stations had lost nearly all their traffic to Highland Omnibuses Limited (a company owned by the British Transport Commission).

On 13 June 1960, passenger services were withdrawn from all the intermediate stations between Inverness and Bonar Bridge, except Dingwall, Invergordon, Fearn, and Tain. Beyond Bonar Bridge, bus services do not parallel the railway to the same extent, and on the northern part of the line only the stations at Rogart, The Mound, Loth, Halkirk, Bower, Watten, and Bilbster were closed. The elimination of 20 stops permitted a substantial saving in journey time between Inverness and Wick[1]. That these economies had

---

[1] The financial saving was £41,000 per annum.

been rather too drastic became evident in March 1961, when Rogart station was reopened as a halt.

The crossing loops at Foulis and at Acheilidh Crossing (between Lairg and Rogart) had been removed before the summer of 1960, but with these exceptions the traffic capacity of the line was maintained by the retention of double-line working between Clachnaharry and Clunes, and the crossing loops at the closed stations.

Also closed on 13 June 1960 was the isolated roadside station of Auldern,[1] some two miles east of Nairn. The original main line of the Highland Railway runs through Nairnshire for about eight miles and is the only railway in that county. For nearly 40 years after the station at Cawdor was closed in 1858, Nairn was the only station on this section of line, and therefore in the county. Auldearn was opened in 1895, and with its closure, 65 years later, Nairn reverted to its unique position.

The most extensive civil engineering works undertaken in the north of Scotland since nationalisation have been the reconstruction of some two miles of the Kyle of Lochalsh line, to enable the level of Lochluichart to be raised in connection with a hydro-electric project. The works included a new bridge of 100 ft span over the River Conon, the formation of rock cuttings and stone-pitched embankments, and the re-siting of Lochluichart station. The new line (only 43yd longer than the old) was opened on 3 May 1954.

THE CENTENARY AND THE FUTURE

A noteworthy post-war development on the southern main line was the restoration, in the autumn of 1955, of the evening train from Perth to Inverness, which now runs throughout the year, and not during the summer only. At first, this train had good connections from southern Scotland, and the north of England, but passengers from London had to leave Kings Cross before 4 a.m. Two years later, the morning 'Talisman' was inaugurated, and the departure time from Kings Cross became 7.45 a.m., but there was an interval of nearly 1½ h. between the arrival of the new express in Edinburgh and the departure of the connection for Perth and Inverness.

It was not until the summer of 1962 that the acceleration to a six-hour schedule of the 'Elizabethan' between London and Edinburgh gave a departure at 9.30 a.m. and an arrival at 9.25 p.m. in Inverness, with 33 m. for changing trains in Edinburgh. In the

---

[1] The signal box and crossing loop had been removed on 5 June.

winter service, a further improvement has enabled an Inverness connection to be given from the 10 a.m. train from King's Cross.

Journeys to and from the Highlands at weekends were facilitated in the autumn of 1957, when for the first time the sleeping cars and through coaches leaving London (Euston) for Perth on Saturday evenings were extended to Inverness, *via* Forres, on Sunday mornings. Not only was a change of train, and a long wait, at Perth eliminated, but arrival times at stations on the Highland line became considerably earlier. A corresponding southbound train left Inverness on Sunday evenings. From the summer of 1959 a sleeping car ran between Edinburgh and Inverness, in addition to the car to and from Glasgow.

The table on pages 193 — 195 shows a summary of services on the main lines from Perth to Inverness and from Inverness to the north at salient dates from the autumn of 1863, when the route through the Central Highlands was opened. At that time, the northern line extended no further than Invergordon, but the figures for 1874 show it open to Wick. The substantial improvements of the summer of 1885 appear in the third section of the table, and the effects of the opening of the shortened route to Inverness in the fourth. The times for August 1914 and August 1939 show the position immediately before the outbreak of the two world wars, and those for 1922 and 1947 the services on the eve of the grouping and nationalisation respectively. The accelerations that have followed the introduction of diesel traction are apparent from the times shown for the summers of 1962 and 1971.

In every case, only trains making the through journey are shown in the summaries, and except for the 'Further North Express' (in the table for August 1914) trains running only on certain days of the week have been omitted. After 1898, trains shown running *via* Forres have been included only because they did not also serve the Carr Bridge lines.

The centenary year (1963) of the opening of the main line from Forres to Perth across the Grampians, passed without further closures, but 1964 saw the local passenger service between Keith Junction and Elgin via Mulben withdrawn and the disappearance from the timetable of a few wayside stations. The Aberfeldy branch ceased to carry passengers in May 1965, only two months short of its centenary, and the old main line between Forres and Aviemore closed to all traffic in October, thus reducing the route mileage of the former Highland Railway by 44 miles 57ch.

The remodelling of the junction at Stanley was only one of a number of signalling and track layout changes which had started after the end of the Second World War. They were, of course, made in the interests of economy—especially of manpower—and were the precursors of intensified rationalisation to follow. This consisted of closure of many signal boxes (in Highland days officially called 'cabins') on both double and single line sections, replacement of two boxes by a single one at larger stations, such as Ballinluig, Blair Atholl, Aviemore and Grantown-on-Spey West, and closure of crossing loops. It should be pointed out that at many wayside stations, particularly north of Inverness, the electric tablet instruments were placed in the station offices, the two 'signal boxes' required to control the North and South loop points and relevant signals being, in effect, only unmanned ground frames. It was not uncommon to see the porter-signalman or stationmaster, cycling along the platform to set the road for the passing of a train. Tablets were exchanged at most boxes by automatic apparatus, but hand exchange was also in force, especially where the instruments were located in the office. Since 1966 the longest single line section has been between Helmsdale and Forsinard, 24 miles 24 chains. Details of these changes appear in the notes to the Distance Tables, Appendix II.

As part of the rationalisation programme, several double line sections were singled and worked at first by electric token system, replaced on the southern main line by the tokenless block system in 1968–71 (see Appendix V). On minor branches still worked by electric tablet, this was withdrawn and 'one engine' working substituted.

Further economies were made during the 1960s by de-staffing of level crossings or providing alternative means of protecting the crossing where there was no longer a signal box from which the gates were formerly worked. In 1966–7 those at Kinloss, Brodie, Gollanfield and Dalcross were equipped with automatic half-barriers actuated by approaching trains. North and West of Inverness, where neither rail nor road traffic justifies such expense, 12 open crossings were created, without gates or barriers, safety being secured either by automatic red and green traffic lights to control road traffic, or a severe speed restriction on passing trains; in some cases the train is brought to a stand and the engine horn sounded before passing over the roadway.

The outlook for the railways in northern Scotland was uncertain in the late 1960s, though efforts were made towards halting the depopulation of the northern counties by introducing industrial development. These are described in the following chapter.

On the passenger side, whilst the main line south of Inverness and the greatly-improved Aberdeen–Inverness services were not in immediate danger, the same could not have been said of the northern lines. Both the Inverness, Wick & Thurso and Kyle of Lochalsh services were and remain grant-aided under section 39 of the Transport Act 1968, the former receiving £584,000 for 1970–72 and the latter £179,000 for 1970–71.

CHAPTER 14

The Oil Years

OIL AND TOURISM RELATED GROWTH IN TRAFFIC

At the beginning of the 1970s, the longer term prospects for the heavily subsidised lines to Wick/Thurso and to Kyle of Lochalsh looked unfavourable. Although the value of both lines as vital links for the local population was beyond dispute, both lines had been existing under a cloud of uncertainty since the Beeching Report of 1963 and the opportunities for reducing the size of the subsidies looked limited; indeed the puzzling decision to make Ullapool the port for the Stornoway ferry instead of Kyle, which necessitated £4m road improvements, was guaranteed to exacerbate matters from the transfer in autumn 1972. The development of the British Aluminium smelter at Invergordon apart, there was little ground for arguing that a sound industrial base could be created to staunch the gradual human drift south in search of better prospects. The constructive and positive relationship that existed in the mid eighties between British Rail, the Highlands & Islands Development Board (established in 1965 and now Highland and Island Enterprise) and the Highland Regional Council (formed in 1975) had not yet been developed, and morale amongst BR staff was inevitably low living under the Sword of Damocles. It is a measure of the transformation wrought by North Sea oil developments that, in contrast to the retrenchment feared in the early 1970s, a proposal for a new line was being considered by district councils in 1978.

However optimistic the plan for a new line between Tulloch and Newtonmore may have been, the fact that councils could seriously address themselves to an examination of a route that roughly followed the ill-fated Glasgow & North Western Railway of 1882–3, is evidence of the hopes induced largely by oil. The story of the Highland lines from 1970 to 1985 can therefore be told largely in terms of the response to the growth in traffic generated by oil-related business and, to a lesser extent, by the lengthening of the tourist season through winter sports and the temporary success of Motorail. More recently efforts have been made to reduce costs on the secondary routes as the benefits of the oil boom recede.

The foremost need for BR was to increase the capacity of the Perth to Inverness line which had been gradually rationalised during the 1960s with a reduction in passing loops and the amount of double track. The most important change had been the singling of the 23¼ miles of double track between Blair Atholl and Dalwhinnie; its restoration was the major improvement proposed in the *Moray Firth Access Transport Study*, prepared for the Highlands & Islands Development Board and published in 1974. The advocated re-instatement of passing loops at Kincraig, Slochd Summit and Moy also became part of the formal BR plans for a £3.7m improvement programme which received approval from the DoE in early 1976. In 1975, ½m tons of oil-related freight was carried over the Highland main line and the line's utilisation had reached a point at which there was only one spare freight path, so clearly to exploit further increases in traffic, extra paths had to be found. Work on the improvements began in earnest in mid July 1976 with the establishment of work sites at Blair Atholl and Dalwhinnie. The second set of metals over the 23¼ miles between these two points, divided into three sections by intermediate block colour light signals and provided with an emergency crossover at Dalnacardoch, was ready for the introduction of the new timetable in May 1978. The other part of the improvement, the resignalling of the 39¾ miles between Kingussie and Culloden Moor, was delayed by two severe winters and was not fully completed until early 1980. Tokenless block had been installed over the line in 1968–9, but the system differed from others on BR in that the instruments and their operation were made as similar as possible to conventional token instruments. Colour light signals now control trains through the loops between Kingussie and Culloden Moor except at Aviemore where mechanical signalling was largely retained to keep down costs. The panel controlling the 39¾ miles is located in what was Aviemore North cabin, now the only signal box at the former junction for Forres. The improvements created three additional passenger and three additional freight paths in each direction, thereby introducing greater flexibility in operation and therefore reducing the impact of any delays. Journey times of both passenger and freight trains were reduced by about ½ hour between Perth and Inverness.

Improved journey times and timekeeping were also helped by the gradual replacement of the older Class 24, 26 and 27 diesels by Class 40s, 45s and 47s over the main line. Double-heading of the less powerful Bo-Bos was the norm, and triple-heading was not uncommon with heavier trains. Class 50s never regularly appeared on the Highland, but the odd one reached Inverness, most typically on a Motorail service. Even a Deltic was seen in the Highland capital; in June 1973 D9004 *Queen's Own Highlander* assisted a Class 24 and a Class 26 with the up Royal Highlander. With the introduction of the new timetable in May 1984, Inverness, Aviemore, Kingussie and Pitlochry became part of the HST 125 network, served by a single train each way from King's Cross, the London-bound train leaving Inverness at 7.20am and arriving at 4.00pm, while the northbound train left the capital at 12.00pm for a 8.50pm arrival in Inverness. (The northbound HST served more stations on the Highland than the southbound.) The intention of the Highland Chieftain, as the new train was called, was to replace the Clansman as the principal train between the Highlands and the English capital. Faster line speeds over the Highland — a section of 100 mph line was created — reduced the Inverness-Perth run to a little over 2 hours. The strongly seasonal nature of passenger traffic over the Highland was reflected in other services: two daytime services each way between Glasgow and three with Edinburgh reduced to one and two respectively for the winter months, and the Friday-only evening service with Edinburgh was also a feature of the summer months only. Nonetheless there was a steady increase in passenger carryings over the main line during the early 1970s; for example, there was an increase of 25 per cent between 1971–4 and a 28 per cent increase in passengers using Inverness station between 1977–9. The attractiveness of rail travel was helped by improved timings and the introduction of air-conditioned Mk 2 stock, maintained in the new £1.3m carriage maintenance depot at Inverness, authorised in 1981 and commissioned in 1983.

On the freight side, oil-related business brought dramatic increases in rail-borne traffic, although it may be argued that the main beneficiary of North Sea oil was the A9 road upon which about £200m was lavished, even before the Dornoch bridge works of the 1990s. (To put this figure in perspective, the BR Scottish Region's investment programme for the whole country amounted to £18.6m in 1981 and to £8.6m in 1982.) An early instance of BR's responsiveness to the needs of oil-work contractors was the installation in 1972 of a ¼ mile siding to serve the MK-Shand pipe-coating plant at Invergordon. Exactly three weeks from the first site meeting, the first train carrying 450 tons of pipes left the siding for Tyneside where they received a bitumastic coating before returning to Invergordon to be encased in concrete. A plant to carry out the

JUNCTIONS

(38) *The junction at the north end of Muir of Ord station, showing the Black Isle branch to Fortrose going off on the right. Note the attractive shunt arm signal in the fork of the junction and the HR water column at the end of the platform.*

(39) *The Mound, with train for Wick and Thurso on the left and one of Drummond's 0—4—4T 'Passenger Tanks' on the right with the Dornoch branch train.*

(40) *Gollanfield Junction looking west, with the branch to Fort George on the right. The bracket signal must have been one of the tallest on the HR.*

(41) *You can feel the damp and spot the flatness of the very far north. The engine has come off the Thurso train on its arrival at Georgemas Junction and the Wick portion will shortly arrive. Note the pressure on the sidings, though Georgemas Junction had already seen its peak traffic in World War I.*

bitumastic coating was under construction at Invergordon which obviated the need for the journey to Tyneside, but the siding was used for the delivery of 150 tons bitumen a week, cement in Presflo wagons from Oxwellmains near Dunbar and other materials. Other places to benefit from oil-related traffic were Fearn and Evanton (Novar until 1937): at Fearn 7,000 tons steel plate were brought in by a nightly service from Dalzell Works at Motherwell for use in the construction of Nigg Bay graving dock; at Evanton a siding was put in to connect the 7 acre depot of Graham Wood Scotland Ltd which handled steel products. For a period in 1976 two trains a day left MK-Shand's siding at Invergordon for Fraserburgh with pipes for the Brent Field gas pipeline.

LATER FREIGHT DECLINE

The *deus ex machina* of the Kyle line, the Howard Doris construction site at Strome Ferry on Loch Kishorn, never realised its full potential or early expectations. Opened in 1975, it had been in prospect for long enough to help the reprieve of the Kyle line; in Autumn 1973 the Minister for Transport stated that the future of the line probably rested with freight. Built partly on reclaimed land, the five sidings were put in to supply the construction site on Loch Kishorn where the master platform for the Ninian field was being built. The initial service of one weekday train carried cement from Oxwellmains, fly-ash pozzolan in Presflo wagons from Alloa, pre-stressing material from Ayr and other materials, some in Freightliner containers. It was hoped that other orders would follow and that traffic might build up to three or four trains a day. Such hopes remained unfulfilled and the site closed at the end of September 1977, the only hope (ultimately vain) being a takeover of the facilities by the Navy which has a torpedo testing base at Kyle and which then received supplies by rail.

Undoubtedly the heaviest single blow to freight traffic in the region — and also to passenger returns — was the closure of the British Aluminium smelter at Invergordon, largely due to an inability to reach a new agreement for cheap electricity which had been a major incentive for the siting of the works. Its closure was a serious blow to the community, already suffering from reduced opportunities in the local oil-supply industries, and to BR which handled £½m freight business a year. This, coupled with the improved road communications as a result of the Kessock Bridge at Inverness, that across Cromarty Firth and upgrading of other stretches, gave BR a difficult task in maintaining freight services to Wick. Nonetheless it fought back with the introduction of a daily container service on passenger trains between Aberdeen and Wick, conveying containers for Sutherland's Transport on the 1.55pm from Aberdeen to Inverness and 5.40pm Inverness to Wick. This was achieved by modifying Freightliner wagons, fitting a steam pipe alongside the standard air and vacuum pipes and plugging up the rear of the air pipe. Mention should also be made of the flow of bulk grain from York and Diss to Muir of Ord, of oil to terminals at Lairg and Invergordon and continuing grain traffic on the Burghead branch. It was hoped that some of the sizeable Wick fish traffic might be won back to rail by conveying containers to Aberdeen to be added to regular Freightliner services, but nothing came of this. Although Inverness was the first of thirteen TOPS responsibility areas in the Scottish Region to be connected with the central computer in London in January 1975, it was not until the end of 1982 that Speedlink air-braked rail freight services to Inverness were inaugurated. A fillip to freight on the Far North line in 1985 was a short-lived flow of agricultural chemicals for the Forestry Commission from Ayr to Altnabreac.

RADIO SIGNALS AND CONTROLS

The particular problems of the Highland lines to Wick/Thurso and Kyle—long, single-track lines through sparsely inhabited country susceptible to disruption during the winter months—encouraged an innovative response from BR engineers in trying to reduce the over-heads and improve operating efficiency. Following the destruction of most of the overhead wires and poles on the 59 miles between Lairg and Forsinard during a severe blizzard in January 1978, it was decided to take the opportunity of replacing wires by radio signals over the 103 miles between Tain and Georgemas Junction. An interface data transmission unit was installed in eight signal cabins which converts the electrical current operating the block bells into a radio signal, and transmits it to the adjacent box where a similar unit decodes the signal to operate the bells and indicators. Locomotives operating over the line are fitted with an aerial and a transmitter/receiver. Road and rail vehicles of the Signals & Telecommunications and Engineers departments are similarly equipped. The system facilitates a much quicker response to any problems that arise as well as reducing maintenance. Another result of the January blizzards was the decision to provide survival hampers on trains running north of

Inverness.

The Far North line was chosen for the pioneer experiment of the open station system, introduced in November 1981, which included Inverness. Few changes have been made to passenger facilities over the Wick/Thurso line since the closure of twenty stations in June 1960. Three of the twenty have been reopened: Alness was re-opened as an unstaffed halt (before the open station system was introduced elsewhere) on 7 May 1973 to serve new housing developments, and Muir of Ord reopened on 4 October 1976,. Dunrobin reopened in 1985 (see Chapter 15). Finally, in response to a request from the Highland Regional Council, the name of the station at Bonar Bridge was changed to Ardgay on 2 May 1977. A five-car DMU of Swindon-built stock off the Edinburgh-Glasgow service was tried out for a day in may 1971, but it was not deemed suitable. Class 24s gradually gave way to the Class 26s by 1976, in turn replaced by Class 37s with the introduction of the new time-table in May 1982. The three Class 37s on the three return work-ings, with a fourth on the Thurso line, enabled about 20 minutes to be saved on the journey to Wick which took 4 hours 21 minutes.

Even more revolutionary than the radio signals of the Far North line was the method of radio control developed by the BR research Department at Derby for the Kyle line. To make a dramatic impact on overheads, it is evident that mechanical signalling, costly to operate and maintain, must be superseded by a system that exploits the potential of microprocessors coupled with radio. Safety was obviously the prime concern in the development of the equipment, and a number of checks are built into it to ensure that a malfunction will become obvious to the operators. The need for conventional signalling was eliminated at the three intermediate stations and at Kyle by a control panel in the signal box at Dingwall which gave a visual display of the entire line with the position of trains, designated by numbers, and their direction of travel. Solid state interlocking at Dingwall governed the issue of electronic tokens by radio to the traction units, supplemented by a verbal authorisation to drivers, followed by a visual display on the unit with which all Kyle-line locomotives are fitted. The driver has to confirm acceptance and may then proceed, knowing that the section ahead cannot be handed over to another driver without his co-operation. Even when he has reached the next loop and released the token, it cannot be issued to a following train until the driver has confirmed verbally that he has left the loop. Notwithstanding the installation costs and the vital provision of point heaters and a stored energy device to hold point blades, savings were made within a remarkably short time, partly because the conventional pole route would have required early renewal. The system was later extended to the Far North line (see Chapter 15).

TRAIN SERVICE CHANGES

The strongly seasonal nature of traffic on the Kyle line, giving a summer/winter ratio of 8:1, encouraged the reintroduction of a Sunday service in summer 1983 with one train each way. It proved so successful — as did the reinstated summer Sunday services on the Wick/Thurso and Aberdeen lines in 1979 — that the experimental period was extended into September. Also revived in 1979 to boost revenue was the observation car, also serving light refreshments, a facility last offered in 1967. Flying Scotsman Enterprises provided GWR saloon No 9004, but it developed a hot box on the way north so Caledonian Railway saloon No 41, built in 1879, was dispatched to Inverness to work the service.

The seasonal passenger ratio was also reflected in the large number of Britrail passes used during the summer months, the remarkable savings achieved by purchasing such tickets in America encouraging the use of rail travel. Excursions and rail-based holidays which used special coaching stock, as for example those organised by Jules Verne Travel, augmented the summer trains. Class 26 locomotives were still in evidence on the line, having taken over from Class 24s in 1975–6, but Class 37s dominated workings. The Kyle of Lochalsh Hotel, together with the Station Hotel at Inverness, ceased to be railway owned with the privatisation of British Transport Hotels in 1983–4.

The passenger service over the Aberdeen-Inverness line was one of the first to be completely dieselised in the Region, in 1959. The long reign of the DMUs came to an end in April 1980 when a full service of locomotive-hauled trains came into operation, usually a Class 27/1 with five or six coaches that included a buffet on most trains.

Accidents were mercifully few and included only one fatality which was not the result of negligence on anyone's part. On 5 November 1973 there was a head-on collision between a passenger and goods train at Dingwall when the 4.20pm Invergordon to Inverness goods overran signals and crashed into a Kyle train that was leaving the station. Two passengers and two train crew were taken to hospital but released the same evening. The fault was attributed to the driver, who was driving at the time and who had failed to control speed through the correct application of the brakes. On 3 February 1983, the last coach of the 1.50pm Aberdeen to Inverness train derailed and overturned near Elgin, resulting in one fatality and ten injured passengers. Evidence at the inquiry suggested that the cause was a rail-end fracture for which no blame was attached, the line having been examined only a short time before the accident. Finally, in the early hours of 24 September 1983, six coaches of the previous day's 11.50pm Inverness to Glasgow/ Edinburgh sleeper derailed on an embankment near Pitlochry. Five of the coaches, which included Mk 1 sleeping cars, slid down both sides of the embankment but their descent was checked by trees. Seven of the twenty-nine people taken to hospital were detained. Of the 96 passengers, 28 were taken to hospital though none was seriously injured. The official report was not published until 1987 and also addressed a similar derailment at Pershore on the Worcester–Oxford line in 1984; both were caused by fractures of deep-skirted fishplates at bullhead joints.

During the 1970s work began on the resurrection of the railway between Aviemore and Boat of Garten by the Strathspey Railway Co. The original proposal for the acquisition of the line came from the Scottish Railway Preservation Society, but opposition to the idea resulted in the scheme being formally abandoned at the EGM in July 1971. A breakaway Strathspey Railway Co was formed shortly after by those feeling that a mistake had been make in dropping the proposal, and a supporting Strathspey Railway Association was established in March 1972. With the financial support of the Highlands & Islands Development Board, the 5¼ mile line, including the 4-road engine shed at Aviemore, was purchased in 1972 for £44,250. The first steam passenger train was run on 6 April 1974 for the benefit of directors and shareholders attending the AGM, and the first train to use the line after restoration was a LCGB special in September 1975 which was hauled by LMS Class 5 4—6—0 No 5025. Opening of the line was delayed by problems over a level crossing which the local authority wanted to install north of Aviemore, but the line finally opened to the public on 22 July 1978 after which Ivatt 2—6—0 No 46464 proved the mainstay of services in the first season. The railway has over a dozen locomotives and an impressive collection of historic rolling stock. The only Highland Railway items are a six-wheel composite of 1909 and four-wheel full-brake No 5, built c1870, which was beautifully restored by the late W. E. C. Watkinson at his Worcestershire home before going to the Strathspey.

Steam also returned to the Highland with a number of rail tours over the Kyle line, operated by LMS Class 5 No 5025, and over the main line from Perth to Aviemore with A4 No 60009 *Union of South Africa* and No 5025.

In addition to the proposal already mentioned for a railway from Tulloch to Newtonmore, an ambitious scheme was promoted for a rack railway from Strathpeffer to the summit of Ben Wyvis that would have shared the trackbed of the Kyle line between Achterneed and Raven's Rock, subject to safety provisions stipulated by BR. Substantial financial support from local councils was promised, but the scheme came to nought.

CHAPTER 15

The final decade of British Rail

The ten years from 1985 have been dominated by the need to reduce costs as government support for the railways has, with the exception of Channel Tunnel-related work, shown a significant reduction from a figure already amongst the lowest per capita in Europe. The principal instrument of cost reduction has been the almost total replacement on all Highland lines of locomotive-hauled trains by diesel multiple units (DMUs), a transformation that has also permitted an acceleration of services. The only regular exceptions are trains between London and the Highlands. However, the switch to a DMU railway has not made it any easier to cope with the large fluctuation in seasonal loadings – adding a coach or two in summer was much easier than obtaining an additional DMU. This difficulty has been compounded by the structure chosen by the government for its privatisation of the railways, in which almost all passenger trains are owned by three rolling stock companies (ROSCOs); it quickly became apparent that paying additional hire charges to accommodate peak demand could seldom be justified on purely financial grounds.

The other theme that spans the decade is the controversy over the Dornoch bridge. This sorry tale is indicative of the obstacles placed in the path of rail investment, in marked contrast to Highland road schemes, which have absorbed an overwhelming proportion of transport spending in the region. Only with the emerging new realism of the mid-1990s is there a waning of the myopic attitude held by some authorities that public money spent on railways is subsidy whereas that spent on roads is investment.

In administrative terms ScotRail became a more autonomous organisation from February 1990, taking over responsibility for operations (known in industry jargon as 'production') which had been retained by the Scottish Region after sectorisation in 1982. This gave ScotRail a brief period of control over all aspects of the railway north of the border before the creation of Railtrack on 1 April 1994 again fragmented the structure. The government intends to franchise ScotRail, but there have been calls for the consideration of micro-

franchises for lines such as Kyle and the Far North. A new Highland
Rail Network Development Partnership was formed in late 1995 at
the behest of Highlands & Islands Enterprise (HIE); it is made up of
the key players in the railway, tourism and economy of the region.
HIE's initiative follows publication of a report it commissioned
which reveals that the Highland's railways generate over 1,700 jobs
and £24m a year for the regional economy.

TRANSFORMING THE TRAINS

The first visit of a Sprinter to the Highlands took place in January
1988 when Metro-Cammell Super Sprinter No 156402 went on
proving trials to Kyle and Wick. The intention was to eliminate
locomotive-hauled passenger trains within ScotRail by 1990, thereby
achieving a 50 per cent reduction in operating costs. Class 158
Express units would operate the service over the Highland main line
and Class 156s would take over the other Highland services. Their
introduction did not prove so straightforward.

Class 156 Super Sprinters were supposed to be introduced with a
new timetable on 23 January 1989, but they were sent to deputise
for Class 155 units withdrawn from services elsewhere in Britain for
modification to door controls. Class 156s were finally introduced on
the Aberdeen line in May 1989, and in October 1989 the same class
of units enabled a reduction in journey time of 40 minutes to Wick,
10 minutes off the Kyle schedule and 20 minutes between Inverness
and Aberdeen.

The following year Aberdeen line trains temporarily reverted to
locomotive haulage by Classes 37 and 47 when the Class 156s were
drafted elsewhere to replace Class 158 Express units. This was
necessitated by problems with Class 158s failing to activate track
circuits, forcing their withdrawal until the fault was rectified.

While these new diesel multiple units have reduced costs and
schedules, their introduction has not been without problems:
overcrowding has been a frequent complaint, in some instances so
severe that a relief bus has had to be organised and in others that
station stops were omitted because there was no room for waiting
passengers; and space for bicycles and backpacks is limited, despite
the obvious need for such accommodation in a tourist area renowned
for outdoor pursuits. However, ScotRail's Class 156s were modified
to take four bikes per two-car set rather than the two south of the
border. The inadequate provision for bicycles was exacerbated by an
attempt to impose a complete ban on their carriage by Class 158

units from 13 May 1991. The outcry was so great that the measure was rescinded.

National newspapers capitalised on this wave of protest in mid-May to illustrate the new bicycle bought   by ScotRail for the signalman at Nairn: the distance between the mechanical cabins at each end of the loop (now a rare feature) had warranted the provision of a bicycle since about 1955.

As a consequence of these various problems, locomotive haulage of some workings persisted on most lines, especially in summer to cope with the tourist loadings and the greater number of bicycles. This was particularly the case on the Kyle line, not least because of the continued operation of the observation car. By May 1992 most Aberdeen trains had switched from Class 156 to 158 operation.

Class 158 Express units took over the main line services on 5 November 1990, but withdrawals were necessary to rectify faults with the door frames and sub-floor mountings. Their first winter was a baptism of snow, since they did not incorporate snowploughs and could not cope with more than 6 inches of snow. Consequently Class 156s from the Aberdeen line had to take over some workings while ploughs were fitted to the 158s.

TRAIN SERVICES

The continuing good loadings of the Clansman after the introduction of the Highland Chieftain in May 1984 encouraged BR to plan two year-round trains between London and Inverness. To improve connections off the northbound Clansman, especially for the Far North line, departure from London Euston was brought forward from May 1986 to 07.45, calling after Perth at Pitlochry and Aviemore and arriving in the Highland capital at 17.22. The southbound working left Inverness at 11.00 for a 20.30 arrival at Euston.

Also new in the timetable of May 1986 was a train between Inverness and Bristol, but this ran for one summer only. Running from May to the end of September, it left Inverness at 08.30 and called at all stations on the Highland main line. Because the service replaced the previous year's 09.20 train to Glasgow Queen Street, the new Bristol train ran via the Glasgow terminus and had to make a complicated reversal at Eastfield to head south. The return working began at Taunton on Mondays to Fridays and at Paignton on Saturdays.

Passenger revenue on the Far North and Kyle lines increased by

11 and 25 per cents respectively during 1987. To stimulate further growth, a Highland Railcard costing £3 was introduced in October 1988 for residents of Inverness and of the areas served by the Kyle and Far North lines. The card entitled the holder to a 20 per cent discount on standard single, return, day return and Saver tickets. The take-up was slow: by late 1994 only 1,200 had been issued, but a strong marketing effort raised the figure to 30,000 a year later.

From May 1990 most trains between Inverness and Edinburgh were diverted to run via Kirkcaldy and over the single line between Ladybank and Perth; the exceptions were the Clansman and trains from King's Cross which continued to run via Stirling.

In summer 1991 a new early morning Invergordon–Glasgow train was timetabled and would have become the first through service for many years from north of Inverness to the lowlands. However it never actually began operation.

The Clansman was discontinued north of Edinburgh from October 1991, largely because a Class 158 service had been timed to leave Edinburgh five minutes before the northbound Clansman (which lingered for 20–25 minutes at Waverley) and arrived in the Highland capital 45 minutes ahead of the Clansman; not surprisingly, everyone aware of this transferred to the faster train.

Strong passenger growth continued on all Highland lines in the early 1990s: in the three years to summer 1992, for example, the percentage increases were 100 on the Kyle line, 90 between Inverness and Edinburgh/Glasgow, 50–60 on Aberdeen services and 18 on the Far North, despite the improvements to the A9. Given the slower journey times and higher fares of trains compared with buses between Inverness and Wick/Thurso, the continuing levels of patronage suggest that passengers prefer the qualities of train travel.

Strong opposition was voiced to the complete withdrawal of all Motorail services from 27 May 1995, which coincided with a furore over the axeing of the Fort William sleeper; the protest saved the latter, albeit with a much reduced capacity, but the London–Inverness Motorail came to an end at a time when the government was saying that the days of building roads to meet demand were emphatically over.

In 1995 Inverness depot assumed responsibility for maintenance of the 64 sleeping car train vehicles, helping to compensate for the depot's reduced workload following the virtual end of locomotive-hauled trains on ScotRail services. This long-heralded termination was again postponed during the summer of 1995 when ScotRail hired a set of Waterman Railways carriages to operate the 10.30

Inverness–Edinburgh and 15.40 return working. The *raison d'être* for this was to increase luggage and cycle capacity and to release three diesel multiple units to strengthen other workings with strong tourist demand.

In 1995 the pattern of services on the main line is three trains between Inverness and Glasgow and five between Inverness and Edinburgh, one of the latter the Highland Chieftain to and from King's Cross. On the Far North line there are three trains a day with the prospect of an early commuter train from Tain to Inverness. All Wick-bound trains now run via Thurso, adding over half an hour to the schedule. The Kyle line also has three trains a day with a fourth in July and August. The Aberdeen line sees 10 trains a day with a working between Inverness and Elgin.

The scenic attractions of the Kyle and Far North lines were exploited by Luxury Days Out excursions such as the Orcadian and Hebridean Heritage; these were operated by the Special Trains Unit until its sale to Waterman Railways in 1995. The Orcadian took in both lines with visits to Skye and the Orkneys from the terminus of each line. The increased costs attributable to such trains in the wake of privatisation makes their continuance unlikely.

FREIGHT TRAFFIC

The decade has seen freight traffic continue to decline, from the high levels of the oil years to almost nothing, before the beginnings of a renaissance in 1995, thanks to the entrepreneurial drive of the Scottish freight company Transrail.

During the mid-1980s the prospects for Dounreay nuclear power plant looked bright, and there was even talk of constructing a new 14-mile branch railway from Scotscalder to facilitate transport of materials. Nirex, the nuclear waste disposal authority, was still looking at the possibility of building the line in 1990, in conjunction with construction of a national low-level waste repository at Dounreay. This would have generated 10–15 train loads a week. However, local opposition to the idea of the repository was strong and it was dropped.

In 1991 a new daily intermodal service was inaugurated by Tiger Rail between Coatbridge and Elgin. Whisky from Keith was one of the southbound traffics. The service had a year to establish itself, requiring a daily load of 200 tons to break even, but it was discontinued in May 1992. Another service introduced in 1991, by Railfreight Distribution, was for grain traffic from King's Lynn and

Eccles Road to Burghead and Roseisle (a terminal on the Burghead branch); beginning in October the weekly service did not last a year and its demise marked the end of rail-borne grain traffic.

In common with the broader picture of rail freight generally, the years 1991–3 were discouraging, marked by cessation of various traffics, such as liquid petroleum gas to Elgin and Inverness, and flows of cement, oil and coal to Inverness. The only substantial traffic to survive was timber out of Inverness and Elgin.

The decline in freight traffic over the Highland lines began to be reversed during the summer of 1995, thanks to the enterprise of the Scottish freight operator, Transrail, one of the three geographically based companies created on 1 April 1994 out of the old Trainload Freight. The first new flow was 550 tonnes of containerised coal from Selby to Inverness, carried on behalf of British Fuels.

But the real accolades from the Highland media, local government and politicians were reserved for the resumption of freight services over the Far North line on 29 September, when a Class 37 left Inverness for Wick and Thurso. It hauled 230 tonnes of coal in containers for British Fuels and dropped off at Georgemas Junction two bogie vans loaded with 100 tonnes of steel for Norfrost's fridge and freezer factory at Castletown near Thurso, the district's largest employer. The train returned with scrap for Ayr and Norfrost products for export from Liverpool.

Since then regular workings have attracted such additional traffic as concrete bridge sections from Swansea, bagged anthracite from Ayr to Wick and Thurso, pipes from Teesside for use in underwater installations being built by Rockwater at Wester near Wick, and timber from Wick to Elgin, conveyed in wagons refurbished with the help of Highlands & Islands Enterprise. Other traffic in prospect at the time of writing is marble from Ledmore Quarry near Ullapool bound for Italy that would be loaded at Lairg, and flagstones from Caithness Stone Industry's quarry at Achscrabster. The hope is that traffic will support at least a fortnightly service.

SIGNALLING

The introduction of Radio Electronic Token Block (RETB) on the Far North line in 1984–5 was not without its problems, due largely to difficulties with radio transmission. It transpired that the allocated frequencies interfered with those used by emergency services in Norway. The changeover to different frequencies on the railway finally took place in November 1992, during which the signalling system was out of action, compelling the use of pilotmen on the Far North line and the temporary closure of the Kyle line.

Completion of the resignalling around Inverness was marked by the unveiling of a plaque in Inverness Signalling Centre on 3 June 1987. Controlling colour light signalling as far as Clachnaharry to the west, Aviemore to the south and Nairn to the east, the centre replaced the mechanical signal cabins, with dates of closure that year, at: Welsh's Bridge (14 February); Loco Box, Millburn Junction and Culloden Moor (7 March); and Rose Street (21 March).

RETB working was extended to the section between Inverness and Dingwall on 12 August 1988, linking up with the systems in use on the Kyle and Far North lines. This entailed closure of cabins at Lentran, Muir of Ord and Dingwall, and the transfer of control of the Kyle and Far North lines from Dingwall to Inverness.

WATERLOO VIADUCT

Disaster struck just after 08.00 on 7 February 1989 when heavy rains and a high tide combined to sweep away Joseph Mitchell's handsome Ness (or Waterloo) Viaduct at Inverness, isolating the Far North and Kyle lines. Mitchell's listed masonry viaduct of 1861–2 had five main spans and four small approach spans; a pier and the two spans it supported were the first to go, followed by two separate collapses of two more spans that evening. By chance, the ScotRail General Manager, John Ellis, was in Inverness and immediately pledged that the bridge would be rebuilt; the only question was, would it be rebuilt with sufficient strength to take freight trains?

At the time, freight traffic comprised oil to Invergordon for the distillery and to Lairg, as well as some seasonal grain traffic to Muir of Ord. However, agreement had nearly been reached for an annual movement of 20,000 tonnes of peat from Caithness to Leicester; the bridge collapse ended hopes of the contract being signed.

Six Class 37s and four sets of coaches were marooned north of Inverness, sufficient stock for the winter service to be maintained, with bus connections between Inverness and Dingwall and a separate bus service to Muir of Ord. A £1/4m facility for traction maintenance was set up at Muir of Ord, while Dingwall was chosen as the base for carriage cleaning and on-train catering. However, a major road transfer operation was carried out from late March to shuffle stock about, 10 Sprinter coaches, 9 Hebridean Heritage coaches and 7 InterCity charter vehicles being sent to Invergordon, while 2 Class 37s and 10 oil tankers were brought south. The Sprinters enabled a four-train service on the Far North line to be inaugurated, while Kyle trains remained locomotive-hauled.

Work on the new £1.85m bridge started in August, construction being undertaken by Fairclough Scotland Ltd to a design by JMP Consultants of Glasgow that would allow locomotive-hauled freights north of Inverness. Between the retained abutments of the old bridge, three spans supported by concrete piers were inserted. It was formally opened on 9 May 1990 by the Secretary of State for Scotland, Malcolm Rifkind.

THE KYLE LINE

The continuing popularity of the Great Western and Caledonian observation saloons on the Kyle line led in 1987 to a Class 101 DMU driving trailer being converted for the role. Fitted with loose seating and carpets, it ran on the 10.15 from Inverness and the 17.10 from Kyle from Monday to Thursday and Saturday, and on both the line's Sunday trains.

The role of Kyle of Lochalsh as a springboard for the western isles has been in decline since 1972, when Ullapool became the port for the Stornoway ferries. A further blow was the opening on 16 October 1995 of the highly controversial Skye Bridge across the kyle that had received approval on 24 June 1992. Many were of the opinion that a large viaduct would irrevocably disfigure the beautiful landscape, but it was the way the bridge was built that evoked the greatest ire. The bridge was an early example of the Conservative government's private finance initiative, whereby public infrastructure is built by the private sector in return for, in the case of roads, toll revenue.

The consequence is that the bridge toll is the most expensive in Europe and nearly as high as the fare charged by the ferry between Kyle and Kyleakin that the bridge replaces; moreover, the ferry company Caledonian MacBrayne has not been allowed to continue operation of the ferry as this competition would jeopardise toll revenue. The impact the bridge will have on the railway remains to be seen, but it is unlikely to be anything but deleterious.

THE FAR NORTH

A number of changes have taken place at stations on the line: Dunrobin station was reopened as Dunrobin Castle on 30 June 1985;

Brora was the last manned station betwen Dingwall and Wick, and lost its final staff member in spring 1992; and in 1993 the station building at Kildary was demolished to make way for road improvements to the A9.

The station at Scotscalder has been renovated by its owner, Daniel Brittain-Catlin, each room being restored in the style of a different decade; the quality of the work was rewarded by the station being judged the overall winner in the Ian Allan Railway Heritage Awards for 1993. In a public-spirited gesture, Mr Brittain-Catlin donated some of the prize money to the purchase of hanging baskets for other stations on the Far North line.

Before the much-lamented departure of ScotRail Director Chris Green, after a distinguished railway career, he put forward in early 1995 the idea of a new curve at Georgemas Junction to permit through running to Thurso. One of the reasons for the suggestion was the closure of Thurso depot in May with the end of train division at Georgemas and the separate service to Wick and Thurso.

The Friends of the Far North Line was formed in 1994 to campaign for better services and the restoration of freight traffic. The organisation held a well-supported conference at the Station Hotel in Inverness in October 1995; the speakers included ScotRail's Director, John Ellis, the Director of Railtrack Scotland, Paul Prescott, the Managing Director of Transrail, Julian Worth, the MP for Caithness and Sutherland, Robert Maclennan, and the MP for Ross and Cromarty, Charles Kennedy. Amongst the pledges were the introduction in May 1996 of a morning commuter train from Tain to Inverness, efforts to reduce the Inverness–Thurso journey to three hours, and a commitment to a regular freight service.

THE DORNOCH BRIDGE

The idea for a joint road/rail bridge across the Dornoch Firth, to derive some benefit from the £300m A9 upgrade, was first considered by British Rail during the winter of 1984–5. The initial proposal was for a new line that would leave the existing route close to the site of Edderton station, cross the firth and swing east to serve Dornoch before following the route of the closed Dornoch branch to rejoin the existing line at the former junction of The Mound.

ScotRail also looked at a modified scheme that would cross the narrows at the mouth of Loch Fleet to rejoin the Far North line just south of Golspie rather than at The Mound, thereby saving further miles. By the time British Rail submitted a Parliamentary Bill for the new line in November 1985, the cost had been put at £12m, three-quarters of which had been identified, leaving just £3m for the Scottish Office and the Department of Transport (DoT) to find.

British Rail had been given a deadline of 1 June 1986 to make a commitment to a joint bridge, but funding remained a problem. The difficulty according to BR was that DoT investment rules insisted that only schemes which would increase revenue could be put forward; the objective of this proposal was to preserve income in the face of the increased bus competition that the bridge would create. By this point the contribution needed by the DoT and the Scottish Office had been revised to £4.5m.

The deadline passed without a decision. A written question in the House of Commons by Caithness and Sutherland MP Robert Maclennan was followed by a round of unseemly buck-passing, in which most parties laid the blame at BR's door. During exchanges, the Scottish Office said it had refused to make any contribution to the rail component of the bridge. In the welter of accusations and counter-accusations, the selection of statistics to justify different standpoints gave pay-back times for the rail bridge varying from 12 to 100 years.

It appears that BR made no applications to Brussels to determine what grants might be available, but equally European Regional Development Fund managers expect an indication of support for a project by the national authorities before they will consider a request for funds; this had not been given. Moreover, it is normally the role of government departments to make such applications.

In February 1987 various internal BR documents were leaked. Amongst them was a memo which revealed that BR had been 'advised' by the Scottish Development Department not to participate in a submission to the Scottish Office for support which had been proposed by the Highland Regional Council in March 1985. The Highlands & Islands Development Board would also have participated. The implication was that BR had been warned to tone down its initial enthusiasm for the scheme.

Whether the failure to build the rail link was due to a lack of vigour and determination on the part of BR, or obfuscation and parsimony by government departments, it remains an illustration of the unbalanced way in which road and rail investment schemes have been repeatedly treated. It was significant that a request in Parliament to the Junior Scottish Office Minister, Michael Ancram, to publish the cost/benefit analysis for the road bridge was ignored.

The £11.25m road bridge across the Dornoch Firth opened in August 1991, cutting the road distance between Inverness and Caithness by 26 miles. The consequence of the three new road bridges on the A9 is that Inverness to Wick is 108 miles by road and 161 by rail. Bus is now quicker by about 45 minutes; had the rail bridge been built, trains could have almost matched the bus schedule. To emphasise the impact of the decision to build only the road bridge, on the opening day a group of cyclists de-trained at Golspie and cycled to Tain 12 minutes faster than the train.

It is unlikely that the sad affair will rest there, though more recent ScotRail comments have been less than supportive of those still campaigning to have the rail link built. This was given fresh hope in 1993 when the European Commission gave the Highlands and Islands Objective 1 status, entitling the region to enhanced status for capital grants.

PRESERVATION AND STEAM SPECIALS

The principal development on the Strathspey Railway has been the start and substantial progress on the northern extension towards Broomhill and Grantown-on-Spey. Tracklaying began in 1994 and is being progressed from Broomhill south; rails had reached Croftnahaven by late 1995. The extension is being supported by Highland Regional Council, both financially and with the thorny problem of a bridge over the A95 to the north of Boat of Garten station. It is expected that the Strathspey Railway will be able to extend slightly to the south to run into the ScotRail station at Aviemore.

In August and early September 1992 Grampian Railtours introduced Sunday steam-hauled excursions between Aberdeen and Elgin, hauled by LMS Class 5 4-6-0 No 44871. Other Class 5-hauled specials have included the occasional trip over the Kyle line and to Helmsdale.

Appendices

AUTHORIZATION AND OPENING DATES

Line	Authorized	Opened to public traffic
Stanley Junction to Dunkeld ...	10 July 1854	7 April 1856
Inverness to Nairn	24 July 1854	6 Nov. 1855
Inverness Harbour Branch	24 July 1854	6 Nov. 1855
Nairn to Dalvey (a)...	21 July 1856	22 Dec. 1857
Dalvey to Elgin	21 July 1856	25 Mar. 1858
Elgin to Keith	21 July 1856	18 Aug. 1858
Kinloss to Findhorn (b)	19 April 1859	18 April 1860
Inverness to Dingwall	3 July 1860	11 June 1862
Dingwall to Invergordon	3 July 1860	25 Mar. 1863
Alves to Burghead (c)	17 May 1861	22 Dec. 1862
Dunkeld to Pitlochry	22 July 1861	1 June 1863
Forres to Aviemore...	22 July 1861	3 Aug. 1863
Aviemore to Pitlochry	22 July 1861	9 Sept. 1863
Ballinluig to Aberfeldy	22 July 1861	3 July 1865
Invergordon to Meikle Ferry (d) ...	11 May 1863	1 June 1864
Meikle Ferry to Bonar Bridge ...	11 May 1863	1 Oct. 1864
Bonar Bridge to Golspie (e) ...	29 June 1865	13 April 1868
Dingwall to Strome Ferry (f) ...	5 July 1865	19 Aug. 1870
Golspie to Helmsdale (g)	20 June 1870	19 June 1871
Helmsdale to Wick	13 July 1871	28 July 1874
Georgemas to Thurso	13 July 1871	28 July 1874
Canal Junction to Muirtown Basin (h)	4 July 1890	9 April 1877
Keith to Portessie (i)	12 July 1882	1 Aug. 1884
Fodderty Junction to Strathpeffer ...	28 July 1884	3 June 1885
Aviemore to Carr Bridge	28 July 1884	8 July 1892
Carr Bridge to Daviot	28 July 1884	19 July 1897
Daviot to Millburn Junction ...	28 July 1884	1 Nov. 1898
Burghead to Hopeman	4 July 1890	10 Oct. 1892
Muir of Ord to Fortrose (j) ...	4 July 1890	1 Feb. 1894
Gollanfield Junction to Fort George	4 July 1890	1 July 1899
Orbliston Junction to Fochabers ...	27 June 1892	16 Oct. 1893
Strome Ferry to Kyle of Lochalsh ...	29 June 1893	2 Nov. 1897
The Mound to Dornoch (k) ...	13 Aug. 1898	2 June 1902
Wick to Lybster (k)	27 Nov. 1899	1 July 1903

(a) Temporary station, near Forres, closed when the Findhorn Viaduct was completed, and the line opened to Elgin.

(b) Regular services withdrawn on 1 January 1869. The rails were subsequently removed.

(c) Old terminus on Burghead Pier, subsequently the goods station.

(d) Temporary station, 4 miles west of Tain, closed in 1869.

(e) Sutherland Railway: authorized from Bonar Bridge to Brora, but only completed to Golspie.

(f) Dingwall & Skye Railway: authorized from Dingwall to Kyle of Lochalsh, but only completed to Strome Ferry, opened for goods traffic 5 August 1870.

(g) The Duke of Sutherland's Railway. Opened from Dunrobin to West Helmsdale on 1 November 1870.

(h) The line was constructed without Parliamentary powers. In 1890 it was deemed advisable to obtain official sanction.

(i) Line closed to passengers on 9 August 1915.

(j) Railway authorized from Muir of Ord to Rosemarkie, but completed to Fortrose only.

(k) Authorized under Light Railways Act of 1896, and nominally independent until the grouping.

DISTANCE TABLES

Distances as at September 1925 with subsequent amendments and additions. All stations on single lines have crossing loops except where otherwise shown.

Perth to Inverness, direct via Carr Bridge

	miles	chains	See note
PERTH	0	00	
Luncarty	4	16	1
Strathord	5	12	1
Stanley	7	18	2
Murthly	10	28	3
Kingswood Crossing	12	71	4
Dunkeld & Birnam	15	45	
Inchmagranachan Crossing	17	77	5
Dalguise	20	23	6
Guay	21	36	7
Ballinluig	23	44	8
Moulinearn Crossing	25	62	9
Pitlochry	28	36	
Killiecrankie	32	16	10
BLAIR ATHOLL	35	20	11

Blair Atholl to Dalwhinnie singled 11 July 1966
Blair Atholl to Dalwhinnie doubled 24 April 1978

Black Island Platform	36	16	12
Struan	39	65	13
Dalanraoch	44	49	14
Edendon box	48	00	15
Dalnaspidal	50	79	16
Druimuachdar Summit	53	00	
Balsporran box	54	69	17
Dalwhinnie	58	48	
Inchlea Crossing	62	44	18
Etteridge Crossing	65	72	19
Newtonmore	68	58	
Kingussie	71	48	
Balavil box	74	18	20

	miles	chains	See note
Kingcraig	77	33	21
Dalraddy Crossing	79	49	22
AVIEMORE	83	26	23
Carr Bridge	90	02	24
Slochd Crossing	95	29	25
Tomatin	98	79	26
Moy	103	10	27
Daviot	107	04	28

Daviot to Culloden Moor singled 31 March 1968

Culloden Moor	111	27	
INVERNESS—			
Millburn box	117	34	29
Welsh's Bridge box	117	50	
Locomotive box	117	62	
Station	117	78	

1 Boxes closed 30 July 1961; **2** Former CR line to Forfar closed passengers 4 September 1967, goods 7 June 1982; **3** Box downgraded to gate box 26 February 1984; **4** Box and loop opened 3 June 1908, closed 15 December 1963; **5** Box and loop opened 8 July 1897, closed 24 August 1947; **6** Box and loop closed 23 August 1964; **7** No loop; **8** South box closed and line singled between South and North boxes 12 November 1967, latter renamed 'Ballinluig'; **9** Box and loop opened 8 July 1897, closed 31 August 1947; **10** Loop opened 9 July 1896, box and loop closed 22 December 1963; **11** North box closed and line singled between South and North boxes 25 August 1968, South box renamed 'Blair Atholl'; **12** Not advertised, closed 11 April 1959; **13** Box closed 13 July 1965; **14** Old box (double line) closed and replaced by new box and loop at 45m 61ch 11 July 1966, 'new' box closed 24 April 1978 when line doubled; **15** (double line) Box closed 16 December 1951; **16** Box closed 24 April 1978; **17** Opened 1 June 1908, reopened on new site 25 October 1942, closed 16 December 1951, then reopened as required for summer traffic and finally closed 28 October 1963; **18** Old box and loop opened 8 July 1897, replaced by new box 9ch further north, box and loop closed 11 January 1966; **19** Box and loop opened 25 June 1911, closed 7 May 1963; **20** Box opened December 1942, closed 31 August 1947; **21** Box and loop closed 10 January 1966; **22** Box and loop opened 28 June 1903, closed 14 September 1937, reopened 20 December 1942, closed 24 August 1947; **23** South box closed 4 April 1971; **24** South and North boxes closed and replaced by new box on up platform 15 December 1957; **25** New box 95m 33ch replacing former South box (which housed the token instruments) opened 23 July 1944, box and loop closed 15 December 1963; **26** South and North boxes closed and replaced by new box ('Tomatin') 11 August 1968, box closed 24 June 1979; **27** South and North boxes and loop closed 15 December 1963; **28** Box and loop closed 14 December 1969; **29** Mileage of old box, new box 117m 18ch.

Aviemore and Keith to Inverness

	From Perth		From Keith		
	miles	chains	miles	chains	See note
AVIEMORE	83	26			
Boat of Garten	88	40			1
Broomhill	92	55			2
Grantown-on-Spey	95	76			3
Castle Grant Platform	98	21			4
Dava Summit	101	46			
Dava	104	32			5
Dunphail	110	58			5
Dallas Dhu Siding	117	64			
KEITH JUNCTION			0	00	6
Tauchers Platform			3	70	7
Mulben			4	75	8
Orton			8	27	9
Orbliston Junction			11	61	10
Lhanbryde			14	54	2
ELGIN			18	05	11
Mosstowie			21	24	12
Alves			23	21	13
Kinloss			27	08	14
FORRES	119	24	30	20	15
Brodie	122	52	33	51	16
Auldearn	126	31	37	27	17
Nairn	128	63	39	59	
Gollanfield Junction	134	28	45	24	18
Dalcross	137	10	48	06	19

Dalcross to Millburn singled 12 March 1967

	From Perth		From Keith		
Castle Stuart Platform	138	23	49	19	4
Allanfearn	140	46	51	42	20
INVERNESS—					
Millburn box	143	31	54	27	
Welsh's Bridge box	143	47	54	43	
Locomotive box	143	59	54	55	
Station	143	75	54	71	

1 South and North boxes closed, double line between them singled and made through section Aviemore–Grantown-on-Spey (GNS) station 6 December 1965; **2** No loop; **3** South and North boxes closed and replaced by one new box 23 November 1952, and this closed 18 October 1965; **4** Private station; **5** Boxes closed 18 October 1965; **6** East and West boxes closed 23 October 1966, and line singled; **7** No loop, platform not advertised until 23 May 1949; **8** East and West boxes and loop closed 19 January 1965; **9** East and West boxes and loop closed January 1947; **10** East and West boxes and loop closed 12 June 1966; **11** New West box 6½ chs nearer Inverness opened 30 April 1951, double line Elgin Centre box (GNS) to West box; **12** Box and loop (opened 1 July 1902) closed 31 October 1948; **13** East and West boxes and loop closed 11 December 1966, and junction with Burghead branch controlled by a ground frame; **14** East and West boxes and loop (opened 30 May 1904) closed 6 November 1966; **15** South box closed 15 August 1966, West box closed and line singled between East and West boxes and new loop provided at East box (renamed 'Forres') 28 May 1967; **16** East and West boxes and loop closed 8 May 1966; **17** Box and loop (opened 3 July 1905) closed 5 June 1960; **18** Junction and East boxes replaced by new Junction box to east and loop (opened 1 July 1899) closed 16 January 1966; **19** Box closed 12 March 1967; **20** Box closed 19 October 1965.

(42) A northbound express passes Luncarty station behind 'Castle' 4—6—0 No 143 Gordon Castle and a 'Loch' class 4—4—0. The photograph was taken in the early 1900s as Drummond's elaborate livery—basically Jones's second scheme with minor modifications—was abandoned after 1902 as an economy measure.

Inverness to Wick and Thurso

	From Perth				
	via Carr Bridge and Inverness station		via Carr Bridge and Inverness Loop		
	miles	chains	miles	chains	See note
INVERNESS—					
Millburn box	117	34	117	34	
Welsh's Bridge box	117	50	117	50	
Locomotive box	117	62		—	
Station	117	78		—	
Rose Street box	118	28	117	72	
Ness Viaduct box	118	41	118	05	1
Clachnaharry box	119	55	119	19	
Clachnaharry station	119	61	119	25	1
Bruichnain box	120	58			2

Clachnaharry box to Clunes singled 2 May 1966

Bunchrew	121	34		3
Lentran	123	45		4
Clunes	125	29		5
Beauly	127	67		6
Muir of Ord	130	61		
Conon	133	78		7
DINGWALL	136	34		8
Foulis	140	51		9
Evanton	142	58		10
Alness	146	25		11
INVERGORDON	149	12		
Delny	152	53		12
Kildary	154	35		13
Nigg	156	79		12
Fearn	158	34		14
TAIN	162	00		
Glenmorangie Siding	163	19		15
Edderton	167	29		16
Mid Fearn Halt	172	78		17
Bonar Bridge	175	43		
Culrain	178	51		18
Invershin	179	07		12
Lairg	184	49		
Lairg Summit	187	05		
Acheildh Crossing	190	22		19
Rogart	194	47		

	miles	chains	miles	chains	
The Mound	198	44			20
GOLSPIE	202	06			21
Dunrobin (Private)	203	72			12
Brora	208	15			
Loth	213	39			12
Helmsdale	219	10			
Salzcraggie Platform	221	70			12
Kildonan	228	52			22
Borrobol Platform	232	42			12
Kinbrace	235	71			22
Forsinard	243	34			
County March Summit	247	39			
Altnabreac	251	56			23
Scotscalder	260	61			24
Halkirk	263	39	miles	chains	12
Georgemas	264	79	0	0	
Hoy			0	75	12
THURSO			6	52	25
Bower	267	59			12
Watten	271	50			22
Bilbster	274	07			12
WICK	279	14			26

1 Closed; 2 Box and loop opened 15 March 1902, became part of double line between Clachnaharry and Bunchrew opened 23 June 1913; 3 Box closed 2 May 1966; 4 Loop opened 2 May 1966; 5 Loop opened 13 June 1904, subsequently formed the end of the doubling from Clachnaharry opened 1 June 1914, box closed 2 May 1966; 6 South and North boxes and loop closed 20 July 1965; 7 Box and loop (opened 29 June 1911) closed 22 November 1961; 8 New North box 130 yards north of former box opened 3 November 1963, North and South boxes converted to ground frames 18 March 1984; 9 Box and loop (opened 4 October 1916, located south of station) closed 24 July 1949; 10 South and North boxes and loop closed 7 June 1962; 11 South and North boxes and loop closed 15 January 1967; 12 No loop; 13 South and North boxes and loop closed 26 July 1965; 14 Box and loop (opened 30 July 1910) closed 9 October 1966, replaced by ground frame to control siding points; 15 Closed June 1970; 16 South and North boxes and loop closed 10 April 1962; 17 Closed to public traffic 1 September 1865, then unadvertised; 18 Box and loop opened 2 June 1902, closed 8 May 1962; 19 Opened 1 July 1909, closed 11 November 1956; 20 Box and loop (goods trains only) closed 25 June 1963; 21 South and North boxes and loop closed 2 October 1966, replaced by ground frame to control siding points; 22 South and North boxes and loop closed 20 November 1966; 23 South and North boxes and loop closed 25 September 1966; 24 South and North boxes and loop closed 17 November 1964; 25 Box closed 9 August 1970, and branch converted to 'one train' working; 26 Box closed 27 April 1977.

Dingwall to Kyle of Lochalsh and Strathpeffer

	From Perth via Carr Bridge				
	miles	chains	miles	chains	See note
DINGWALL	136	34			
Fodderty Junction	138	56	138	56	1
Strathpeffer			141	14	
Achterneed	141	07			2
Garve	148	23			3
Lochluichart (new station)*	153	44			4
Achanalt	157	74			5
Achnasheen	164	24			
Loan Crossing	170	44			6

* Distances from Lochluichart onwards as amended from 3 May 1954.

	miles	chains	See note
Glencarron	172	52	4
Achnashellach	176	66	7
Strathcarron	182	23	8
Attadale	184	49	4
Strome Ferry	189	42	9
Duncraig	193	36	10
Plockton	194	49	4
Duirinish	194	03	11
KYLE OF LOCHALSH	200	06	12

1 Box closed 1936, reopened 23 June 1940, closed 20 August 1944; **2** Box and loop closed 24 March 1966; **3** East and West boxes closed 1 April 1984; **4** No loop; **5** East and West boxes and loop closed 23 March 1966; **6** Opened 1 February 1918, closed 1920, removed by 1922; **7** Box and loop (opened 1 June 1900) closed 22 March 1966; **8** East box closed 17 June 1984, West box downgraded to gate box 17 June 1984; **9** East and West boxes and loop closed 20 March 1966; **10** Formerly private platform, made public from 23 May 1949; **11** No loop but box opened 28 April 1940, closed 28 October 1945; **12** Box closed 3 June 1984.

Aberfeldy branch

	miles	chains	
Ballinluig	0	00	
Balnaguard Halt	2	11	No loop
Grandtully	4	27	No loop
Aberfeldy	8	59	

Black Isle branch

	miles	chains	
Muir of Ord	0	00	
Redcastle	3	58	No loop
Allangrange	5	39	No loop
Munlochy	8	02	No loop
Avoch	11	25	No loop
Fortrose	13	45	

Dornoch Light Railway

	miles	chains	
The Mound	0	00	
Cambusavie Halt	1	28	No loop
Skelbo	3	60	No loop
Embo	5	33	No loop
Dornoch Level Crossing	7	31	
Dornoch	7	51	

Wick & Lybster Light Railway

	miles	chains	
Wick	0	00	
Wick Junction	0	19	
Thrumster	4	32	No loop
Welsh's Crossing Halt	6	52	
Ulbster	7	47	No loop
Mid Clyth	9	52	No loop
Roster Road Halt	10	09	
Occumster	12	32	No loop
Parkside Halt	12	72	
Plantation Level Crossing	13	26	
Lybster	13	63	

Portessie branch

	miles	chains	
Keith station	0	00	
Keith Junction West	0	18	
Aultmore	2	37	No loop
Enzie	7	63	No loop
Drybridge Platform	10	03	No loop
Rathven	11	29	No loop
Buckie	12	26	
Portessie	13	64	
Junction with GNSR	13	71	

Fochabers branch

	miles	chains	
Orbliston Junction	0	00	
Balnacoul Halt	2	19	No loop
Fochabers Town	3	00	

Hopeman branch

	miles	chains	
Alves	0	00	
Coltfield Platform	2	20	No loop
Burghead	5	05	
Burghead Old Station	5	37	Known as 'Harbour Extension'
Hopeman	7	05	

Fort George branch

	miles	chains
Gollanfield Junction	0	00
Fort George	1	38

Invergarry & Fort Augustus Railway
(worked by the Highland Railway 1903 to 1907)

	miles	chains
Spean Bridge	0	00
Gairlochy	2	58
Invergloy Platform	7	29
Invergarry	15	12
Aberchalder	19	34
Fort Augustus	23	19
Fort Augustus Pier	24	16

APPENDIX 3

CLOSURES OF LINES AND STATIONS

Line	Miles	Closed to passengers		Closed entirely	
Inverness Harbour branch	$\frac{3}{4}$	June	1867		
Kinloss to Findhorn	3	1 Jan.	1869	c. 1880	
Burghead to Burghead Harbour[1]	$\frac{1}{2}$	10 Oct.	1892	7 Nov.	1966
Keith to Aultmore	$2\frac{1}{2}$	9 Aug.	1915	3 Oct.	1966
Aultmore to Buckie	$9\frac{3}{4}$	9 Aug.	1915	9 Aug.	1915
Buckie to Portessie	$1\frac{1}{2}$	9 Aug.	1915	1 April	1944
Alves to Burghead	$5\frac{1}{2}$	14 Sept.	1931		
Burghead to Hopeman	2	14 Sept.	1931	31 Dec.	1957
Orbliston Junction to Fochabers Town	3	14 Sept.	1931	28 Mar.	1966[2]
Gollanfield Junction to Fort George	$1\frac{1}{2}$	5 April	1943	11 Aug.	1958[3]
Wick to Lybster	$13\frac{3}{4}$	1 April	1944	1 April	1944
Fodderty Junction to Strathpeffer	$2\frac{1}{4}$	23 Feb.	1946	26 Mar.	1951[4]
Muir of Ord to Fortrose	$13\frac{1}{2}$	1 Oct.	1951	13 June	1960
The Mound to Dornoch	$7\frac{3}{4}$	13 June	1960	13 June	1960
Keith Junction to Elgin (via Mulben)[5]	18	18 Dec.	1964		
Ballinluig to Aberfeldy	$8\frac{3}{4}$	3 May	1965	3 May	1965
Dallas Dhu Siding to Forres East	$1\frac{3}{4}$	18 Oct.	1965	21 May	1967[6]
Aviemore to Boat of Garten	$5\frac{1}{4}$	18 Oct.	1965	16 June	1969
Boat of Garten to Dallas Dhu Siding	$29\frac{1}{4}$	18 Oct.	1965	18 Oct.	1965
Forres West Curve	$\frac{1}{4}$	18 Oct.	1965	15 Aug.	1966
Invergordon Harbour branch	$\frac{1}{4}$	—		31 May	1971

[1] Including Burghead first station.
[2] Cessation of traffic, officially closed 12 June 1966.
[3] Cessation of traffic, officially closed 28 December 1961.
[4] Cessation of traffic, officially closed 12 August 1951.
[5] Local passenger service only withdrawn and intermediate stations closed.
[6] Cessation of traffic, officially closed 30 June 1967.

Station	Closed to passengers	Closed to goods
Aberfeldy	3 May 1965	25 Jan. 1965
Achanalt		2 Nov. 1964
Achnashellach		27 Jan. 1964
Achterneed[1]	7 Dec. 1964	18 May 1964
Allanfearn[2]	3 May 1965	27 Jan. 1964
Allangrange	1 Oct. 1951	13 June 1960
Alness[3]	13 June 1960	
Altnabreac		15 Aug. 1966
Alves	3 May 1965	7 Nov. 1966
Attadale		15 Aug. 1966
Auldearn	6 June 1960	7 Sept. 1964
Aultmore[4]	9 Aug. 1915	3 Oct. 1966
Avoch	1 Oct. 1951	13 June 1960
Ballinluig	3 May 1965	
Balnacoul Halt	14 Sept. 1931	
Balnaguard[5]	3 May 1965	
Beauly	13 June 1960	25 Jan. 1965
Bilbster	13 June 1960	13 June 1960
Black Island Platform[6]	11 April 1959	
Blair Atholl[7]		7 Nov. 1966
Boat of Garten	18 Oct. 1965	2 Nov. 1964
Bonar Bridge[8]		
Borrobol	29 Nov. 1965	15 June 1964
Bower	13 June 1960	18 May 1964
Brodie	3 May 1965	28 Dec. 1964
Broomhill	18 Oct. 1965	25 Jan. 1965
Buckie	9 Aug. 1915	9 Aug. 1915
Bunchrew	13 June 1960	27 Jan. 1964
Burghead (1st station)	10 Oct. 1892	
Burghead (2nd station)	14 Sept. 1931	7 Nov. 1966*
Cambusavie Halt	13 June 1960	
Carr Bridge		27 Feb. 1967*
Clachnaharry	1 April 1913	
Clunes	13 June 1960	27 Jan. 1964
Coltfield Platform[9]	14 Sept. 1931	
Conon	13 June 1960	11 Oct. 1965

1 Opened as Strathpeffer, renamed 1 June 1885.
2 Opened as Culloden, renamed 1 November 1898.
3 Reopened as unstaffed halt 7 May 1983.
4 Opened as Forgie, renamed 1 January 1899.
5 Opened by LMS Railway 2nd December 1935.
6 Not advertised.
7 Opened as Blair Athole, renamed 7 September 1893.
8 Renamed Ardgay 2 May 1977.
9 Opened as Wards, renamed 1865.
* Except private siding.

Station	Closed to passengers	Closed to goods
Culloden Moor	3 May 1965	27 Feb. 1967*
Culrain		18 May 1964
Cummingston	1 April 1904	1 April 1904
Dalcross	3 May 1965	15 June 1964
Dalguise	3 May 1965	27 Jan. 1964
Dalnaspidal	3 May 1965	27 Jan. 1964
Dalvey[1]	25 Mar. 1858	
Dalwhinnie		27 Feb. 1967*
Dava	18 Oct. 1965	27 Jan. 1964
Daviot	3 May 1965	7 Sept. 1964
Delny	13 June 1960	15 June 1964
Dornoch	13 June 1960	13 June 1960
Drybridge Platform	9 Aug. 1915	
Duirinish		1 Feb. 1954
Duncraig[2]	7 Dec. 1964	
Dunkeld & Birnam		4 Aug. 1969
Dunphail	18 Oct. 1965	2 Nov. 1964
Dunrobin (private)[3,9]	29 Nov. 1965	2 Nov. 1964
Edderton	13 June 1960	2 Nov. 1964*
Embo	13 June 1960	13 June 1960
Enzie	9 Aug. 1915	9 Aug. 1915
Evanton[4]	13 June 1960	2 Nov. 1964
Findhorn	1 Jan. 1869	c. 1880
Fochabers Town[5]	14 Sept. 1931	28 Mar. 1966
Forsinard		15 June 1964
Fort Augustus Pier	1 Oct. 1906	July 1924[6]
Fort George	5 April 1943	11 Aug. 1958
Fortrose	1 Oct. 1951	13 June 1960
Foulis[7]	13 June 1960	13 June 1960
Glencarron	7 Dec. 1964	
Gollanfield[8]	3 May 1965	7 Sept. 1964
Grandtully	3 May 1965	25 Jan. 1965
Grantown-on-Spey West	18 Oct. 1965	5 July 1965
Guay	3 Aug. 1959	3 Aug. 1959

1 Inverness & Aberdeen Junction Railway at closure.
2 Formerly private station made public 23 May 1949.
3 Goods depot public.
4 Opened as Novar, renamed 1 June 1937.
5 Opened as Fochabers, renamed 1 July 1894.
6 Approximate date.
7 Opened as Fowlis, spelling altered 20 March 1916.
8 Opened as Fort George, renamed Gollanfield Junction 1 July 1899, and Gollanfield, March 1959.
9 Reopened as Dunrobin Castle 30 June 1985.
* Except private siding.

Station	Closed to passengers	Closed to goods
Halkirk	13 June 1960	29 Mar. 1965
Hopeman	14 Sept. 1931	30 Dec. 1957
Hoy	29 Nov. 1965	29 Nov. 1965
Inverness Harbour	June 1867[1]	
Invershin		27 Jan. 1964
Kildary[2]	13 June 1960	25 Jan. 1965
Kildonan		2 Nov. 1964
Kildrummie[3]	Jan. 1858[1]	
Killiecrankie	3 May 1965	28 Oct. 1963
Kinbrace		29 Mar. 1965
Kincraig[4]	18 Oct. 1965	18 May 1964
Kingussie		11 Oct. 1965
Kinloss	3 May 1965	7 Nov. 1966
Lentran	13 June 1960	7 Sept. 1964*
Lhanbryde	7 Dec. 1964	2 May 1966
Lochluichart (1st station)	3 May 1954	3 May 1954
Lochluichart (2nd station)[5]		27 Jan. 1964
Loth	13 June 1960	18 May 1964
Luncarty[6]	18 June 1951	23 May 1966
Lybster	1 April 1944	1 April 1944
Meikle Ferry	1 Jan. 1869	1 Jan. 1869
Mid Clyth	1 April 1944	1 April 1944
Mid Fearn[7]	1 Sept. 1865	1 Sept. 1865
Mosstowie	7 Mar. 1955	28 Dec. 1964
Moy	3 May 1965	27 Jan. 1964
Muir of Ord[8]	13 June 1960	
Mulben	7 Dec. 1964	20 April 1964
Munlochy	1 Oct. 1951	13 June 1960
Murthly	3 May 1965	4 Aug. 1969
Nigg	13 June 1960	28 Dec. 1964
Occumster	1 April 1944	1 April 1944
Orbliston[9]	7 Dec. 1964	20 April 1964

[1] Last appearance in timetable.
[2] Opened as Parkhill, renamed 1868.
[3] Opened as Cawdor, renamed 1857.
[4] Opened as Boat of Insh, renamed 1871.
[5] Opened by British Railways 3 May 1954.
[6] Caledonian Railway station used by Highland passenger trains.
[7] Continued in use unadvertised.
[8] Reopened 4 October 1976.
[9] Opened as Fochabers, renamed Orbliston Junction 16 October 1893, Orbliston 12 September 1960.
* Except private siding.

Station	Closed to passengers	Closed to goods
Orton	7 Dec. 1964	20 April 1964
Parkside Halt[1]	1 April 1944	
Plockton		7 Sept. 1964
Rafford	31 May 1865	31 May 1865
Rathven	9 Aug. 1915	9 Aug. 1915
Redcastle	1 Oct. 1951	13 June 1960
Rogart[2]		18 May 1964
Rohallion	Oct. 1864[3]	
Roster Road Halt[1]	1 April 1944	
Salzcraggie	29 Nov. 1965	
Scotscalder		27 Jan. 1964
Skelbo	13 June 1960	13 June 1960
Stanley[4]	11 June 1956	6 Dec. 1965
Strathord[4]	13 April 1931	2 Nov. 1964
Strathpeffer	23 Feb. 1946	26 Mar. 1951
Strome Ferry		15 June 1964
Struan	3 May 1965	27 Jan. 1964
The Mound	13 June 1960	27 Jan. 1964
Thrumster	1 April 1944	1 April 1944
Tomatin	3 May 1965	
Ulbster	1 April 1944	1 April 1944
Watten	13 June 1960	15 June 1964
Welsh's Crossing Halt	1 April 1944	1 April 1944
West Helmsdale	19 June 1871	

[1] Opened by LMS Railway 27 January 1936.
[2] Closed to passengers 13 June 1960, reopened 6 March 1961.
[3] Last appearance in timetable.
[4] Caledonian Railway station used by Highland passenger trains.

SUMMARY OF TRAIN SERVICES

Date	No. of trains		Fastest train		Slowest train	
September 1863						
Perth and Inverness (via Forres, 144 miles)						
	north	2	6 h		6 h	50 m
	south	2	5 h	55 m	7 h	30 m
Inverness and Invergordon (31¼ miles)						
	north	4	1 h	25 m	1 h	50 m
	south	4	1 h	30 m	1 h	40 m
August 1874						
Perth and Inverness (via Forres)						
	north	4	5 h	15 m	8 h	
	south	4	5 h	15 m	9 h	30 m
Inverness and Wick (161¼ miles)						
	north	2	7 h	5 m	7 h	25 m
	south	2	7 h	10 m	7 h	30 m
July 1885						
Perth and Inverness (via Forres)						
	north	5	4 h		7 h	20 m
	south	5	4 h		9 h	
Inverness and Wick						
	north	2	6 h		8 h	
	south	2	6 h	30 m	9 h	30 m
November 1898						
Perth and Inverness (via Carr Bridge, 118 miles)						
	north	5	3 h	15 m	4 h	20 m
	south	5	3 h	20 m	4 h	23 m
					6 h	35 m[1]
Inverness and Wick						
	north	2	6 h		6 h	45 m
	south	2	6 h	30 m	6 h	45 m

[1] Via Forres.

Date	No. of trains		Fastest train		Slowest train	
August 1914						
Perth and Inverness (via Carr Bridge)						
	north	9	3 h	20 m	4 h	36 m
					4 h	39 m[1]
	south	8	3 h	16 m	4 h	30 m
					6 h	15 m[1]
Inverness and Wick						
	north	3	5 h	30 m[2]	7 h	
			6 h	10 m		
	south	3	5 h	11 m[2]	6 h	55 m
			6 h	40 m		
December 1922						
Perth and Inverness (via Carr Bridge)						
	north	5	3 h	35 m	4 h	42 m
	south	5	3 h	16 m	4 h	45 m
Inverness and Wick						
	north	2	6 h	30 m	7 h	15 m
	south	2	6 h	50 m	7 h	30 m
August 1939						
Perth and Inverness (via Carr Bridge)						
	north	9	3 h	25 m	4 h	25 m
					5 h	38 m[1]
	south	7	3 h	21 m	5 h	
Inverness and Wick						
	north	3	4 h	49 m	6 h	9 m
	south	3	5 h	10 m	6 h	2 m
December 1947						
Perth and Inverness (via Carr Bridge)						
	north	7	3 h	22 m	4 h	34 m
	south	5	3 h	8 m	5 h	16 m
Inverness and Wick						
	north	2	6 h	1 m	6 h	33 m
	south	2	5 h	53 m	6 h	19 m

[1] Via Forres.

[2] 'Further North Express', Wednesdays and Fridays from Inverness, and Thursdays and Saturdays from Wick.

Date	No. of trains		Fastest train		Slowest train	
August 1962						
Perth and Inverness (via Carr Bridge)						
	north	8	3 h	16 m	3 h	45 m
					5 h	9 m[1]
	south	7	3 h	18 m	5 h	5 m
Inverness and Wick						
	north	4	4 h		5 h	8 m
	south	3	4 h		5 h	6 m
May 1971						
Perth and Inverness						
	north	4	2 h	20 m	3 h	35 m
	south	5	2 h	34 m	5 h	
Inverness and Wick						
	north	3	4 h	39 m	4 h	50 m
	south	3	4 h	43 m	4 h	49 m
September 1984						
Perth and Inverness						
	north	8	2 h	24 m	3 h	40 m
	south	9	2 h	8 m	4 h	
Inverness and Wick						
	north	3	3 h	55 m	4 h	15 m
	south	3	4 h		4 h	5 m

[1] Via Forres.

SINGLE LINES AND SIGNALLING ARRANGEMENTS

Doubling of single line sections

Between	Opening date
Blair Atholl and Dalnacardoch box	2 July 1900
Dalnacardoch box and Dalnaspidal	13 May 1901
Dalnaspidal and Druimuachdar Summit	10 June 1901
Druimuachdar Summit and Balsporran box	1 June 1908
Balsporran box and Dalwhinnie	17 May 1909
Clachnaharry and Bunchrew	23 June 1913
Bunchrew and Clunes	1 June 1914

Singling of double line sections

Between	Date
Boat of Garten North box and Boat of Garten South box	6 Dec. 1965
Clachnaharry and Clunes	2 May 1966
Blair Atholl and Dalwhinnie	11 July 1966
Keith Junction East box and Keith Junction West box	23 Oct. 1966
Dalcross and Inverness, Millburn box	12 Mar. 1967
Forres East box and Forres West box	28 May 1967
Ballinluig North box and Ballinluig South box	12 Nov. 1967
Daviot and Culloden Moor	31 Mar. 1968
Blair Atholl North box and Blair Atholl South box	25 Aug. 1968
Aviemore North box and Aviemore South box	4 April 1971

Replacement of electric token working by Tokenless Block system on the Perth and Inverness main line

Between	Date
Stanley and Murthly	8 June 1969
Murthly and Ballinluig	1 June 1969
Ballinluig and Blair Atholl	11 May 1969
Blair Atholl and Dalnaspidal	27 April 1969
Dalnaspidal and Newtonmore	20 April 1969
Newtonmore and Aviemore South box	9 Mar. 1969
Aviemore South box and Aviemore North box	4 April 1971*
Aviemore North box and Tomatin	10 Nov. 1968
Tomatin and Culloden Moor	11 Aug. 1968

Doubling of single line sections

Blair Atholl and Dalwhinnie	24 April 1978

* On abolition of double line between these boxes.

PRINCIPAL ALTITUDES ABOVE SEA LEVEL

	Feet		Feet
Druimuachdar Summit	1,484	Carr Bridge station	914
Slochd Summit	1,315	Kingussie station	745
Dalwhinnie station	1,174	Grantown-on-Spey station	737
Dava Summit	1,052	Boat of Garten station	712
Tomatin station	1,029	County March	
Dava station	985	(Sutherland/Caithness)	708
		Lairg Summit	484

(43) *The last of the 'Strath' class 4—4—0s to be built, No* 100 Glenbruar *in what is thought to be Kyle of Lochalsh shed. Jones's patent cylinder lubricator may be seen to advantage; these were sometimes repositioned on the front of the smokebox.*

OFFICERS

Inverness & Nairn Railway
Merged with the IAJR on 17 May 1861

Chairmen:
| | 1854–6 | Cluny Macpherson |
| | 1857–61 | Eneas William Macintosh |

General manager:
| | 1855–61 | Andrew Dougall |

Secretaries:
| | 1854–6 | Messrs G. & P. Anderson (Inverness)* |
| | 1857–61 | Andrew Dougall |

Locomotive superintendent:
| | 1855–61 | William Barclay |

Engineer:
| | 1854–61 | Joseph Mitchell |

Inverness & Aberdeen Junction Railway
Amalgamated to form the Highland Railway on 29 June 1865

Chairman:
| | 1856–65 | Alexander Matheson |

General manager:
| | 1856–65 | Andrew Dougall |

Secretary:
| | 1856–65 | Andrew Dougall |

Locomotive superintendent:
| | 1856–65 | William Barclay |

* Secretary and solicitors

Engineers:
    1856–63   Joseph Mitchell
    1864–5   Joseph Mitchell & Co

Traffic managers:
    1860–63   Thomas Mackay
    1864–5   William Roberts*

Inverness & Perth Junction Railway
Amalgamated to form the Highland Railway on 29 June 1865

Chairman:
    1861–5   The Hon T. C. Bruce

General manager:
    1861–5   Andrew Dougall

Secretary:
    1861–5   Andrew Dougall

Locomotive superintendent:
    1861–5   William Barclay

Engineers:
    1861–3   Joseph Mitchell
    1864–5   Joseph Mitchell & Co

Traffic managers:
    1863   Thomas Mackay
    1864–5   William Roberts*

Inverness & Ross-shire Railway
Merged with IAJR on 30 June 1862

Chairman:
    1860–62   Alexander Matheson

General manager:
    1860–62   Andrew Dougall

Secretary:
    1860–62   Andrew Dougall

* Designated passenger superintendent

Locomotive superintendent:
        1862   William Barclay

Engineer:
        1860–62   Joseph Mitchell

Traffic manager:
        1862   Thomas Mackay

Sutherland Railway

Merged with the HR on 28 July 1884. The railway was worked by the HR

Chairman:
        1865–84   The Duke of Sutherland

Secretary:
        1865–84   Andrew Dougall

Engineers:
        1865–7   Joseph Mitchell & Co
        1868–70   William Baxter

Sutherland & Caithness Railway

Merged with the HR on 28 July 1884. The railway was worked by the HR

Chairman:
        1871–84   The Duke of Sutherland

Secretary:
        1871–84   Andrew Dougall

Engineer:
        1871–4   Murdoch Patterson

Caithness Railway

Authorized in 1866, but never commenced

Chairman:
        1866–71   The Earl of Caithness

Dingwall & Skye Railway
Merged with the HR on 2 August 1880. The railway was worked by the HR

Chairman:
1865–80	Alexander Matheson

Secretary:
1865–80	Andrew Dougall

Engineers:
1865–7	Joseph Mitchell & Co
1868–70	Murdoch Patterson

Perth & Dunkeld Railway
Merged with IPJR on 28 February 1864. The line was worked by the SNER

Chairman:
1854–64	The Earl of Mansfield

Secretaries:
1854–7	Archibald Reid
1858–9	C. D. Cranstoun
1860–64	Thomas Fyfe

Engineers:
1854–9	J. W. Stewart
1860–64	John Willet

Findhorn Railway
Worked by IAJR from 1862

Chairmen:
1859–66	Peter Brown
1867–70	James Forbes
1871–81	John Binning

General manager:
1860–62	Alexander Hutchison

Secretary:
1859–81	John D. Davidson

Engineer:
1859–62	Joseph Mitchell

The Highland Railway

Formed by the amalgamation of the IAJR and IPJR on 29 June 1865

Chairmen:

1865–84	Alexander Matheson
1885–91	The Hon T. C. Bruce
1892–6	Eneas Macintosh
1897–1900	Sir George MacPherson Grant
1901	J. D. Fletcher
1902–12	William Whitelaw
1913–15	R. M. Wilson
1916	William Whitelaw
1917–22	W. H. Cox

General managers:

1865–96	Andrew Dougall
1897–8	Charles Steel
1899–1910	Thomas Wilson
1911–22	Robert Park

Secretaries:

1865–96	Andrew Dougall
1897–1901	William Gowenlock
1902–10	Robert Park
1911–22	George Cornet

Locomotive superintendents:

1865–9	William Stroudley
1870–96	David Jones
1897–1911	Peter Drummond
1912–15	Fredrick Smith
1915–22	Christopher Cumming
1922 (April to Dec.)	David Chalmers Urie

Superintendents of the line:

1865–75	William Roberts
1876–90	Thomas Robertson
1891–1900	William Garrow
1901–22	Thomas McEwen*

* Designated traffic manager

Engineers:

1865–9	J. W. Buttle	(a)
1870–74	Peter Wilson	(b)
1875–97	Murdoch Patterson	(c)
1898–1913	William Roberts	(d)
1914–22	Alexander Newlands	(d)

(a) Designated superintendent of permanent way
(b) Designated resident engineer
(c) Designated resident engineer until 1893, then chief engineer
(d) Designated engineer

THE ILLUSTRATIONS

Locomotive & General Railway Photographs, plates 1, 2, 3, 4, 5, 6, 7, 11, 12, 13, 14, 19, 20, 21, 25, 26, 27, 28, 29, 31, 32, 33, 38, 39, 40, 41, 42, 43; Locomotive Publishing Co, plates 23, 24; Photomatic, plates 18, 22; Anthony J. Lambert Collection, plate 30; Anthony J. Lambert, plates 34, 35, 36, 37.

COLOUR ILLUSTRATIONS

J. M. Jarvis – Colour-Rail, A; Colour-Rail, B; T. J. Edgington – Colour-Rail, C; N. Spinks – Colour-Rail, D; J. M. Jarvis – Colour-Rail, E; K. H. Leech – Colour-Rail, F; Colour-Rail, 6; Derek Cross – Colour-Rail, H.

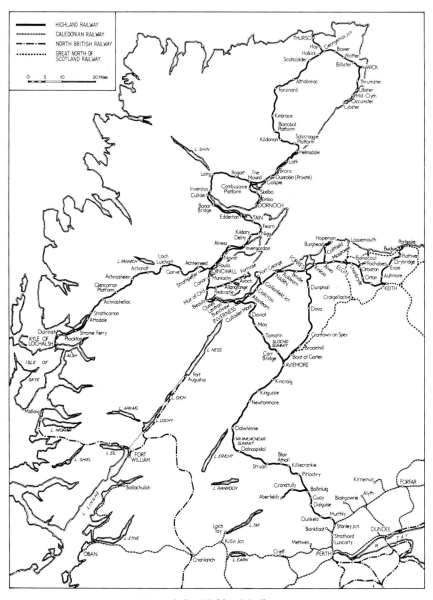

Map of the Highland Railway

Index